EZRA POUND, IDENTITY IN CRISIS

EZRA POUND, IDENTITY IN CRISIS

A fundamental reassessment
of the poet and his work

ALAN DURANT
University Fellow in English Literature,
University of Wales

THE HARVESTER PRESS · SUSSEX
BARNES & NOBLE BOOKS · NEW JERSEY

First published in Great Britain in 1981 by
THE HARVESTER PRESS LIMITED
Publisher: John Spiers
16 Ship Street, Brighton, Sussex

and in the USA by
BARNES & NOBLE BOOKS
81 Adams Drive, Totowa, New Jersey 07516

© Alan Durant, 1981

British Library Cataloguing in Publication Data

Durant, Alan
    Ezra Pound, identity in crisis.
    1. Pound, Ezra—Criticism and interpretation
    I. Title
    811'.5'2   PS3531.082Z/

    ISBN 0–7108–0036–3

Barnes & Noble Books
ISBN 0–389–20197–9

811
P87xdu

Printed in Great Britain by
Bristol Typesetting Co. Ltd.,
Barton Manor, St. Philips, Bristol

Contents

Note on quotation from the 'Cantos'

Quotations from the *Cantos* are made throughout in the form of two numbers, which are separated by a colon, and of which the first is italicized. These appear in parentheses after quoted material. The first number is that of the Canto. The second is a page number in the current Faber edition of the *Cantos*, 1–117 (London, 1975). Thus,

(35 : 172)

is a reference to Canto 35, page 172 in the red Faber edition.

I have used this edition as it is the first single English text to offer all of the poem that is presently available to the public. It has the further advantage that its pagination corresponds with that of American editions (New Directions, New York), from 1970 onwards. This text accordingly becomes the most convenient form of reference to the poem, displacing forms more appropriate when the *Cantos* were still a work in progress, or when collected editions were still unavailable.*

* The most prevalent form of reference before the publication of this edition is that employed by Hugh Kenner, and explained in *The Pound Era* (Faber, London, 1971), pp. xiii–xiv.

Abbreviations

Collected Shorter Poems	Ezra Pound, *Collected Shorter Poems* (Faber, London, 1952; reprinted 1973).
Écrits	Jacques Lacan, *Écrits* (Seuil, Paris, 1966).
Écrits: A Selection	Jacques Lacan, *Écrits: A Selection*, translated by Alan Sheridan (Tavistock Publications, London, 1977).
Four Fundamental Concepts	Jacques Lacan, *The Four Fundamental Concepts of Psycho-Analysis*, translated by Alan Sheridan (Hogarth Press and the Institute of Psycho-Analysis, London, 1977).
Gaudier-Brzeska	Ezra Pound, *Gaudier-Brzeska: A Memoir (1916)* (New Directions, New York, 1970).
Le Séminaire XI	Jacques Lacan, *Le Séminaire XI* (Seuil, Paris, 1973).
Letters	Ezra Pound, *The Letters of Ezra Pound: 1907–1941*, edited by D. D. Paige (Faber, London, 1951).
Life	Noel Stock, *The Life of Ezra Pound* (Routledge & Kegan Paul, London, 1970).
Life (Penguin)	Noel Stock, *The Life of Ezra Pound* (Penguin Books, Harmondsworth, 1974).
Literary Essays	Ezra Pound, *Literary Essays of Ezra Pound*, edited with an

introduction by T. S. Eliot (Faber, London, 1954; reprinted 1968).

Pound/Joyce

Pound/Joyce: The Letters of Ezra Pound to James Joyce, with Pound's Essays on Joyce, edited by Forrest Read (Faber, London, 1968).

Selected Prose

Ezra Pound, *Selected Prose: 1909–1965*, edited with an introduction by William Cookson (Faber, London, 1973).

Standard Edition

Sigmund Freud, *The Standard Edition of the Complete Psychological Works of Sigmund Freud*, edited and translated by James Strachey *et al.*, 24 volumes (Hogarth Press, London, 1953).

Chapter One

Pound currency and its devaluation

THE writing of Ezra Pound (1885–1972) has always presented literary criticism with especial difficulties, not all of which are related to the evident inability of that discourse to keep abreast of exploration and innovation. Indeed, Pound's innovations are often only intelligible in terms of an ultra-conservatism, an effort to reconstitute a version of tradition.

Pound's childhood environment in Hailey, Idaho, was that of a developing, if provincial, frontier territory; on going to university in Pennsylvania in 1901, the aspiring poet's attentions focused temporarily on the work of Arthur Symons, Ernest Dowson and Fiona McCleod. But Pound was to turn away from this early influence towards an alluring European tradition, a tradition made available to Americans all the more by the precedent of illustrious expatriate Henry James. During his long life, Pound would have working and social relationships with many now celebrated fellow writers, including James Joyce, T. S. Eliot, Wyndham Lewis, William Carlos Williams and E. E. Cummings. He would also vigorously encourage a set of aesthetic and social criteria (to be produced from the works of Fenollosa, Frobenius, Gourmont, Agassiz, Douglas, etc.), and hold up for renewed public esteem the works of artists he thought to embody necessary virtues, artists including Homer, Dante, Cavalcanti, Villon and Robert Browning. This working over of the European literary tradition and of established co-ordinates of intellectual history Pound explains as an effort towards the resumption and transplantation of certain features of European culture indispensable for an American Renaissance.

Predictably this enterprise, and Pound's undoubted influence upon fellow writers, has ensured for him a constant and necessary inclusion in versions of twentieth-century literary history, both as

1

an exponent of certain important and developing writing practices (Pound's contribution to Imagism, to Vorticism, his use
of the Ideogram, and so on), and as an advocate and occasional
editor of the works of others, including T. S. Eliot. Both the
emphasis of this new writing and of his encouragement of
certain currencies in the writing of others Pound came to support
with definite forms of philosophical and cultural explanation,
seeking during a period of several decades a decisive transformation in the appearance of the artistic and social world.

This radical context of Pound's writing is also the area of the
critical difficulty he engenders. Unlike Eliot's espousal of a set
of social perspectives moulded from Irving Babbitt's humanism
and largely compatible with prevailing currents in Anglo-Saxon
moralism, Pound's political and cultural notions—similarly fixed
on the idea of a cultural restitution, and particularly accentuated
by despair over Western civilization after the First World War
—take on in the 1930s the less respectable appearance of an
allegiance to Italian Fascism. This led, of course, to the poet's
internment after the Second World War, found unfit to plead
on a charge of treason when indicted for wartime broadcasts on
Rome Radio to invading American troops. These broadcasts
might be thought the most energetic form of denunciations of
American society which had continued throughout the preceding
decade.

Criticism of Pound's work—retarded by an understandable
post-war vilification of Fascist sentiments and sympathizers—has
consistently failed to confront questions concerning the interrelation of his literary prescriptions and developing political
theories. The late emergence in the 1950s of a revitalized and
more openly sympathetic interest in Pound, even if made more
difficult by the virtual continuity between his incarceration and
expatriation (Pound left America for Italy once more almost
immediately upon release from St Elizabeths Hospital in 1958),
produced a formidable biographical and exegetical machinery.
But it came little closer to these particular problems.

In addressing the question of the success of Pound's writing,
and in particular of his long and unfinished poem the *Cantos,*
available commentaries continue in a reluctance to pose contingent questions as to the theoretical conditions for that success
or failure. Effectively an unacknowledged complicity with Pound's

founding aesthetic principles (often to do with notions of precision in language, and tissues of necessary relations obtaining between bodies of facts) has substantially vitiated many of these criticisms. This can be quite clearly seen in referential or cartographical approaches, which seek to elucidate the *Cantos* by explaining allusions in the poem to an extra-linguistic world.

What damages this kind of project is the ease with which it moves from the written page itself to an external circumstantial world and back again, as if by learning to see through the language of the poem the world, its culture and its history will become transparently available to the reader. Subsequent reservations about Pound's specific theories, facts and hypotheses are in consequence limited to disagreement within a general conception of the relation of writing to the world, which, for the purpose of reading Pound's work, has already been implicitly agreed. Protocols of judgement in such a scheme become a kind of expertise with various knowledges. Such criticisms appeal to a conception of knowledge violently opposed by the emphases of Pound's own didacticism, even if, as we shall see, his own provision of alternative facts confronts this kind of knowledge precisely upon its own ground of empirical factuality.

Referential commentaries in general—the differing views of Pound expressed in the works of Donald Davie and Hugh Kenner are perhaps the best known—are not concerned to consider relations between the domain of writing (its techniques, effects, production), and that of politics (Pound's lamentable affiliation). Politics is thought to be a distinct social level secondary to and removed from forms of individual experience. Pound's adoption of a specific politics is thought to be effected by means of a choice made from an already established, coherent, and autonomous area of individual experience, which has itself no political character. Language is an instrument which purveys or expresses meanings selected by this central anthropological origin, consciousness. Mind, language and politics are divided off from one another, and consciousness accorded priority as the progenitor of self-expression and political opinion.

Such a disjunction of the fields of writing and experience allows for such commentaries a definite conception of literature as consisting in formal artefacts removed from the social level except where this latter is specified in terms of a *content*, as subject matter. It is, significantly, this disjunction which makes possible an evaluation of artistic worth which is at least ostensibly removed from canons of political pertinence. This follows from the consideration of political opinions in literary works as arguable constructs distinguishable and separate from the realm of creativity, expression and subjectivity. The result is the possibility of valuing and praising Pound's forms of writing and his social commitment, whilst retaining the freedom to express reservations or offer apologies for his politics.

If works of literature are valorized in this debate over the merits of various cultural opinions, they are also decisively measured according to their properties of relative formal beauty, the evaluation of expression held in distinction from what is expressed. This form of evaluation employs an analogous division, closing off the quality of self-expression from questions of the relation between language and the domain of the self, as well as from the realm of what is expressed. In this aesthetic measurement politics becomes merely an irksome parenthesis, grafted onto a notion of the naturally given experience of the self mediated through a secondary linguistic expression.

What the above theoretical shortcoming in much criticism of Pound's work appears to make presently necessary is an attempt to trace in his texts questions of the interrelation of forms of writing and notions of culture, not in terms of an investigation of a content or set of cultural opinions—although these will frequently intervene—but in the very terms of production of the writing.

To undertake such an examination is to place in question the notion of a privileged intention (such as is assumed in the above conceptions of the centrality of consciousness), arguing that this in itself is less important than the sites and conditions in which particular readings may be produced. Pound's intentions are dislodged from their traditionally accorded priority by an analysis of the conditions and relations of reading which may be established across his work. This is not simply to replace an individual writer's truth with a truth of social conditions (in the manner of assessments of appropriations of texts at given historical moments), but seeks to argue that forms of writing define possible reading relations, and forestall other types of assumption of a text. Such an examination considers the places assigned to writer and reader in the production of language : it is, therefore, of necessity an examination of forms of subjectivity in relation to language.

Arguments along these lines might claim both to assess the theoretical space occupied by Pound's writing and social hypotheses, and to consider the theoretical (and thereby social) problems these raise. I will argue that Pound's adopted modes of writing bespeak a particular conception of language which *necessarily* spills into a set of cultural perspectives.

Pound's work has a particular current importance in its clear suggestion of this compact between forms of writing and notions of culture and politics. Whereas the poet's espousal of Fascism has frequently led commentary into embarrassment and forms of special pleading on a cultural rather than explicitly political platform, I will argue that Pound's unmistakable attachment to Fascist doctrines and devotion to Fascist practices of which he was aware (no matter if in some measure recanted in the mid-1960s) can provide a means of understanding certain conditions necessary for the emergence of this phenomenon. These conditions relate to forms of subjectivity on the terrain of language, and are not exhausted by accounts in the history of ideas.

In arguing that political forms disclose a contribution made by specific constructions of language and subjectivity, the foregoing argument evidently rests on the postulation that Fascism is a phenomenon whose configurations are not immutably given historically, but are adaptable to differing political conditions. This is a postulation ever more frequently vindicated by contemporary events. To follow such an argument is to assume conceptions of Fascism as being articulated at the level of economic conditions and in multiple political determinations, but to insist upon a surplus beyond these social causes.

Conceived in this way, Pound's politics cannot acceptably be made reducible to a set of largely Social Darwinist prejudices prevalent in the United States at the turn of the century, even if these do make their contribution; neither can his anti-Semitism be fully accounted for as that which gained widespread popularity in America following the implementation of the Open Door Immigration policy, nor his desire for a centralized cultural administration be explained as redress for feeling a colonial backwoodsman in cultured European society. I will suggest that there is an irreducible element of psychological causation in Fascism, and further and in particular, that this is engendered at the level of

determinate modalities of our individual assumptions of subjectivity and language.

Pound's writing becomes important precisely because it sets these
elements in play, and so exposes them. Much of Pound's work has
attained popularity from forms of miscalculative appropriation
which produce versions of his writings based on a conception of
formal pleasure that openly disavows intended political emphases.
More importantly, however, I will suggest that Pound's popularity
among careful readers shows in exemplary fashion how im-
minently codes of writing and notions of subjective identity which
are publicly revered can bring us upon forms of extreme reaction.

If I have suggested an element of psychological determination
in Fascism, it is immediately necessary to specify the theoretical
domain in which alone that concept can operate. It is important
that this psychological element should not be here understood in
relation to received notions of the psyche as a repository of
occluded identity, and the practice of psychoanalysis as accordingly dealing with a content of the unconscious. Such notions
conceive our subjective development as a single and decisive
childhood event. Psychical determination is rather to be understood in relation to work in Freudian psychoanalysis which has
stressed that the fundamental terrain of the unconscious is language. Such work takes up Saussure's linguistics, and develops across
Jakobson's readings of this work. It is established and recognized
most frequently in the work of French psychoanalyst Jacques
Lacan, and of those directly or indirectly associated with his work.

The specific concerns of this version of psychoanalytic theory
can possibly be best approached by means of Jakobson's distinction
between two kinds of aphasia. These consist respectively in impairments of the linguistic faculties of selection or substitution, or of
combination and contexture.[1] Finding their most condensed expression in the rhetorical tropes metaphor and metonymy, these
impairments assume a constitutive role in the production and
distribution of discourse.

When Jakobson notes how two polar functions operate in
semiotic systems of all kinds and locates these linguistically in the
tropes metaphor and metonymy, he further notes a pressing need
to examine this recognition in various other disciplines, and cites
Freud's finding of similar mechanisms at work in his analysis of
dreams.[2] It is, then, one mode of entry into the complex teaching

of Lacan to consider that in broaching this question he has promulgated an analogous operation of these two tropes in the constitution of our discourses as of our dreams, claiming in short
that the unconscious is structured like a language.[3]

It has been argued above that what is problematic with classic
accounts of Pound's work is the ease with which language is considered merely as a secondary instrument of communication which
itself has no constitutive value and merely transmits a content.
Lacan's work is a fundamental questioning of this assumption.
What alone can sponsor such an assumption is that language
involves a perfect correspondence between spoken or written signs
and a defined and homogeneous area of personal experience,
such as is assumed by Donald Davie or Hugh Kenner, for example. This field of experience is in its turn guaranteed by the
philosophical category of the unitary individual or subject, sanc-
tioned in simple self-evidence since the celebrated *cogito ergo sum*
of Descartes. From this unproblematically assumed position the
conditions for a representation of a field of experience and a
communication by way of language are made possible.

But the Cartesian sponsorship of this notion of the subject is
also its definition as the product of a particular investigative procedure, obscured only by being so pervasively at work in our own
contemporary world. Lacan has referred to Freud's assessment of
his discovery of the unconscious as being analogous to the revolu-
tionary Copernican view of the universe, suggesting that a similar
displacement of man from a central position is its concern.[4] For
Freud the unconscious is another scene which becomes evident in
dreams, jokes, slips of the tongue or pen, and so on, and the
analytic situation establishes a silence of the analyst against which
the discourses of the analysand are exposed. This surrounding
silence enables to become apparent those breaks which most
vigorously assert the reality of that other scene.

But it is not the clinical practice of psychoanalysis which is in
question here. What is involved is rather an adoption of what
has been learned in the metapsychological theory of that practice
in consideration of literary texts. What is crucial in Lacan's contribution to that theory is that the unconscious appears not simply
in the substance of what we say or omit to say, but in the disposition of metaphor and metonymy in the very constitution of
our discourses. The application of such a theory to literature dis-

places an analysis of the represented symptoms of great writers, which has traditionally been the domain of psychoanalytic accounts of texts, by an examination of their discursive organization.

In order to offer any introductory account of Lacan's reworking of Freud, it is necessary to consider his representation of infantile entry into the world of adults. This comprises a description and theoretical development of those stages recognized as crucial by Freud in which accession to the world as a sexed and speaking subject is achieved. These stages have been formalized in psycho-analytic theory as the oral, anal and phallic phases. At erotogenic zones of the body a baby recognizes presence and absence in the course of articulations of demands to another, generally the mother, or in the case of toilet training answers demands from this other person. In the instance of psychical effects theorized as an anxiety over the possibility of castration, a recognition of a physical division of the sexes takes place, but is articulated around the presence or absence of the penis, which accordingly takes on a central significance in any infantile accession to sexuality. This is so far a traditional, if condensed, account of fundamental elements of Freudian theory.[5]

In taking up Ferdinand de Saussure's division of the linguistic sign (proposed in lectures of 1907–11 that were collected by his students as the *Cours de linguistique générale*) into signifier, the acoustic or written matter of language, and signified, the concept which can appear to become attached to that signifier,[6] Lacan has suggested a revised presentation of the Freudian discovery, now in terms of such a linguistic foundation:

I have been led to certain results: essentially, to promulgate as necessary to any articulation of analytic phenomena the notion of the signifier, as opposed to that of the signified, in modern linguistic analysis. Freud could not take this notion, which postdates him, into account, but I would claim that Freud's discovery stands out precisely because, although it set out from a domain in which one could not expect to recognize its reign, it could not fail to anticipate its formulas. Conversely, it is Freud's discovery that gives to the signifier/signified opposition the full extent of its implications: namely, that the signifier has an active function in determining certain effects in which the signifiable appears as submitting to its mark, by becoming through that passion the signified.[7]

For Lacan the unconscious is constituted by the fact that in order to speak, our selected signifiers can only become operative in a differentiation from all those others which are absent from what we say, but which must necessarily exist elsewhere in order for the symbolic system, the tissue of differences which Saussure postulates collectively form language, to be workable. Accordingly Lacan proposes that the unconscious is forged not as an exclusion from an already constituted consciousness following the process of a repression, but rather in our very accession to the system of language on the trace of those other effects of language whose signification precipitates what we have come to know as subjectivity. In entering the linguistic system, the subject is necessarily split or divided, as it takes up possibilities within a given set of formal oppositions or differences.

In this reformulation the unconscious is not considered as a repository for what has been expelled from a prior consciousness by virtue of being traumatic and unbearable, but as an exclusion of signifiers necessary to make discourse possible at all. It can therefore only be grasped as a mobile surface which is constantly rearticulated and whose structures will appear in the organization of each utterance. Since each enunciation produces new articulations of signifiers, and since we only appear as meaningful subjects by way of signification, any notion of a fixed and defined personality can be maintained only in terms of a consistency of representations of the self. Following such a thesis there can be no longer even any question of our appearing as a consistency which is finally determined at the level of a closed range of representations known as symptoms. Lacan argues that our representations which appear in this way do not record a fixed, traumatic event sealed in the past, but make manifest, as Freud had recognized in the concept of *Nachträglichkeit*, or deferred action,[8] a present conflict articulated in relation to a history.

At this point Lacan's work takes up Jakobson's formulation of the operation of the two axes of language, the tropes metaphor and metonymy. He argues that our discourses are distributed between these two poles and that our combination of these tropes regulates the flow of signifying elements, and so poses the limits of what we can experience. What replaces the notion of a fixed identity from which intended meanings are delivered is the claim that the limits of subjectivity are set according to the range of possibilities which can be taken up in the system of language.

The application of psychoanalysis to literature, then, cannot follow the model of a biography of a writer's symptoms in the way that in its early days it *was* used, even by Freud himself.[9] Such a use retains the notion of a representation of discrete symptoms, and so merely substitutes for the classic relation of intending author to text a reformulated relation of unintending author to the same text. What Lacan's work has made possible is rather a radical recasting of this relation to language, examining how positions are produced or closed off in the act of speaking or writing. Limitations written into a text of course impose restrictions on positions available in reading, effectively delimiting possibilities of textual experience. In this way possibilities of meanings are determined at the formal level of the constitution of discourse.

This is not exclusively a formal matter, however. Our accession to language takes place at the level of sexuality in those constitutive experiences of separation from the breast, the faeces, and from any unequivocal possession of the phallus in the experience of sexual difference formalized as castration. Since these separations both set up the terms of difference necessary for the emergence of signification and also give birth to our experience of desire, any text will be organized also at the sexual level. At this level substantive and formal concerns will be enlaced. To debate a text is thus both to consider aspects of its formal constitution which establish positions available to a reader, and to give a related account of occupations in content which interrelate with this construction.

In offering such a description of the ways in which psychoanalysis may be called upon in the study of literature, it is immediately necessary to say that such a psychoanalysis has, of course, its own historical conditions of existence, and its current theoretical difficulties. Such a psychoanalysis cannot be appealed to as a complete or enclosed discipline, though neither can it be simply criticized for not being such. Its relevance consists in an ability to trace forms of human subjectivity to a historical causation, specifically to a division in language. This division, and the modalities of subjectivity it establishes, prompt at the level of discourse effects which in our culture are generally hidden and contained, and whose exposure is widely thought subversive of forms of personal identity and of existing social institutions. Manifestations of the unconscious accordingly take on such forms as hastily disguised slips, jokes and failures. In inaugurating a radical analysis of the production of subjectivity, Lacan's reworking of Freud can only have important repercussions on our notions of what is involved in literature and art, in science, in philosophy, and in politics.

It is specifically by working across certain texts by Freud that Lacan introduces his comments about the politics of Fascism in concluding remarks to his 1964 seminar. This seminar has been translated into English as *The Four Fundamental Concepts of Psycho-Analysis*.[10] To consider Lacan's argument here it is necessary very briefly to consider the positions Freud adopts in these papers.

Freud argued, in his 1921 paper 'Group Psychology and the Analysis of the Ego', that participation in forms of social collectivity can be considered by means of an examination of the particular constitution of individual subjects within the group in question. On these grounds Freud suggests that in forms of collective fascination—such as Fascism, as Lacan points out, even if Freud's local context is the Church, the Army, hypnosis and love—a common object is put in the place of our narcissistic infatuation with fabricated versions of ourselves, with our *ego ideal*.[11]

In commenting on anti-Semitism in the 1938 paper 'Moses and Monotheism' shortly before his death, Freud suggests that among the multiple determinants of anti-Jewish feeling are the following: that Jewish culture in principle refuses to accept (and so through our Saviour, the Son, be absolved for) the killing of the primal Father, God; that sacramental circumcision among Jews carries the trace of a primaeval castration which other races vehemently disavow; that Aryan races assert in their hostility towards the Jews their polytheistic resistance to a historically recent imposition of monotheism.[12]

Whereas it might be evident that these latter concerns relate to recurrent elements in Pound's theories (as will be demonstrated below), it may not be quite so clear how the structural description of collective fascination offered by the earlier Freud paper can assist in our understanding either of Pound, or of Fascism. Lacan's concern with this text serves to elucidate this importance, and in doing so redirects the ways in which the evident links suggested by the latter paper may be grasped.

The emphasis of Lacan's work has been to stress that sub-jectivity emerges in a symbolic field from which we are con-stituted by being cut out. In this field we are produced on the trace of a series of necessary lacks which we seek to occlude or recapture with an illusion of completeness and sufficiency. The means and extent of this occlusion generally orientate our pro-duction of symptoms, and the forms of our self-representation or identification. Lacan signifies this lack by what he calls the *objet petit a*, an eternally lost and unassimilable object, the lower case 'a' indicating that it is both other and absent. What is crucial about the *objet petit a* is that it refers to an irretrievably lost object. Even if partially encountered at the mother's breast, for example, it can never have been fully possessed. This eternally lacking object situates the subject in an unalterably lacking condition, rather than in a painful separation in weaning from a preceding condition of plenitudinous contentment.

In forms of collective fascination our establishment of a narcissistic image in the place of this lacking object closes off symbolic production, and endows us with a dissembling autonomy. Nevertheless the manifestations of the unconscious continually disclose the insufficiency of this disavowal, and in doing so reveal a continual yet unsatisfiable desire. In Fascism, Lacan argues, the uncontrollable desire established by our lacking relation to this symbolic field is constantly propitiated with sacrifice, in an effort to satisfy what appears its voracious appetite, namely its perma-nent and radical unassimilability within our represented images of ourselves as powerful and all-controlling beings. Thus restricted in our assumable attributes, we adopt in religious ceremonies and certain forms of mass politics various kinds of sacrament and sacrifice, to solicit well-being from a determinacy which is else-where and irreducibly Other.[13]

The theoretical framework of Lacan's arguments on this topic (even if his comments about Fascism in particular occupy little more than a page) offer the most developed available account of a psychical element in this phenomenon. What is significantly deficient about his account is its omission of any reference to historical determinants which, even if arguably amply demon-strated in available studies, nevertheless clearly contribute to the particular construction of subjects in given social formations. There is evidently still need, for example, of theorization of the relations that obtain between the role of the father in the nuclear family in given forms of social relations, and the symbolic function of the father (in Lacan's general, formal account, the Name-of-the-Father) to announce the symbolic field which irrupts into the narcissistically focused world of the infant. This join in the theory effectively closes off questions of the intermesh between social relations of production and the formal construction of subjectivity in relation to irreducible lack.[14]

The arguments which follow seek to show that Pound's writing constantly attempts to foreclose the possibility of lack, and to take upon itself assumed powers of control and authority which can only be conferred in exactly such a disavowal. Nevertheless, Pound's work itself, of any period, cannot be taken as in any way representative of a general class of Fascist discourse, even if certain of its recurrent themes typify concerns of other writings more usually associated with Fascism. To ascribe to Pound's work such a theoretical role would be to ignore historical specificity, and in particular to neglect literary considerations such as inherited genres and artistic movements which imposed definite limits and conditions on his work.

The arguments about Pound which follow, then, do not aspire towards a general aesthetic, nor a definitive critical evaluation of individual poems. The specificity of an individual history with definite configurations of personal circumstance and prevailing political conditions ensures that ways of reading Pound cannot be transposed by homologous relations into the form of a general literary methodology. What follows is a study of Pound and his particular discourses, not of the structures of language itself, nor of Fascism itself. No canons of literary success or failure will be offered, merely the affirmation that the very practices of writing Pound adopts work towards the securing of particular aesthetic and social objectives. To assess these it would be necessary to appeal to a given or unstated political position; no general, trans-historical, or apolitical assessment is possible.

My criticisms of Pound's own conceptualization of his activities (which will be frequent and extensive) need, however, to be considered in the context of an initial ascription to his work of a historical and contemporary importance. This follows from

Pound's ability and determination to challenge entrenched features of American society, and to introduce economic and political questions as immediate and central concerns of artistic expression. It might be said, too, that innovations made by Pound have also, despite themselves, contributed to substantial and desirable developments in literary writing: such developments, as we shall see, might be thought to spring from possible transgressions of the subjective positions the poet's writing constantly seeks to assign to its readership.

Whilst disclaiming any pursuit of critical evaluation, I will nevertheless argue that the forms of writing adopted by Pound are beset by problems as regards their realization of his theoretical prescriptions. Indeed, they cannot be held to vindicate those intentions unless in an extreme disavowal of properties of written discourse. This disavowal has, of course, been facilitated by Pound's own abandonment of the *Cantos*, which left the residual possibility of artistic unity and triumph if only the poet might have continued to live.

In opposition to this, I will argue that elements constantly repressed in Pound's writing surface to threaten the authority upon which his imperative crusade against obfuscation is based. The importance of the poet's project of a cultural redemption offered in the *Cantos* by means of a re-establishment of lost origins in a new world will, I suggest, be in consequence displaced. The rejection of such elegiac projects I feel to be a necessary preliminary to any significant development either in practices of writing or theories of culture.

Notes

1 R. Jakobson, 'Aphasia as a Linguistic Trope', in *Selected Writings*, 2 vols (Mouton, The Hague and Paris, 1971), pp. 229–38; and 'Two Aspects of Language and Two Types of Aphasic Disturbances', in *ibid*. pp. 239–59.

2 *Ibid*. p. 258.

3 Passim; for example, Jacques Lacan, *Écrits: A Selection*, translated by Alan Sheridan (Tavistock Publications, London, 1977), p. 147. In French, Jacques Lacan, *Écrits* (Seuil, Paris, 1966), p. 495. When referring to the writings of Lacan, I shall cite translations by Alan Sheridan as available, in order to preserve the continuity of the text. In order to facilitate reference to the original French, I shall also cite page numbers from the appropriate French editions. In cases where no published translation exists, I shall give

my own version, and quote the French in full in a footnote. To avoid extensive repetition, these two editions of Lacan's work will be referred to respectively as, *Écrits: A Selection*, and *Écrits* in all subsequent references.

4 *Écrits: A Selection*, p. 165; *Écrits*, pp. 516–17.

5 A fuller account of these aspects of Freudian theory has been given by Juliet Mitchell, in *Psychoanalysis and Feminism* (Penguin, Harmondsworth, 1974; reprinted 1976), pp. 5–119.

6 See Ferdinand de Saussure, *Cours de linguistique générale*, edited by Charles Bally and Albert Sechehaye (Payot, Paris, 1964), pp. 97–103; in English, *Course in General Linguistics*, edited Charles Bally and Albert Sechehaye, translated by Wade Baskin (New York, Toronto and London, 1960), pp. 65–70.

7 *Écrits: A Selection*, p. 284; *Écrits*, p. 688.

8 All references to works by Freud are to *The Standard Edition of the Complete Psychological Works of Sigmund Freud*, edited and translated by James Strachey, in collaboration with Anna Freud, and assisted by Alix Strachey and Alan Tyson, 24 vols (Hogarth Press, London, 1953). Discussion by Freud of *Nachträglichkeit* occurs in a long footnote in 'Further Remarks on the Neuro-psychoses of Defence (1896)', *Standard Edition* vol. III, p. 167n. This edition is referred to hereafter as *Standard Edition*.

9 See, for example, Freud's suggestions in 'Creative Writers and Day Dreaming', *Standard Edition*, vol. IX, or in 'Delusions and Dreams in Jensen's *Gradiva*', *ibid*.; Freud's attention to other arts follows largely the same pattern. See 'Leonardo da Vinci and a Memory of his Childhood', *ibid*. vol. XI, or 'The Moses of Michelangelo', *ibid*. vol. XIII.

10 Jacques Lacan, *The Four Fundamental Concepts of Psycho-Analysis*, translated by Alan Sheridan (Hogarth Press and the Institute of Psycho-Analysis, 1977); in French, *Le Séminaire XI* (Seuil, Paris, 1973). These editions are abbreviated hereafter to *Four Fundamental Concepts*, and *Le Séminaire XI* respectively.

11 *Standard Edition*, vol. XVIII, especially pp. 105–16.

12 *Standard Edition*, vol. XXIII, pp. 90–2.

13 Lacan's distinction between 'other' and 'Other' is made more difficult by the analyst's own diachronic movement from one to the other. The lower case 'other' refers to what is reflected of the subject's own form in objects, and can be encountered as the ego, the imaginary image, or the specular image. The upper case 'Other', as here, refers to what is radically opposed to the subject, namely the locus of signifiers, the symbolic field in which, as subject, it is articulated.

14 It might be remonstrated that Wilhelm Reich attempted such an interrelation in his *The Mass Psychology of Fascism*, translated by Theodore P. Wolfe (Orgone Institute Press, third edition, New York, 1946). Reich's arguments, however, merely suggest that the father in the family is a reflection of the industrial boss, and so prepares within the context of the nuclear family suitable attitudes towards labour. In consequence, infantile development is thought to be determined finally at the level of social oppression, mediated by behavioural suppression in the family. The Oedipus complex is thus made simply a reflection of mode of production, and the whole question of the unconscious by-passed. Such an account is further unable to offer any explanation of the emergence and insinuation of Fascism within an already functioning social mechanism with no theoretically specified requirement for or means of development or supercession. See, especially, pp. 45–9.

Chapter Two

Early writing: the self of the poetry

THE first collection of Pound's poems carries the title *Personae*, and is remembered by the poet in the essay 'Vorticism' as a casting-off of complete masks of the self in each poem.[1] This appears to be a movement away from any simple disclosure of personal experience. Although this multiplication of selves explicitly serves the design of a quest for ' "sincere self expression" ',[2] and so is situated at least in intention within a search for a true or essential self, nevertheless one remarkable feature of Pound's poetic writing —at least until the composition of the *Pisan Cantos*—is its virtual exclusion of an avowedly confessional first person. It has accordingly become a commonplace of Pound criticism that this early collection contains multiple images of selfhood, or more exactly that its poems are framed as revelations of experience.

That experience is not, however, aligned explicitly with the writer's own self, but bespeaks dramatically constructed selves who are on occasion named. As if to reinforce this referentiality to specific speech acts, a subservience of discourse to a world of empirical evidence is often announced, the emphasis of demonstratives such as 'thus' in 'And thus in Ninevah', or 'Guido invites You Thus'.[3] In 'Cino' and 'Na Audiart',[4] too, prefatory inscriptions locate the discourses which follow in determinate historical moments. The delimitation constrains the terrain of the poems' intelligibility to the context of a world extrinsic to language itself. In alluding to particular speech acts in given historical instances, and in presenting these in sets of consistent linguistic practices as stylistic imitations, the poems of *Personae* frequently construct enclosed ideological spaces which may be understood as consistent representations of the world. Although casting these off as merely masks of the true self, the poet nevertheless both animates these representations, and fixes them in a kind of

16

proprietary control, becoming the supporting condition of their existence. Pound's efforts at mastering this creation of ideological spaces constitutes a quest for control over the qualities of language which confer social position. This is certainly one element of the assertion, in the essay 'The Serious Artist', that ' "Good writing" is perfect control',[5] even if another sense of that affirmation concerns the stylistic level of purely technical accomplishments of versification.

This interest in the construction of social positions in language is further part of an occupation with the negotiation of a social position for language—what can be seen in terms of Pound's biography as a dismay with the condition of literature and of the writer in what he calls in *Hugh Selwyn Mauberley* a 'half savage country'[6]—and a search for a position for himself in sociality. When the early poems constantly return to the troubadour social milieu, where according to Pound in the essay, 'Troubadours—Their Sorts and Conditions' writing occupied a position of 'social prestige', at least one way of looking at this is as a concern for the establishment of professional identity.[7] In the world of the troubadours the execution of writing could command, as in the poem 'The Eyes', the deployment of a large and organized workforce.[8] In 'Marvoil' the importance of poetry to the intercourse of the wealthy is suggested in its adoption as a unit of currency, Arnaut in this poem exchanging a poem for a lady's kiss:

> As for will and testament I leave none,
> Save this: 'Vers and canzone to the Countess of Beziers
>
> In return for the first kiss she gave me.

He further considers his own professional engagement in terms of contractual duration:

> The Vicomte of Beziers's not such a bad lot.
> I made rimes to his lady this three year:
> Vers and canzone . . .

His work is specifically on behalf of another, and addressed to still another:

> A-jumbling o' figures for Maître Jacques Polin.[9]

Clearly at one level the solicited movement from text to external world links the text with a given mode of social organization in which the poet has a prominent position, and Pound's reconstruction of these poems implicitly invokes a homologous literary condition. But inasmuch as these depictions of a self are being cast off, aspects of a self not to be disclosed *in propria persona* as it were, it is evidently not at this level that the intervention of the self is to be found. Rather that intervention is traceable to the very practice of fixing images of the self or of other selves, to the closure which appears to punctuate intelligibility in a series of identifications of seemingly coherent subjects. In this act of representation these subjects are precluded from any further alteration, and pinned in a world of identity confirmed only in the assumption of the power of representation and the truth of appearance.

Whilst the *Personae* collection might be thought to excise explicit mention of the self, and so to diffract the tradition of confessional complaint into a multiplicity of removes and identifications, nevertheless that subjective self is not finally expunged, but is only disguised. The self persists in its appropriation of the capacity of representation, its manufacture of a condition of writing in which language is considered secondary to but yet coincidental with experience, and in which the world is delivered up for discrete and finished meanings.

If in *Personae* the self can be seen to fade only at the level of explicit thematic proclamation and to function, though veiled, as the articulating sponsor of discourse, the first efflorescence of Pound's innovative practice in the poetics of Imagism undertakes a much more fundamental exclusion of the subject from the field of language. In this poetics the subjective process is considered to be extinguished before the objective operations of a world which engenders emotional responses from concrete experience. This concept of a receptivity to the immanent forms of a world beyond individual experience founds both the epistemological basis of the ideogrammic method of much of the later writing, and also the science of poetry promulgated in the essay 'The Serious Artist', roughly contemporaneous with the inaugurative phase of Imagism.[10] In order to approach either of these practices it is necessary first to consider Pound's establishment in this essay of certain methodological precepts.

In 'The Serious Artist' poetry is likened to a scientific discipline in its aspiring accuracy to empirical data, for poetry 'lasting and unassailable data regarding the nature of man, of immaterial man, of man considered as a thinking and sentient creature.'[11] Of this nature, Pound affirms:

From the arts we learn that man is whimsical, that one man differs from another. That men differ among themselves as leaves upon trees differ. They do not resemble each other as do buttons cut by machine.[12]

Nevertheless, observations made about the immaterial nature of man, the root which nourishes these heterogeneous leaves, can recommend modes of social behaviour and organization:

As our treatment of man must be determined by our knowledge or conception of what man is, the arts provide data for ethics.[13]

It is this derivation of principles from generalized observations which in the later essay, 'How to Read' will require of artists that they preserve the 'solidity and validity' of words for use by 'governor and legislator'.[14] Whilst Pound here regards the human species as differing one from another, the individual is considered to have a static and definable existence (the emphasis of 'what man is'). It is by application to this fixed identity that the variations become, to specify the prime means of their registration, visible. Precision to the nature of man in this light becomes a faithfulness to an observed condition of things, and produces the kind of typological representability which characterizes the *Personae* collection.

Whereas art is the source of ethics and law, its own existence is of a natural rather than a cultural order:

Now art never asks anybody to do anything, or to think anything, or to be anything. It exists as the trees exist, you can admire, you can sit in the shade, you can pick bananas, you can cut firewood, you can do as you jolly well please.[15]

This allegedly natural existence for art is effectively a claim of natural auspices for a tendency of extreme conservation, which seeks to maintain the essential identity of things by preserving the way they appear. The differing innate essences of human

beings which separate them from buttons are held to a genesis
in an unspecified immateriality which claims parenthetical articulation to 'man considered as a thinking and sentient creature'
in the above quotation. Empirically attestable inequalities among
humankind may in consequence be endorsed as features of nature.

This allegedly scientific programme for poetry is further
returned to the domain of classic subjectivity, in its sense of differing apprehensions sustained and valued by differing subjects, by
reliance upon a truthfulness to the 'inner nature and conditions
of man' which can only be ascertained in acts of individual perception.[16] Such a reliance is encountered in Pound's 'ultimate
attainments of poesy' in a letter to William Carlos Williams of
October 1908. Of these attainments the first among others is, 'To
paint the thing as I see it'.[17] Difficulties emerge for this understanding of truth in the evident possibility of a plurality of truths
in a state of contradiction, and Pound's efforts to resolve these fall
back upon a final verification as inner or personal truths which,
so long as that guaranteeing self is preserved, remain unshakeable :

If an artist falsifies his report as to the nature of man, as to his own
nature, as to the nature of his ideal of the perfect, as to the nature
of his ideal of this, that, or the other, of god, if god exist, of the life
force, of the nature of good and evil, if good and evil exist, of the
force with which he believes or disbelieves this, that or the other, of
the degree in which he suffers or is made glad . . . then that artist
lies.[18]

The cadential force of this last clause, anticipatory of the condemnatory assurance of much of the later essay writing, is pre-
pared in a gradual transition from areas of extreme speculation
whose final truthfulness is dissipated in contingent conditional
clauses, towards the domain of feeling over which, in this general
epistemological framework, the subject has privileged knowledge.
The paradox of a lie as to one's own nature when that nature
is only to be discerned by self-observation is passed without
examination. The truth of art becomes its accurate representation
of the artist's perceptions at any artistically disposed moment :

Purely and simply . . . good art can NOT be immoral. By good art I
mean the art that bears true witness, I mean the art that is most precise.
You can be wholly precise in representing a vagueness. You can be

wholly a liar in pretending that the particular vagueness was precise in its outline.[19]

Precision, the central aspiration of Pound's later writing and a founding condition of Imagism, is given to lie in the accuracy with which any state of mind can be transcribed to paper. Beauty is to be ascertained, and held distinct from imitation, by a similar empirical process:

I am not now speaking of shams. I mean beauty, not slither, not sentimentalizing about beauty, not telling people that beauty is the proper and respectable thing. I mean beauty. You don't argue about an April wind, you feel bucked up when you meet it. You feel bucked up when you come on a swift moving thought in Plato or on a fine line in a statue.[20]

Not only is the proper condition of beauty here held to be unproblematically bound to its name ('I mean beauty'), but the generalizing of subjective impression into a world of reified fact is traced in the shift from this 'I' of 'I mean' to the general 'you' of 'You don't argue'.

Pound's general epistemology, then, is an empiricist one, relying upon deliberations on a world of objects and events by a subject assumed to have an already given set of faculties, including experience and judgement. These facilities themselves lie outside the domain of investigation of the epistemology, and must be relied upon as prior affirmations, or else assumed to be given by a superior form of knowledge which cannot itself be investigated. This restriction on the scope of possible investigation has the important consequence that the empiricist subject is never placed in question, but is taken to exist outside the totality of what can be tested, complete and assured in its assessments of what constitutes knowledge.[21] The identity of the Poundian subject is not the traditional poetic self expressive of personal emotion, but rather the space of these assumed capacities which situate the subject distinct from the world and able to effect correspondences and judgements according to an assumption of discriminatory powers.

Language is relegated in this conception to a position of imitation or representation, aspiring to an accuracy to the real world facing the subject. Accordingly, Pound praises 'clarity' in

writing, and enthuses about the qualities of prose in verse, which
are held to be a directness achieved in transcribing objects and
events in the world into linguistic reconstructions. In the essay
'The Prose Tradition in Verse' Pound exalts Ford Madox Hueffer
for exactly this quality of directness, 'his insistence upon clarity
and precision, upon the prose tradition; in brief, upon efficient
writing—even in verse.'[22] Efficiency here is a measure of the convergence of language and reality, and an aspiration towards their
complete congruence. In an essay on Joyce in *The Future*, in
1918, Pound endeavours to substantiate this claim for realism,
now in relation to the novel, by quoting in its entirety the preface
by the brothers Goncourt to *Germinie Lacerteux*, claiming that
this is 'the whole case for realism'.[23] In another essay, 'Ulysses'
Pound argues that the Cyclops episode of that work is 'a measuring of the difference between reality and reality as it is represented in various lofty forms of expression.'[24] Not only does
this claim presuppose a reality preceding linguistic formulation,
from which 'lofty' expression diverges by infusing a surplus,
elevating decoration, but is also an appeal to a neutral discourse
directly imitative of the world.[25]

The disparity between 'lofty' forms of expression and the
transparent discourse of reality itself prompts in Pound's investigations a search for a prime language of total efficiency. His
prognosis for the correction of what he considers the excesses
and shortcomings of poetry contemporaneous to his own early
work accordingly becomes a desire for the elimination of those
aspects of language which reveal or even indulge the fact of its
own plasticity, or of its own material production. To be stressed
instead are those elements of language which appear to offer up
meanings immediately, and of themselves:

As to Twentieth century poetry, and the poetry which I expect to see
written during the next decade or so, it will, I think, move against
poppy-cock, it will be harder and saner, it will be what Mr. Hewlett
calls 'nearer the bone'. It will be as much like granite as it can be, its
force will lie in its truth, its interpretative power (of course, poetic
force always does rest there); I mean it will not try to seem forcible
by rhetorical din, and luxurious riot. We will have fewer painted
adjectives impeding the shock and stroke of it. At least for myself,
I want it so, austere, direct, free from emotional slither.[26]

Not only are certain kinds of discourse deprecated in this passage in such formulations as 'poppy-cock' and 'luxurious riot' for their alleged periphrasis of reality, but truth and interpretative power are synonymized in what is an assertion of a singularity of interpretation, and the emergence of a realm of the factual, real, or true. Signification for Pound at this time is characterized as a practice in which signifiers with most 'interpretative power'—and hence most poetic force—are those which come closest to a pre-existent truth, or signified.

It is in this context of a truth pre-existing language as a primary signified, a truth revealed to the subject who then expresses it in language, that the intended poetics of Imagism lie. Indeed, this commitment to a homogeneous subject outside language and able to confer meanings upon it is implied in Imagism's three tenets, described in Pound's essay, 'A Retrospect', and elsewhere by Aldington and Flint.[27]

Pound's formulation of the first Imagist tenet concerns 'the direct "treatment" of the thing', where an act of treatment is one conducted upon an already existing body. In this way, the tenet can be seen to address itself to a condition of language in which the work entailed in signification, as the subject's coming into a position where the aspects of the sign appear coincidentally, is obliterated in the notion of directness or immediacy. This obliteration attempts to situate the subject outside language, which can then be considered an expressive instrument serving to transmit meanings which are already established and possessed, rather than being produced exclusively in discursive organization. The attachment of language to pre-existing thought is further considered in Imagist poetics to be reversible, such that given a linguistic unit, an anterior concept may be ineluctably deduced. Pound's exhortation to avoid 'abstractions' because they 'dull' the image, and his bestowal of priority upon the 'concrete' affirms that the naming of the object is to be the sufficient symbol of the experience.[28]

The second clause of the Imagist canon, too, 'to use absolutely no word that does not contribute to the presentation'[29] asserts the prior existence of the signified to the signifier, even though its first intended aim appears to have been the correction of what Pound calls in *Gaudier-Brzeska: A Memoir*, 'mushy technique'. This technique is held to produce 'dull and interminable

B

effusions'.[30] Nevertheless, quite apart from this intervention in literary history, the affirmation of inactivity of language in a text, not at the level of composition where words may yet be changed for others thought to be more suitable to conduct intended meanings but at the level of effectivity once written, returns language to intention and to the assumption of pre-existent meanings. If language itself produces meanings rather than being instrumental of intended meanings, then every element of a text is actively determining, whether its significations conform to authorial intention or not.

Finally, the third Imagist directive, 'as regarding rhythm: to compose in the sequence of the musical phrase, not in sequence of the metronome',[31] argues further the dependence of language upon the sponsorship of a speaker in its exhortation to reflect rhythmically the very patterns of human enunciation. The virtue of Pound's 'musical phrase' is its fidelity to the emotionally expressive intonations of a speaker, and indeed Pound stresses this capacity of rhythm to convey emotion in his formulation of 'absolute rhythm', where only one rhythm is considered able to carry a particular emotion.[32] But the prevalent Imagist practice of reconstructing rhythms from classical Greek poems immediately disrupts this notion of rhythmic expressivity in destroying the specificity of the relation between the plastic material of a particular language and intonation. This appropriates the musicality of one language to convey the meanings of another, as if the emotionally conductive qualities of rhythm are realized exclusively in a privileged relation between intonation and meaning. In this translingual exercise the force of the 'phrase' as constitutive part of a discourse is lost, and rhythmic composition falls back simply upon a new and different metronome, in so far as cadential emphases are clearly influenced by lexical and syntactic constraints in any given language. They cannot be interchanged from language to language with anything more than a musical connection.

There are further features of Imagism which have an important place in the establishing of the writing practices which will inform Pound's later composition of the *Cantos*, and to consider these it is necessary to turn to other writings by Pound at this time. The ascription of the term 'laconic speech' to the work of the Imagists, initially applied to a piece by H. D. in a letter by Pound covering some of her work sent to Harriet Monroe,[33] endorses Pound's own contemporaneous attention to the 'haiku' or 'hokku' form as being emblematic of concision. Features of experiments with this form have an enduring influence upon Pound's later work. The anecdotally recorded composition of 'In a Station of the Metro' announces that not only is the 'direct treatment of the "thing" ' a procedure which is held to strip the originary experiential stimulus of any surplus linguistic effects, but operates also as condensation of that sensation to its smallest possible form.[34] From the minimal linguistic unit the reader is to constitute the sensation once more by a reversal of the reduction process, and so recover the nexus of impressions which the selection of the image seeks to express. The efficacy of the 'hokku' image can be seen to rely upon a presumed logic which governs both the reduction and the extrapolation processes so that they are as far as possible identical.

Yet Pound recognizes in *Gaudier-Brzeska* the ineffectuality of this process in the comment, 'I dare say it is meaningless unless one has drifted into a certain vein of thought', here conceding that the communicative precision of the image depends upon an extra-lingual sympathy in the reader rather than upon any equation taking place in the language itself.[35] Nevertheless, he elsewhere asserts an importance for this extrapolation process from a linguistic ellipsis. In the *ABC of Reading*, for example, he observes, and separates from the typographical lay-out of the text as if to emphasize the observation, that 'Dichten=condensare', and explains that 'Dichten' is the German verb corresponding to the noun 'Dichtung' meaning poetry.[36] Poetry is to be condensation, and the strength of the Imagist practice is to lie in its compression. Indeed, Pound repeats this equation between 'Dichten' and 'condensare' in the later work *A Visiting Card*, linking it there to a proposed reform of the universities 'by the infusion of certain known facts condensable into a few pages'.[37] And in the same work he recalls a saying of T. E. Hulme that, ' "All a man ever *thought* would go onto a half sheet of notepaper. The rest is application and elaboration" '.[38]

In the early writing this recovery of wider meanings from minimal evidence is considered to be a legitimate scientific procedure, and is formalized as such in the second part of the essay, 'I Gather the Limbs of Osiris':

I mean, merely, a method not of common practice, a method not yet clearly or consciously formulated, a method which has been intermittently used by all good scholars since the beginning of scholarship, the method of the Luminous Detail, a method most vigorously hostile to the prevailing mode of today—that is, the method of multitudinous detail, and to the method of yesterday, the method of sentiment and generalization. The latter is too inexact and the former too cumbersome to be of much use to the normal man wishing to live mentally active.[39]

This method consists in certain 'facts' or signs which 'give one a sudden insight into circumjacent conditions, into their causes, their effects, into sequence and law.' Whilst 'these facts are hard to find', once found they are 'swift and easy of transmission. They govern knowledge as the switchboard governs an electric circuit.' The confidence with which Pound introduces this method with the phrase, 'I mean, merely, . . .' is reflected in the assurance of its presumption to invade adjacent areas, and to determine their 'law'. This 'law' is a simultaneous defining and confining, and is thought to be capable of establishment not by examining the specific area itself, but by looking at an area to which this area of application is 'circumjacent'. This practice is a misunderstanding of the legitimate boundaries of substitution or metaphor, since to substitute generalities for specifics in this way mistakes its proper condition as synecdoche and consequently metonymy. The Luminous Detail and the 'hokku' are early instances of this fundamental misunderstanding by Pound of the functioning of these relations, which, as the two poles of language recognized by Jakobson as controlling the activity of language, have important consequences upon the writing of the *Cantos*, as we shall see below.[40]

Another feature of the elliptical construction of the 'hokku' poems needs to be considered here. Alongside their compression, these poems are remarkable for their extreme simplification of the rhetoric of an articulating syntax, a simplification clearly contributory to the 'direct treatment of the "thing"'. If name and thing are indissolubly linked, then the thing is most directly revealed by the unadorned invocation of its name. The poem 'In a Station of the Metro', for example, is composed of two parallel syntactic units which are juxtaposed paratactically, and is to this extent representative of several of Pound's other 'hokku' studies, notably 'April' and 'Gentildonna'. It appears on the page:

> The apparition of these faces in the crowd;
> Petals on a wet, black bough.[41]

The two lines do not relate to one another by an appeal to a voice outside the text to articulate them, but by an associative play of the kind which links 'apparition' to 'black' by way of their common allusion to death, or which opposes pastoral and urban in the appearance of 'petals' in the setting of a 'Metro' station. The two lines are further related not by a syntax which binds them together but by grammatical parallelism, as plural nouns dependent upon a singular noun by a preposition of place.

The associative freeplay which this invites ('apparition' for example is still a noun from the verb 'to appear', if it is also allusive to death) is not for Imagism a liberation from the exigencies of fixed meaning, but the very token by which language can reflect the world objectively, in that syntax is considered as a mediating voice by which the primal condition of language as the correspondence of word and thing becomes merely subjective. The dissolution of syntactic articulation undertakes to restore this first condition of language by presenting the unified sign as such. Signs may then be juxtaposed paratactically to create constellations of contiguous signification, and hence fabrications of objective meaning. Poetic sensibility is considered to be passive to 'the precise instant when a thing outward and objective transforms itself, or darts into a thing inward and subjective'.[42] Collocation of images creates the emotional response, although individually these images simply imitate the objective world.

Certain of these important features of Imagism are maintained and extended in Pound's next allegiance, to the largely Wyndham Lewis dominated doctrine of Vorticism, in which Pound's main role appears to have been to contribute the name, from one of his *Osiris* series of 1912, as well as certain theoretical speculations added late in the preparation of the first of the two issues of *Blast*.[43] Whilst both issues of this magazine contain poems by Pound, it is nevertheless difficult to speak of a specifically Vorticist poetic, since the force of these poems derives largely from the

energy of their vituperation. They consequently owe little to
Vorticist theory beyond its commitment to polemic and social
indictment. Any consideration of the Vortex in particular regard
to poetry becomes inevitably confused with Imagism, in that
Pound's explanation of Vorticism proposes precisely the continued practice of the doctrine of the image. Indeed in the first
issue of *Blast* the poetic Vortex is described simply as 'the
IMAGE'.[44]

If the importance of Vorticism can in this way be seen not
to reside in poetic practice, its infusion of a theory of contradictory energies reconciled in a central stasis none the less informs
Pound's philosophical speculations of this period, and bears
directly both upon the later readings of the work of Ernest
Fenollosa and upon the composition of the *Cantos*. The article,
'Our Vortex', delivered in the first issue of *Blast*, is itself composed of paradoxes and contradictions:

Our Vortex desires the immobile rythm of its swiftness.

And,

The Vorticist is at his maximum point of energy when stillest.

And,

Our Vortex is white and abstract with its red-hot swiftness.[45]

The Vortex pattern of energies reconciles these contradictions in
a condition of static tension. The Vortex is a cluster of energies,
'from which, and through which, and into which, ideas are constantly rushing',[46] and finds its expression in images such as the
whirlpool or the knot. It is illustrated by Lewis five times in the
first issue of *Blast* as a graphic representing a cone mounted on
a wire running through its longitudinal axis.[47]

The existence of this wire, however, indicates that the Vortex
is not a field of endlessly transformable relations, such as the
suggestion 'rushing' implies, but is rather a pattern defined by
and convergent upon a central point. This point, which is considered to incorporate most energy whilst being stillest, is postulated as a node attestable in the natural world in the form of

the effect of a magnet upon iron filings, or the central suction of a whirlpool. Deducing from this a notion of human culture as consonant with or even mimetic of the natural world, the Vortex is exalted by Pound, for example in the essay 'The Renaissance' of 1914—the year of *Blast*—as a desirable cultural phenomenon.[48]

The Vortex pattern of energies repeats itself in many areas of Pound's thought in the form of a qualitative distillation, the best being whatever gravitates to the centre. Pound's arrival in England is specifically a move to conquer London, which lodges the 'Great English Vortex' of *Blast* magazine.[49] In 'a rather longish article . . . announcing the College of Arts' described in a letter to Harriet Shaw Weaver in October 1914, Pound claims that, 'London is the capital of the world', and that ' "Art is a matter of capitals" '.[50] In 1913 he had likened London to Rome as 'a vortex, drawing strength from the peripheries',[51] and in the essay 'The Renaissance' explains exile from America in terms of America having 'as yet no capital'.[52] The postulation of a superior centre nourished by its 'peripheries' is simultaneously a relative dismissal of those peripheries, and Pound alludes to a 'natural spreading ripple that moves from the civilized Mediterranean centre out through the half-civilized and into the barbarous peoples'.[53] Similarly, 'Mary Queen of Scots . . . held but a barbarous, or rather a drivelling and idiotic and superficial travesty of the Italian culture as it had been before the débâcle of 1527.'[54] The drive towards a centralized culture contributes to the elitism of Pound's article for the second issue of *Blast* in which he rejects and derides 'homo canis'.[55] In the essay, 'How to Read' this elitism finds its counterpart to derision in praise for 'the men who tried to civilize these shaggy and uncouth marginalians.'[56]

Induction from outer zones of the Vortex into its core predicates that these circumambient energies are all disposed around a primary presence which articulates them and resolves their contradictions. In his memoir for *Gaudier-Brzeska* Pound calls this centre, 'THE POINT ONE AND INDIVISIBLE' and describes it as 'ABSOLUTE', a 'VORTEX of FECUNDITY', capitalizing these formulations in the text. Later in the same work, the structure of a circle is defined as 'the universal, existing in perfection, in freedom from space and time',[57] and in *Blast*, the Vortex 'plunges to the heart of the Present'.[58] The first clause of one of the Vorticist manifestos is, 'Beyond Action and Reaction

we would establish ourselves', a desire that energies should collapse into a central essence rather than engage in any further
permutation.[59]

Instead the Vortex operates to reclaim forces from any process
of increasing eccentricity to an originary presence which is necessarily posited as at the centre of but at the same time outside and
transcending the interacting energies. This is clearly the case
both in the natural models cited by the Vorticists (the iron filings
only form a pattern when confronted with the power of the
magnet, and the whirlpool is fixed by external geological determinants) and in the model of the axial cone drawn by Lewis,
which is only symmetrical around the particular axis illustrated
by the wire. The authority of the Vorticist patterns is only
achieved in a systematicity which depends upon application to
an exterior for its support. It cannot be analysed by examination
of the model alone except if that exterior agency is previously
accepted by an initial affirmative act, or *fiat*.

In a paper delivered to an international symposium at the
Johns Hopkins Humanities Centre, Baltimore, in 1966, and
written up in *The Structuralist Controversy*, Jacques Derrida has
situated this conception of a structure focused on an originary
centre in the context of metaphysics, arguing that in general the
history of Western metaphysics has been the substitution of centre
for centre, as essence, substance, subject, and so on.[60] This centre
is involved in the paradox of being both that point at which the
substitution or transformation of elements is no longer possible
and so an internal point of focus, and yet simultaneously in itself
not conforming to that structurality, being outside the structure as
a node of transcendence. For Derrida a decisive moment has come
in the history of knowledge in the discovery of language, which
in being constituted by Saussure as a set of absences without any
presence or centre forestalls the possibility of any continuing
assumption of transcendental signifieds such as are evidently
operating in the history of metaphysics. It is clearly this latter
assumption which sustains Pound's promulgation of the Vortex.
But Derrida points out that since the prevailing form of that
supportive centre is in the present day the category of the Cartesian
subject of experience, any realization of language must involve,
at least in part, a questioning of the assured powers of that subject.

The suggestion of the possibility of a personal Vortex, exemplified in the titles of sections of *Blast* such as 'Vortex, Pound', and 'Vortex, Gaudier-Brzeska',[61] is a claim that the opposing energies of human beings are reconciled in a still centre, and is to this extent a reaffirmation of the coherence of the subject. The space of the homogeneous subject is endowed with power to control contradiction, such that its discourses can be what are called in *Gaudier-Brzeska*, 'lords over fact'. These discourses are 'the thrones and dominations that rule over form and recurrence. And in like manner are great works of art lords over fact, over race-long recurrent moods, and over tomorrow.'[62]

The foregoing has argued that Pound's early writing practices are organized around the assumed supporting effect of a subject. Yet the operation of this endorsing capability can nevertheless be seen to be disturbed in certain moments when the instrumentality of language functions with a complexity in excess of the writer's presumed powers. This excess agency of language engenders the possible multiplication of meanings which has made Pound's poetry an object of such difficulty for a criticism concerned to trace particular and definable meanings in the various texts.

Such a surplus agency has already been directly encountered above in an ambiguity attached to the 'thus' of referentiality to a world extrinsic to the language of the text in certain poems of *Personae*.[63] This 'thus' clearly also alludes to the constitutive language of the poems, and so to its own existence as the product of an enunciation. It is a 'thus' in whose very enunciation attention is drawn to the words which are being enounced. The ambiguity of the 'thus' undermines its function of establishing a contextual referentiality for dramatic monologues by posing the question of language itself which has to be ignored in order to ensure communicative instrumentality. But even in this radical protest of the 'thus' it is to some extent absorbed within the framework of the *Personae* once more, as a reference to the language of stylistic imitation central to this early enterprise. Indeed, a profit is sought from allusions to the constitutive matter of language in the poem 'The Return', where the return addressed in the title—that of the Classical poets, 'Gods of the winged shoe'—is inscribed in the course of the poem as a series of allusions to metrics, the 'slow feet', the 'tentative/Movements', the 'uncertain/Wavering', and the 'trace of air'.[64]

In *Hugh Selwyn Mauberley* this rupture of definite meanings by the operations of language beyond the control of the writer becomes more evident. In at least one section of the poem, the third section of the 1919 sequence, a break of meaning occurs which is created precisely by the adoption of paratactic juxta-position in preference to syntax, despite the fact that Pound remembers the poem, in his 1932 essay, 'Harold Monro', as a 'remedy' to the 'general floppiness' of *vers libre*, and a return to 'rhyme and regular strophes'.[65] This section of the poem fore-grounds and explores the process of change occurring through time, a change represented as chronologically disparate but juxta-posed images. The third strophe proposes, and then immediately discountenances the dialectic of this process:

> All things are a flowing,
> Sage Heracleitus says;
> But a tawdry cheapness
> Shall outlast our days.[66]

A retraction of dialectical transformation is effected here in the rhetorical and cadential vigour which invests its renunciation. The displacement of one element irreversibly by another also informs all until the last strophe, and is contained in verbal forms such as 'outlast', ' "replaces" ', 'supplants', 'follows', 'made way for', 'casts out', 'defects', and 'not for us . . . we have'.

Accompanying this understanding of change as irretrievable displacement is an element of nostalgia, a sense of loss. In the elegiac ode for 'E. P.', the first section of the 1919 sequence, the aim of maintaining the sublime 'in the old sense' is only 'wrong' in its incompatibility with present circumstances:

> Wrong from the start—
>
> No, hardly, but seeing he had been born
> In a half savage country, out of date.[67]

Here the fundamental correctness of conservation is emphasized

in the metrical stress accorded to 'No, hardly . . .' by its position
at the beginning of a line and of a strophe.

The final poem of this sequence, the italicized 'Envoi', reproaches the process of change and exhorts the preservation of
'Beauty' which is alone in successful resistance to the consuming
passage of time.[68] 'Change' is accused of destruction in a discourse
which has already exalted 'longevity' ('And build her glories in
their longevity'). Its agency is considered exclusively in its face
of extinguishing energy, and in this lament for temporal mutability that function of change also inscribed in the word 'tran-
sience', as a passage through to something else which has been
formalized as dialectics, is neglected. 'Envoi' carries this conservatism even to its last line, 'save Beauty alone', where the
archaic sense of 'save' as 'except' embraces another 'save', that of
desperate preservation. Similarly, in the earlier section, 'Siena mi
fe; Disfecemi Maremma', preservation through pickling in the
first line allows the insurgence of the participle 'perfecting' in the
second.[69] In this way the poem establishes a literary retrospect
delivered at the level of its content in a series of epigrams and
yet refuses the possibility of fluid movement which might trans-
form these conditions. The energy of 'Envoi' is one of vain
resistance. Its proposals of future practice are constructed in
'I would' verbal forms which predicate, within the archaic currency of the poem, a set of real wishes, but within English contemporary to the poem's composition, by a mutation of verbal
forms, a set of possible but obstructed wishes.

In the last strophe of the third section of the 1919 sequence
the kinds of enclosure enjoined by these features of writing
are radically subverted. This strophe is not articulated by the
verbally defining relation which characterizes all the preceding
strophes :

> O bright Apollo,
> τίν᾽ ἄνδρα, τίν ἥρωα. τινα θεόν
> What god, man, or hero
> Shall I place a tin wreath upon![70]

From the repeated structure of the earlier strophes it is possible

to read this as a further cultural displacement, and indeed it has
frequently been read this way. A devaluative change is thought
to exist in the parallel which compares the line of Greek (for
which the Loeb edition gives, 'What god, what hero, aye, and
what man shall we loudly praise') and the last two lines which
roughly translate the Greek and rhyme with it.[71] The 'tin wreath'
may be taken to connote little value because of a cultural assignation to that metal of an unsuitability for making wreaths and
its relatively low place on an agreed hierarchy of metallic value.
But the devaluative comparison is only made possible by an
address to a further body of social semiotics, since the opposition
of 'tin' and the line of Greek can only be sustained in an accrued
social status afforded to what is Greek. The poem invokes a
predetermined social status for the quotation in order to articulate
the comparison, and yet at the same time laments precisely an
opposite condition, the abandonment of the proper social esteem
for Greek culture.

The dissolution of the defining constraints of the verb form
which structure earlier strophes offers a plurality of positions for
the reader to assume relative to the juxtaposition. This not only
deconstructs any simple monological effectivity for the strophe,
but, in reinstating language as something material which has to
be worked to be read, brings attention to the purely formal
assonance of 'τίν' and 'tin'. The emergence of an articulation
which has to take place in the act of reading throws into question
any possibility of an easy access by language to a world of
finalized meanings.

The risk run in *Hugh Selwyn Mauberley* is that the possible
relations opened in this counterpoint cut across the kinds of
domination over meaning sought by the writer to make of the
poem a vehicle for certain apprehensions. It is not, then, as it
has been for much Pound criticism, a question of discovering
where the self can find a place in the discourses of the poem, but
of how the self can only find a place by restraining the intrinsic
possibilities of the language of its own discourses which continually seek to escape that suppression.

The question of the self finding a place in language only by
closing off linguistic possibilities is in effect posed in reverse
in *Homage to Sextus Propertius*. A wide range of diverse discourses are set up in mutual contradiction, and none appears to

have any special privilege for defining the world. The transmissive effectuality of language is only saved from collapse by
the token following of the thread of an already established text
of Propertius. Creating the illusion of subjectivity, these various
discourses are conflated into a seemingly continuous and grammatically unified piece of writing, and mediated by a first person
pronoun, even though they refuse the subject evidently predicated
by that pronoun any consistency. The contradictoriness of these
discourses disclaims any consistent social position, and so takes up
the conflict between poetry's celebratory concerns and its personal
or intimate concerns in the formal presentation of poetic voice.
The contradictoriness of the discourses appears in a constant
interpenetration :

> Out-weariers of Apollo will, as we know, continue their
> > Martian generalities,
> > We have kept our erasers in order.
> A new-fangled chariot follows the flower-hung horses;
> A young Muse with young loves clustered about her
> > ascends with me into the aether, . . .
> And there is no high-road to the Muses.[72]

Here the fragmentation of rhetorical eloquence into a diversity
of codes is so extensive that it is impossible to assign positions
to interjections or to a dominant discourse which offers them
hospitality, a dominance necessary to accommodate the devices of
the ironist. In so far as an easy access to consistent subjectivity
and to a world dependent upon that subjectivity for its meanings is in this way denied, and since it is this access which elides
away language itself in favour of a transparent instrumentality,
the diffraction of *Homage to Sextus Propertius* into these inter-
mixed linguistic codes can be seen as an appeal to the fact of
language in the production of meanings.

Whilst earlier adaptations from troubadour poetry could forge
for Pound out of technical exercises an opportunity for soliciting
by historical precedent a place for the poet in sociality, the debate
in *Propertius* concerning the occupations of poetry hinges instead
upon the poet's quest to find a language in the available discourses of society. It is at this point that Pound appears to recog-

nize most clearly that social meanings are primarily produced in language. It is therefore also at this point that conflicts in his early writing place his work most in jeopardy, in as much as for the poet to pursue the elaboration of specific social meanings is at the same time to diverge from the investigation of language itself. That this dilemma over finding a place in an infinity of possible ideological constructs all making claims upon the world does not exclude the poet and his writing from the political forum during the composition of the *Cantos* is, as we shall see below, largely traceable to Pound's belief in the work of Fenollosa, and in a notion that of all these meanings some may be properly derived from the processes of nature.

Pound's own comments about this poem, however, describe its occupations quite differently. In responding to the storm following publication, his defence turns upon retracing those diffractions of language to a reference point in the work of *Propertius*, even to Propertius's intentions for that work. In a letter to Felix E. Schelling, 8 July 1922, Pound claims that Propertius was writing a rejoinder to the magniloquence of Virgil and Horace, that he was 'tying blue ribbon' in their tails.[73] Similarly his claim that, 'my job was to bring a dead man to life, to present a living figure'[74] focuses upon the same subordination of the complexities of language to the presence of a writer who knows what he is saying. In these defences writing is made reflective of experience, and Pound claims, 'If the reader does not find relation to life defined in the poem, he may conclude that I have been unsuccessful in my endeavour.'[75] But this simplificatory apology for the complex effects of the language of the poem—possibly necessary to pacify objections of the particular kind made against it—is far removed from the order of difficulty the poem presents for reading. In this respect, Pound's defence of *Homage to Sextus Propertius*, and the kinds of criticism it has precipitated, prefigure in at least one important way the traditional issues of the *Cantos*. The direction of attention towards an originary presence thought to inhere in a body of classics is precisely an abandonment of the questions about language raised in the *Propertius* poem itself.

Notes

1 The essay 'Vorticism' was published in the *Fortnightly Review*, in September 1914; Pound thought fit to reprint it in its entirety in *Gaudier-Brzeska: a Memoir (1916)* (New Directions, New York, 1970), pp. 81–94. This work will be referred to hereafter simply as *Gaudier-Brzeska*. Pound's description of this casting-off of masks occurs p. 85.

2 *Gaudier-Brzeska*, p. 85.

3 These poems appear in *Collected Shorter Poems* (Faber, London, 1952, reprinted 1973), on p. 38 and p. 39 respectively. This edition of the poems will be referred to subsequently as *Collected Shorter Poems*.

4 *Collected Shorter Poems*, p. 20 and p. 22 respectively.

5 In *Literary Essays of Ezra Pound*, edited with an introduction by T. S. Eliot (Faber, London, 1954; reprinted 1968), p. 49. Referred to subsequently as *Literary Essays*.

6 *Collected Shorter Poems*, p. 205.

7 *Literary Essays*, p. 94.

8 *Collected Shorter Poems*, p. 49.

9 *Ibid.* pp. 36–7.

10 This essay was first published in the *Egoist*, in 1913.

11 *Literary Essays*, p. 42.

12 *Ibid.* p. 42.

13 *Ibid.* p. 46.

14 *Ibid.* p. 21.

15 *Ibid.* p. 46.

16 *Ibid.* p. 44.

17 *The Letters of Ezra Pound: 1907–1941*, edited by D. D. Paige (Faber, London, 1951), p. 39. Referred to subsequently as *Letters*.

18 *Literary Essays*, pp. 43–4.

19 *Ibid.* p. 44.

20 *Ibid.* p. 45.

21 This criticism of empiricist epistemologies has become familiar in recent years through the individual and collaborative works of Barry Hindess and Paul Hirst; these writers have recently summarized some of their arguments on this point, in *Mode of Production and Social Formation: An Auto-Critique of Pre-Capitalist Modes of Production* (Macmillan, London, 1977), p. 17.

22 *Literary Essays*, p. 377. Printed also in *Polite Essays* (Faber, London, 1937), pp. 57-66.

23 'Joyce', in *Literary Essays*, pp. 410–17; this citation is made pp. 416–17. See also, *Pound/Joyce: the Letters of Ezra Pound to James Joyce, with Pound's Essays on Joyce*, edited by Forrest Read (Faber, London, 1968), pp. 140–1. Referred to hereafter as *Pound/Joyce*.

24 *Literary Essays*, p. 407.

25 Recent analyses have suggested that this view taken by Pound is a fundamental misreading of Joyce's writings, arguing that the concern of these texts is with the interrelation of various discourses available in a language and which establish the possibilities of meaning, precisely a project directed against the privilege of a finally realistic metadiscourse; see, for example, Colin MacCabe, *James Joyce and the Revolution of the Word* (Macmillan, London, 1978).

26 See, 'A Retrospect', in *Literary Essays*, p. 12.

27 For Pound's version of these tenets, see, *Literary Essays*, p. 3. For a dis-

cussion of the other versions, particularly those of F. S. Flint and Richard Aldington, see Glenn Hughes, *Imagism and the Imagists: A Study in Modern Poetry* (Stanford, 1931; reprinted New York, 1972), pp. 24–42, and William C. Wees, *Vorticism and the English Avant-Garde* (Manchester University Press, Manchester and Toronto University Press, Toronto, 1972), p. 126.

28 *Literary Essays*, p. 5.

29 *Ibid.* p. 3.

30 Pound makes this claim of 'mushy technique' in *Gaudier-Brzeska*, p. 85; its speculated effects are quoted from his article in *Poetry*, 10 December 1912, cited by Noel Stock in *The Life of Ezra Pound* (Routledge & Kegan Paul, London, 1970), p. 127. The title of this work is abbreviated to *Life* in all subsequent references. But to facilitate reference to the edition published by Penguin Books, Harmondsworth, 1974—the edition much more widely available—I shall also give page numbers to this edition, abbreviated as *Life* (Penguin). In this instance, *Life* (Penguin), p. 159.

31 *Literary Essays*, p. 3.

32 *Ibid.* p. 9.

33 *Letters*, p. 45; an excerpt from this letter is quoted by Noel Stock, *Life*, p. 121; *Life* (Penguin), p. 152.

34 See Pound's account of his attempts to condense the experience behind this poem into as brief a piece of writing as possible in *Gaudier-Brzeska*, p. 89.

35 *Ibid.* p. 89.

36 Ezra Pound, *ABC of Reading* (Routledge & Kegan Paul, London, 1934; reprinted Faber, London, 1951), p. 36.

37 See Ezra Pound, *Selected Prose: 1909–1965*, edited with an introduction by William Cookson (Faber, London, 1973), pp. 297–8. Referred to hereafter as *Selected Prose*.

38 *Selected Prose*, p. 298.

39 *Ibid.* p. 21; also quoted by Noel Stock, *Life*, p. 108; *Life* (Penguin), pp. 136–7.

40 For a discussion of Jakobson's description of these tropes, see above, chapter 1, p. 6; for further discussion in relation to the *Cantos*, see below, chapter 4, pp. 78–9.

41 *Collected Shorter Poems*, p. 119; 'April' and 'Gentildonna' are both printed in this edition on p. 101. It might be noted that this procedure for composition by way of ellipsis and paratactic juxtaposition also characterizes Pound's editing of *The Waste Land* early in 1922. His suggestions for this poem are consistently towards the omission of other forms of subordinating structure; kinds of language which most directly offer up the feeling self are either excised altogether, or else revised in favour of a counterpoint of allusions. This is particularly clear in Pound's editing of the first section, 'The Burial of the Dead'. See T. S. Eliot, *The Waste Land: A Facsimile and Transcript of the Original Drafts including the Annotations of Ezra Pound*, edited by Valerie Eliot (Faber, London, 1971), especially pp. 4–9.

42 *Gaudier-Brzeska*, p. 89.

43 William C. Wees has argued that Pound focused energies already directed towards the production of *Blast*, by providing the concept of the Vortex and the name Vorticism itself. He claims further that this contribution by Pound was made late in the preparation of the first number of the magazine. See Wees, *op.cit.*, pp. 161–2, and p. 163n. See also Hugh Kenner, *The Pound Era* (Faber, London, 1971), p. 238.

44 *Blast: Review of the Great English Vortex*, numbers 1–2, 1914–1915 (Kraus Reprint Corporation, New York, 1967), 1, p. 154.
45 *Ibid.* number 1, pp. 148–9.
46 *Gaudier-Brzeska*, p. 92.
47 See *Blast*, 1, p. 9., p. 12., p. 20., p. 128. and p. 149.
48 *Literary Essays*, p. 220.
49 This designation formed part of the title of the magazine; see above, this chapter, n.44.
50 *Letters*, p. 81., and p. 81n.
51 Quoted by Kenner, *op.cit.*, p. 238.
52 *Literary Essays*, p. 214.
53 *Ibid.* p. 35.
54 *Ibid.*
55 *Blast*, 2, pp. 85–6.
56 *Literary Essays*, p. 35.
57 *Gaudier-Brzeska*, p. 91.
58 *Blast*, 1, p. 147.
59 *Ibid.* p. 30.
60 J. Derrida, 'Structure, Sign, and Play in the Discourse of the Human Sciences', in *The Structuralist Controversy: The Languages of Criticism and the Sciences of Man*, edited by Richard Macksey and Eugenio Donato (Johns Hopkins Press, Baltimore, Maryland, 1970; reprinted 1977), pp. 247–72.
61 *Blast*, 1, pp. 153–4, and pp. 155–8 respectively.
62 *Gaudier-Brzeska*, pp. 91–2.
63 See above, this chapter, p. 16.
64 *Collected Shorter Poems*, p. 85.
65 'Harold Monro', *Polite Essays*, 3–16 (p. 14).
66 *Collected Shorter Poems*, p. 206.
67 *Ibid.* p. 205.
68 *Ibid.* p. 215.
69 *Ibid.* p. 210.
70 *Ibid.* p. 207.
71 Pindar (Olympian Odes, II, 2).
72 *Collected Shorter Poems*, p. 225.
73 *Letters*, p. 246.
74 A comment by Pound to Alfred Orage, quoted by Noel Stock, *Life*, p. 224: *Life* (Penguin), p. 281.
75 In a letter to the editor of the *English Journal*, 24 January 1931, *Letters*, p. 310.

Chapter Three

The changing face of the 'Cantos'

IN important ways, Pound's writing of the *Cantos* inherits both the qualities and the problems of these early experiments and allegiances. Yet by ensuring that the poem's intelligibility will only be possible in a long-term accretion of incrementally published, tentative or fragmentary sections, its particular manner of composition has suspended any serious questioning of larger issues until a deferred moment of completion. This moment, of course, never arrived. In consequence, the *Cantos* remain an endless text which, being constructed as the trajectory of a finite long poem but actually encountered as a huge textual ellipsis, both sets up and denies limits for itself simultaneously.

There are, however, features of the poem from its earliest conceptualization which suggest that this absence of a projected closure was at least to some extent a deliberate artifice. It will be the object of this chapter to demonstrate how an ambiguity between an enclosed and static text, and an unfinished piece of writing requiring further work, is an integral feature of the construction of the *Cantos*, and to indicate some of the ways this inevitably affects the ways in which the poem can be read. Pound returns to one of these features, the ability of a poem based on the model of Browning's *Sordello* to contain anything the poet chooses (a compositional homage first made as part of one of the three retracted drafts published in *Poetry*), in an interview with Donald Hall in the *Paris Review* in 1962, suggesting that it is in the context of a general inclusiveness that the poem is to be read.[1] Both at the very inception of the project of the *Cantos* and in its capitulating stages, the poem is described by Pound, if not in terms of a physical interminability, at least of a theoretical interminability according to which it could go on absorbing material for so long as its author continued to live.

40

It is such an open-endedness which has made possible the prevalent homogenization of the various different discourses of the *Cantos* over the fifty or so years of their composition. But this manner of assimilation as a textual unity relies upon the supportive continuity of the author, and the limits of the text become merely that it shall include only what he chooses for it. The various discourses which comprise the poem are only rendered continuous and homogeneous by considering them as expressive of the meanings of the writer. Within such a view internal contradictions of the text, caused in the differing writing practices of its composition, are treated as reflections of an authorial shift of direction or attention. Investigations of the poem are then made questions of biography.

However, an explicit construction of the *Cantos* in juxtapositions and parallelisms (features of what Pound will theorize as the ideogrammic method), and in ambiguities which require of reading a process of articulation, undermines any unproblematic capacity of the writer to preside over his discourses, in much the same way as that described in the discussion of juxtaposed antinomies representing change and transformation in *Hugh Selwyn Mauberley*. This necessity of reading as a work rather than as a passive consumption is also a questioning of the agency of a subject outside the structure of a text as its effective guarantor of unity. The poem's intelligibility has now to be rethought. It can no longer be reliant upon a relation of discourse to author—the relation which holds the text to its author's affirmed and unquestioned unity—but instead depends upon interrelations of the discourses themselves, and upon the various positions relative to language these discourses inscribe for a reader.

Such a reading process restores contradiction as an element of the text, and so inaugurates forms of reading no longer presuming the coherence provided by the category of an author whom language subserves. The effectivity of the *Cantos*, then, lies in relations forged in and across positions made available by the discourses of the text, rather than in a series of acts of recapturing Pound's intended meanings for the poem. But before this remoulding of the difficulties posed by the *Cantos* can in any way seriously be taken up, it is necessary to examine more closely those elements of the poem which inhabit this ambiguity between enclosure and continuous production, and to

consider how its various sections and stages are fused into an
appearance of continuity and unity only by recourse to an external
support.

Pound's pursuance of the traditional aspect of the poet, initially
revealed in his ascription to writing of the ensemble of terms
and practices conventionally attached to a trade or profession,
prompted in the early years of this century the enterprise of a
magnum opus, first conceived, according to Pound's own recollection of a conversation with his Anglo-Saxon teacher Professor
Ibbotson, as a trilogy on Marozia, the wife of Alberic I, Prince
of Rome.[2] At this early stage, the primary features of such a work
were considered to be its size, by which it should approach the
order of length and scale of the classical epic, and the quantity
of endeavour—a lifetime's dedication—necessary to actualize it.
In 1906, in 'Scriptor Ignotus', the poet promises a 'great forty-
year epic'[3] and in a letter to John Quinn, of January 1917, Pound
speaks of work on 'a new long poem (really LONG, endless,
leviathanic)'.[4] In another letter, to Milton Bronner, 21 September
1915, Pound describes his latest project as that of a 'cryselephan-
tine poem of immeasurable length which will occupy me for the
next four decades unless it becomes a bore.'[5] On 17 March 1917
the poet writes in a letter to Joyce, 'I have begun an endless
poem, of no known category. . . . Probably too sprawling and
unmusical to find favour in your ears.'[6] This description of the
poem as 'of no known category' disclaims any approximation to
an already established genre, and instead avers that its form will
be created in the process of its own composition, setting a literary
precedent. The formulation 'endless' disavows any moment when
its internal contradictions are to be rendered coherent in an
instant of closure. The poem, according to these early sentiments, will pioneer an unknown trail, and will seek no
end.

Indeed, its first stages record a hesitancy which is never retro-
spectively endorsed in a surety of direction. The first published
section of the poem, discounting the retracted and later revised
Three Cantos of 1917, but embracing *A Draft of XVI Cantos
of Ezra Pound for the Beginning of a Poem of some Length*, as
well as the later, extended *Draft of XXX Cantos* which opens
more recent editions, retains the word 'draft' as part of the title.
The last section of the poem, far from legitimizing these tentative

sections in certainty, returns to this formula with its title *Drafts and Fragments of Cantos CX–CXVII.* In this way the *Cantos* close as a work still in progress, even though writing for the poem ceases with the publication of this section.

Incremental composition and publication reinforce the notion of the poem as a continuous production, with the result that its structure can only be understood—until a conclusion—in relation to the passing of time. Structure and further production become interdependent. This continuous act of production, punctuated by intermittent publication, clearly employs dialectical movement as counterpoint in its advance. In a letter to John Lackay Brown, of April 1937, Pound remarks of the progress of the poem, 'not only are the LI Cantos a part of the poem, but by labeling most of 'em draft, I retain the right to include *necessary* explanations in LI–C or in revision.'[7] Whilst these first sections of the poem are only to be grasped in relation to later writing, the later writing will come to be intelligible, owing to its allusiveness, only with regard to the early sections, the poem at first anticipatory and then later retrospective.

The renunciation in the *Cantos* of finality and enclosure is further accentuated in the material incompleteness of certain parts, a fragmentary aspect of the poem quite apart from titular denomination. Not only do lacunae appear in omissions accounted for by the present laws of libel (lacunae which postdate composition but nevertheless constitute an enforced part of reading in current, censored editions), but also in the lack of Cantos 72 and 73.[8] Whilst both these lacks are clearly determined in exterior historical conditions, they nevertheless stress that, even within the terms of its own programme, the actual text falls short of completeness and is a synecdoche of Pound's conjectured epic.

That the poem is such a synecdoche of an imagined completeness is insinuated in another face of these constitutive elements. 'Draft' composition may be read not to cherish open-endedness and the possibility of further transformation, but to advertise in advance the poem's aspiring but presently unattained completeness and coherence. This coherence may then be thought to have been interrupted not by features of the project itself, but by biographical determinants such as the enforced collapse of the poet at Pisa and his loss of powers in old age. In order to avoid seeing the poem in this way as a design of the poet which would have been fulfilled if not sadly interrupted, it is necessary not only to consider both these opposing readings of the poem's formal constitution, but to examine ways in which this alternative is operated within the poem, and so to analyse how at specific stages one reading or the other concurs with dominant concerns at other levels of textual organization. But it is first necessary to establish this ulterior character of the poem in which terminability and coherence are proclaimed.

Against the notion of 'draft' as an inscription of continuing process, a 'draft' can also be held to be a temporary expedient, not a finished piece of writing which nevertheless recognizes further dialectical activity but rather the short-term precursor of a fixed and static text. Publication during the process of composition can be considered not as the launching of a complete part of the text to be followed later by others, but as the provisional distribution of work which may be recalled for revision at a later date. This strategy is implicit in Pound's letter to John Lackay Brown of 1937 cited above. Serial publication can be thought to be the progressive emission of a finally complete poem of one hundred Cantos, an appearance made all the more likely by the popularity of this mode of publication contemporaneous to the distribution of the early *Cantos*, with *Tarr* and *Ulysses* as well-known instances.[9]

Such a view of the poem finds some substantiation in Pound's letters. In one to John Drummond, of 18 February 1932, he promises the completion of the *Cantos* in ' "about 100" '.[10] Similarly, in a letter to Felix E. Schelling of 8 July 1922, the poem is described as of about this length, and indeed during his internment at St Elizabeths Pound reiterates this intention to Charles Olson.[11] Pound urges Hubert Creekmore, in February 1939, 'As to the *form* of *The Cantos*: All I can say or pray is: *wait* till it's there. I mean wait till I get 'em written and then if it don't show, I will start exegesis. I haven't an Aquinas-map; Aquinas *not* valid now.'[12] This assertion not only expresses an aspiration towards completeness in its pronominal reference to Cantos not in existence ('wait till I get 'em written'), which postulates a definite extension in the circumscribed area of the pronoun "em', but inscribes the possible failure of such a scheme by invoking divine intervention in order to be sure of finishing it ('all I can say or pray is'). This suggests that realization of such an aim is dependent upon forces external to the writer, and in so far as these forces need to be propitiated, not entirely within his control.

Deferral of the moment of closure, and the problems it presents to the fabric of the *Cantos*, is discernible also in the already quoted letter to John Lackay Brown, where Pound claims, 'Part of the job is *finally* to get all the necessary notes into the text itself.'[13] This view is reflected in an earlier article on obscurity in the *New Review* in 1931, where Pound writes, 'The "poem" should theoretically in its final stages, swallow its notes.'[14] The description of these 'notes' as 'necessary' indicates that they are to be exegetical notes rather than projective structural ones, and this, coupled with the tentativeness of 'theoretically', suggests that the motions which are to render the poem coherent are as yet unplanned. Despite this, the allusion to the poem's 'final stages' and the emphasized '*finally*' endorse Pound's other claims of the envisaged termination of the poem in a moment of completeness. Not only is this postulation of completeness and coherence (presented materially as incompleteness and contradiction) firmly located in the realm of synecdoche, but its claim that unity lies outside and beyond actual practice invokes the support of a transcendental intention in order for that unification to be made possible. This is clearly analogous to the instance of the Imagist 'hokku' as a condensate of emotional sensation from which a fully constituted experience might be extrapolated.

The tendency towards synecdochic expression can also be traced in Pound's essay writing, where it occurs as an assertion of the irrelevance to present concerns of contingent and larger areas of speculation, or as a stenographic urgency which attempts to meet pressing exigencies. In the essay 'The Tradition' Pound declares, 'This is not the place for . . .' and 'Space forbids a complete treatise on melody at this point. . . .'[15] These suggest that completeness is readily available, and is obstructed simply by immediate requirements. The completeness of the 'treatise' in this quotation resides in—and indeed relies upon—an ambiguity between its completeness as an example of the genre of treatises, or its completeness in subsuming the question of melody. The evident possibility of the first of these two conditions precludes doubts as to feasibility exclusively in terms of the second. In *Guide to Kulchur* Pound provides another exemplary instance, when he argues 'Space does not permit me to give an exhaustive study of the Italian school system', where the exhaustion of the topic intertwines with a sense of the exhaustive labours of the writer.[16]

In 'How to Read', Pound urges, 'Let us also cut loose from minor details and minor exceptions: the main fact . . .', 'Say, for sake of argument . . .', 'admit'.[17] These invoke a fixity of argument which can remain unmodified by its 'exceptions', that is, by its internal contradictions. In 'Translators of Greek: Early Translators of Homer', Pound appends a note apologizing for the essay's unfinished appearance, which persists, as is the case of the *Cantos*, even in its physical completion. In this note, Pound writes:

P.S. I leave these notes, rough as they are, to indicate a block of matter needing examination, the indication being necessary if a reader is to gauge the proportions and relations of other subjects here outlined.[18]

The assertion of infinality is immediately contradicted by Pound's reference to a 'block of matter', 'subjects here outlined', and the notion of 'proportions'. These concepts all presume circumscribed wholes which then only need to be filled in.

In these various formulations, as indeed in the form of the *Cantos*, finality is transfigured into a prerogative of the writer which is not being exercised in the text's existing form. In so far as this prerogative exists as authorial intention, the coherence of a piece of writing becomes a function of this intention, and failure to complete a work can be thought an effect of historical circumstances. It is only if this external plenitude may be presumed in synecdochic writing practices, rather than being tested following the declaration of a piece of writing as finished and complete in itself, that a text such as the *Cantos* may be considered in terms of a biographically foreclosed cohesion. The explicit structuring of the poem around promises of further writing has the effect of putting into question the very possibility of the totalities which the poem aspires to reach, and having reached, to explain.

The absence of a formal demonstration of certain of the tendentious aims of the *Cantos* is not an isolated concern, but contributes to a more general difficulty at the level of the poem's recurrent motifs. These motifs share the kind of oscillation described above concerning 'draft' composition, incrementality, and synecdoche, and create a variety of contradictory possible meanings.

The voyage of Odysseus, for example, is presented both as translations of certain parts of Homer's text *The Odyssey* (the poem embarks with a version of the beginning of Book XI), and as isolated allusions to the text in the form of proper names. Its specific recall of Homer's narrative, in repeated references to the vicissitudes of Odysseus's journey, functions not only as a retelling of this story and so as to pay homage to and recirculate the work of this poet, but as the connoting of a process of discovery which is not governed by a predetermined plan, and instead finds and marks out geographical terrain on the trace of its own progress. Odysseus is compelled to navigate his way through all kinds of contrary forces, and at any stage of the voyage is unable to view its whole scheme or itinerary, which is governed by the gods. This clearly reflects the overall structuration of the *Cantos* in so far as both are articulated by partial vision and by the irreducibility of their continuous movement.

But the story of Odysseus in Homer, and even in the dislocated form it assumes in the *Cantos*, includes features which crucially modify this pattern. In that Odysseus's voyage is not a willingly undertaken adventure, but specifically an endeavour to return home to Ithaca and to Penelope, the voyage is motivated with a goal, a point of return at which the hero's tribulations, and his frequently renegotiated position in the world where he continually suffers pain and attack and enjoys temporary delights by turn, will be finally resolved. In so far as what Odysseus has lost is his home, the future goal is identical with his lost origin, a loss to be closed in an act of refinding. The intermediate stages of his journey involve a passage to hell (indeed this is the part of Homer's narrative which receives most attention in the *Cantos*) as a totally undesirable interlude before reaching home. Immersion in the contrary and contradictory conditions of the world entailed in the interruption of fixed social position is characterized as a hell which can be overcome or escaped only in the restoration and elucidation of the world in a system of law and fixed positionality. Whereas

Odysseus on his voyage can observe: 'I am Noman'—as Pound also will observe in the *Pisan Cantos* (74:426, and 80:499)—refinding the lost origin of Ithaca is a resumption of fixed social order in kinghood and power. Pound's own hesitant shift towards the Paradiso of the *Cantos*, even after the collapse of the extreme social order of his espoused Fascism, goes through a section entitled *Thrones*. Oscillation between these two opposing modes of intelligibility for the Odysseus narrative gravitates towards one of its poles, that of the quest for a lost origin whose discovery will resolve the world's complexities and opacities.

Such a primacy accorded to the more stabilizing pole of the ambiguity may also be discerned in the presentation of the notion 'periplus' or 'periplum' (Pound consistently gives the latter). This notion is introduced in Canto 40, and is alluded to in the Cantos which follow, most densely in Canto 74. Whilst Canto 40 itself does not make explicit that its later stages are a rendering of Hanno's *Periplus*, the translation which follows the capitalized 'PLEASING TO CARTHEGINIANS: HANNO' records a coasting voyage around certain parts of the Mediterranean, specifying that journey in terms of a navigation in which geographical location is held to be deducible from information gained concerning the passage already travelled.[19] Two lines in Canto 59 indicate that at least one significance of such a passage is to connote a voyage of continuous discovery:

> periplum, not as land looks on a map
> but as sea bord seen by men sailing.   (59:324)

This suggestion is reinforced by a line in Canto 40 itself, 'for 12 days coasted the shore' (40:200), since this reaffirms the partiality of a point of vision in which a coast is visible, but which is at the same time deprived of any overview either of hinterland or of general topography.

But the context of this translation in Canto 40 installs at least one other sense. The Hanno passage is introduced and followed by the words 'Out of which things seeking an exit' (40: 199 and 201), placing the section as a desired alternative to what precedes it, but as an undesirable alternative to what follows, namely:

To the high air, to the stratosphere, to the imperial
calm, to the empyrean, to the baily of the four towers
the NOUS, the ineffable crystal :
Karxèdoniōn Basileos
hung this with his map in their temple.   (*40* : 201)

The seeking of exits and the transformations which follow them
chart a movement towards a realization of fixity and stasis, and
an emergence from partial vision and contradiction. The 'periplum' dwells in an ambiguity between a voyage of continuous
discovery, and one of conquest and annexation, the latter notion
furnished in Canto 40 as a taking of captives. The insinuated
sense of conquest anticipates the 'imperial calm' of untroubled
domination, and of the 'baily of the four towers', from which
point of martial elevation the inadequacies of imperfect vision
may be overcome. The exaltation of resposeful domination cul-
minates in the 'NOUS', the 'ineffable crystal'. This crystal situates
such stasis once more in the realm of extra-lingual transcendence
in its description as 'ineffable'. This adjective contains the manifest contradiction of disclaiming the very possibility of verbal
description, but at the same time is used precisely to qualify a
noun, and so describe it. Later in the *Cantos* the priority of the
sense of 'periplum' which is drawn towards unity and stasis is
restated in its reappearance in Canto 74. Here ' "the great periplum brings in the stars to our shore" ' (*74* : 425). This is a
suggestion that processive discovery gravitates on a fixed and
stationary point. The 'periplum' is subject to a magnetism generated from a privileged site, in this case from 'our shore'. Recon-
ciliation in stasis is appropriated by a first person adjective.
     On the implication in the 'NOUS' of a universal reason insisting
in this static calm hinge the particular investments of another
related and ambivalent motif. This is the notion of metamorphosis.
Whilst metamorphoses may be taken to record moments of
transformation, and to stress continuous fluctuation or mutability
of relations, their presentation in the *Cantos* also avouches a revelation in the physical, empirical world of a transcendental realm
of the divine. The penetration of the world by a supernatural
presence is regularly associated with a performance of divine
justice, as is the case in Canto 2 in the assertion by Dionysus of

his proper identity after being abducted by pirates. Here metamorphosis not only announces the god with the growth of vine shoots on the ship's rigging, but also carries out the punishment of the pirates, who are turned into porpoises. Conversely Baucis and Philemon are rewarded for their hospitality by being transformed into oak trees, whilst Actaeon is punished for the transgression of watching Artemis bathing by being turned into a stag.

Although at one level metamorphoses invite the possible rearticulation of the world by way of transformations, at another level this possibility of transformation is confined within the limits of a divine arbitration. The penetration of the world by gods renders continuous the realm of the empirically evident and of the divine, and so is an important conjunction for the *Cantos* in that it makes possible an empirical certainty about the conditions of the divine by a visual attention to instants of physical change. The notion of a universe governed by gods who make occasional appearances prompts Pound's contemplation of a mechanistic recurrence within an otherwise infinite variability of transformation. From this purview generated by a devoted attention to metamorphoses may be predicated a theory of culture as a series of historical rhymes, of human beings charged by an immanent and unchangeable essence, and of a physical nature of seasoned cyclism rather than of evolutionary mutation.[20]

The subordination of fragmented or partial vision to a global overview, and its concomitant resolution of dialectic in a moment of total knowledge, can be seen to be analogous to the model of the Vortex, in so far as it postulates an immanent order to which excentric energies return. The revelation of a divine realm in a world of the senses appropriates transcendental order within the framework of personal possession, in so far as what is empirically evident is judged according to individual experience. In this way the affirmation of a celestial order presiding over the world is an amplification of earlier postulations examined above of a truth to be found in the poet's own sensations.

In the *ABC of Reading* Pound makes quite explicit his subsumption of the dialectical investments of these ambivalences in the adoption of a narrative from *The Odyssey*, of Hanno's 'periplus', and of metamorphosis, by professing that in general the overview of a totality is the summation of successive individual acts of discovery. Whilst singly these appear to trace an open system, their proliferation for Pound gradually adumbrates, and so delimits, an overall, mechanistic structure. Accumulation establishes transcendence, and Pound claims:

It doesn't, in our contemporary world, so much matter where you begin the examination of a subject, so long as you keep on going until you get round again to your starting point. As it were, you start on a sphere, or a cube; you must keep on until you have seen it from all sides.[21]

Not only is it postulated without explanation that subjects in our contemporary world have structures similar to a 'sphere, or a cube', but these structures are 'seen' by a perceiving being who is necessarily placed outside the realm of what is being seen. It is only from this transcendent and exterior position that the finite extent of the discoverable can be gauged, and from which complete and insular objects can be predicated.

Within such a conception of knowledge, discovery is only possible within definite limits set by the attributes of the presiding subject of this act of witnessing; the expression of these discoveries serves merely to reconstruct that subject's own perspective. The production of this perspective itself is placed beyond question. In terms of the celestial and world view this supports, the effect of the concept of accumulative summation is to anchor the uncertainty of dialectic and processive transformation, limiting these to the status of mere component parts in a supreme mechanism which is itself motionless. Yet this understanding of structurality inevitably retains the contradiction of establishing a privileged spectator somewhere outside the totality being witnessed. This totality cannot in consequence be total and embrace everything, since there must always be another realm from which this external subject can cast a gaze.

The *Cantos* cannot, however, be collapsed into a unified project even at the level of the intentions of an extra-lingual writer making deliberations from a static point of overview. One further significant feature of the long-term composition of the poem is its inclusion of a reflective commentary on the shifting relation between writer and the task of writing. This might be most simply recognized as a series of confessions, such as those which pervade the *Pisan Cantos* in a kind of introspective scrutiny, or

those which prepare for the abandonment of the poem with the
Drafts and Fragments in admissions of error and defeat. This
altering stance is related, often across contradictions, to the shifting body of discursive practices in which the *Cantos* are constituted. In order to substantiate the claim that the interminability
of the poem does not derive from an accident of personal biography, but is an inevitable effect of certain of its founding aims
and so implicated from the very outset, it is necessary to examine
these changing practices, as well as their interrelation with the
various pronouncements made about the writing of the poem
during its successive stages.

It is clear that in the early *Cantos* Pound considered that the
poem should be committed to the exposure of usury and bad
government, and should herald an earthly paradise to be achieved
in the cultural coherence of an actual political regime. In the
essay 'An Introduction to the Economic Nature of the United
States', written in 1944, the poet writes of his intention to begin
the *Cantos* ' "In the Dark Forest" ', and for them to end 'in the
light'.[22] In the notes for Canto 117 he records a former desire
'to make a paradiso/terrestre' (*117*:802). The early Cantos are
written as a kind of elucidation of history, which is presented in
a series of documentary extracts and allusions. By means of their
alternately celebratory and polemical propulsions (polarized for
example in the indictment of usury in Canto 45, and the appropriation of time itself in the Fascist formula 'XI of our era'
(*41*:202), these lessons in history urge the re-fashioning of
material reality in political action.

This epic and celebratory tendency is interwoven with a concern to restore lost kinds of social order, the goal of political
practice looping back upon a monumental past. The poem contains in this nostalgia an elegiac disposition, the emphasis of
' "those days are gone by for ever" ' in Canto 19 (*19*:87), or
the commemorative opposition between the past and the present
in Canto 7 :

> That, Fritz, is the era, to-day against the past,
> "Contemporary." And the passion endures.   (7.25)

In the early Cantos this sentiment is portrayed in a series of transcribed documents which serve both to inform the present, and to set out a prospectus for transformation of the future. This kind of historical reference is made more evident in the early Cantos than later in the poem by a consistently greater length of translations and excerpts.

The inclusion of historical scripts appears as an attempt to bind discourse to an external real world which it reflects or to which it corresponds. But in this practice of historical writing, the fundamental questions of language and its production of meanings are neglected. Whilst transcription may be thought to authenticate an effectivity of a piece of writing at a certain historical moment, exactly how that text might have been read by various persons at that moment, or—more importantly—in what ways it may be read in the circumstances of its reduplication cannot be made in any way certain. Rather, reading of these extracts needs to be understood as an articulation of historically given linguistic material whose own history cannot itself stabilize or homogenize a diversity of possible reading relations.

The shifting effectivity of texts has its own force for the conservatism of the *Cantos* in an accrued veneration attached to ancient texts, a veneration exemplified in the inscription in Canto 1, ' "In officina Wecheli, 1538, out of Homer" ' (*1* : 5). Here the address to enduring qualities of a body of classics contributes to a lament for our contemporary loss of origins, but simultaneously marks an endeavour to 'make it new' in a reworking, since the passing of time has shifted its effectivity. The *Cantos* call upon both a trans-historical fixity of interpretation for quoted texts, and yet also a historical mutability to be resisted in the project of 'making new'. This 'making new' can only be achieved by a writer who, controlling the effects of his writing through all the heterogeneous instances of reading, is able by reworking ancient texts to align new effects with those from an original historical conjuncture. In this respect, the project relies upon both a domination over the effects of language, and a definitive perspective of history.

Such presumed domination is sought in these early Cantos largely in a set of artifices which attempt to regulate the kinds of relation which can be made across juxtaposed discourses, and so to enforce a fixed position for them within a larger structure predicated by a privileged and articulating voice. To this voice is traceable the didactic character of the early stages of the poem. In the essay 'The Teacher's Mission' such didactic sponsorship is proposed in a pattern of metaphors of vegetative process, a claim of natural auspices similar to Pound's elaboration of a derivation of ethics from art in the essay 'The Serious Artist' :

Until the teacher wants to know all the facts, and to sort out the roots from the branches, the branches from the twigs, and to grasp the MAIN STRUCTURE of his subject, and the relative weights and importances of its parts, he is just a lump of the dead clay in the system.[23]

This choice of metaphor is repeated in a letter to Henry Swabey, of April 1940, as '. . . but get to the *root* and leave the twigs',[24] and reappears in Canto 109 as ' "phyllotaxis" ' (*109* : 774), the arrangement of leaves or other lateral members upon a stem. Since nature is held to endorse hierarchical structures in its own patterns of growth, the reflection of these patterns in discourse may be considered a practice which is mimetic of, and consonant with, a natural matrix, and the teaching of perceived proportions, either in the world or in discourse, to be the direct implementation of the natural order of things, a hierarchy fixed in preordained equilibrium.

But there are other operations in the text, signs and marks, which support and sustain the hierarchy of discourses. Emphases in typographical lay-out, italicization, capitalization, repetition, and other visual marks give prominence to certain linguistic forms, and reduce the relative prominence of others. Vertical lines in the left margin of the page accentuate certain passages in Canto 67 (*67* : 391) and Canto 71 (*71* : 416), and parts of Canto 46 are differentiated from their surroundings by underlining (*46* : 233). In a letter to Hubert Creekmore, of February 1939, Pound suggests these markings indicate constraints upon reading :

ALL typographic disposition, placings of words *on* the page, is intended to facilitate the reader's intonation, whether he be reading silently to self or aloud to friends.[25]

The link between reading and the patterning of the voice clearly at one level alludes to the poem's own musicality, but in that gesture also places the text's intelligibility in the presence of a speaker. The intentions of that speaker serve in delivery to negotiate ambiguities and complexities—in short all the recalcitrance of writing—by way of inflection. It is this control over the play of meanings which is being written into the poem in these typographical indications, which then contribute to the shift from a sequence of verbal marks on the page to a subjectivity and a lyricism.

Such a dissimulation of writing as speech has other effects, however, which have nothing to do with the musicality of poetry. In the *Cantos*, as elsewhere in Pound's writing and particularly in the letters to Joyce, the conventions of written language are subordinated to the conventions of speech in a mimesis of acoustic properties in spelling. If presented consistently this creates the appearance of subjects having certain distinctive characteristics. In the instance of regional dialects, or of enunciations in English invaded by the properties of other languages such as the French-English and the Russian-English of Canto 16, the Gibraltese-English of Yusuf in Canto 22, and the Jewish-English of Canto 35 and elsewhere, these constructions indicate levels of facility in language. In that proper ethics, law and conduct all depend, according to Pound, upon the preservation of language in given and definite forms, linguistic deviations from these forms contaminate the exercise of social order, and may be thought to comport with deviant relations to public authority.

These linguistic competences are not, within the framework of an empiricist epistemology, effects of a complex historical causality, but are thought essential facts about the subjects in which they are discovered, and so may predicate forms of behaviour and attitudes towards these subjects. This incidentally reveals how disjunct from the field of empirical examination is the subject of that epistemology, since whilst the linguistic practices of other subjects are revealed for judgement, Pound's own deviant spellings and so on do not incur the same response. They are not simply marked off by their lack of consistency—by their intermixing of codes analogous to that adopted for a public voice in *Homage to Sextus Propertius*—but by the fact that judgement for the empiricist subject excludes analysis of the self from any position other than as the assured source of judgement.

The ethnocentrism of these pastiches in the *Cantos* is evident in their recurrent creation of linguistic and social practices of subjects for whom English appears to be a second language. Not

C

only is this, within the circumscribed terrain of use of a particular language, a recipe for xenophobic nationalism, but in its relation to history fails to confront political determinations such as mercantilism or, more importantly, imperialist expansion, which have made an exigency of capabilities in additionally acquired languages. In such stylistic imitations, the poem's construction insinuates undercurrents at a level of content which are very obviously related to the kinds of control over language it attempts to monopolize. The *Cantos* in this respect inscribe at the level of thematic concerns the various problems of their composition to such a degree that any attention to the poem which attempts to treat form and content separately, or in contradistinction, only analyses individual elements of a much larger issue.

The form of the *Cantos* has other features which contribute to their means of establishing meanings. This is apparent in the instance of titles within the poem which, by being typographically and spatially emphasized, confer names upon objects of impending discourse, and so prefix or prescribe an area of identity for that discourse which may or may not then be endorsed in a reading. Such titles offer reading as a process which enfolds the language it traverses into a coherence which may be summarized as the wording of a title. Canto 77 has its own appendix entitled 'Explication' (77 : 476), where an elucidation of a number of ideograms is proposed. This title combines senses of explanation and finality, this latter already familiar from the colophon to the first thirty Cantos, 'explicit Canto/XXX' (30 : 149). This notion of explication not only proposes to complete or finalize meaning, but implies a transmission of material already in the possession of the writer, who can offer final explanation of what has been written.

Such an assumption of control is explicit also in Canto 52, which begins:

> And I have told you of how things were under Duke
> > Leopold in Siena
> And of the true base of credit, that is
> > the abundance of nature
> with the whole folk behind it.
>
> > > > (52 : 257)

Here truth is appropriated as a function of the first person of the verb, and the repeated verb 'to be' proclaims that these are not tentative speculations, but are to stand as facts. The Canto is then able to proceed, 'Know then: . . .' (52:258), where knowledge is simply whatever certitudes appeal to the writer.

But what prevents any easy distancing from these stylistic devices is their absorption within the poem's articulating rhetoric. In Canto 50, for example, quotations from Zobi are elided with interpolations by means of an omission of the marks elsewhere used to demarcate them. Quotation is initially notated in this Canto by a single inverted comma, and a verb of saying:

> 'Revolution' said Mr Adams 'took place in the
> minds of the people
> in the fifteen years before Lexington',
>
> (50:246)

and,

> found there was *'Un' abbondanza che affamava'*
> says Zobi
>
> (50:246)

Fourteen lines after this second verb of saying occur the words 'saith Zobi, sixty years later' (50:247), following a line of Italian but without inverted commas. Then follows immediately:

> 'Pardon our brief digression' saith Zobi:
> America is our daughter and VashiNNtonn had civic virtues.
> and Leopoldo meant to cut off two thirds of state debt,
> to abolish it
>   and then they sent him off to be Emperor
> in hell's bog, in the slough of Vienna, in
>   the midden of Europe in the black hole of all
> mental vileness, in the privvy that stank Franz Josef,
> in Metternich's merdery in the absolute rottenness,
> among embasterdized cross-breeds,
>
> (50:247)

Since the colon which follows 'saith Zobi' is clearly as much an indication of ensuing quotation as the absence of differentiating marks which accompanies 'saith Zobi' in the preceding line, Pound is able to subjoin a passage of his own epideictic language to extracts from Zobi, and so by calling upon the status of the prophetically archaic form 'saith', to claim in a subtle merging of discourses this same authority for his own writing.

Credulity is solicited further by a play between rhetorical assurance and self-deprecating admissions which make minimal concessions,

> and so on the 30th of October Lord Minto
> was in Arezzo (I think Bowring had preceded) and the
> crowd cried EVVIVA
>
> (50:249)

Whereas the acknowledgement of speculative uncertainty concerns Bowring, who is not mentioned elsewhere in the Canto, the reinforcement it offers to the supposed factuality of the section concerns Minto, around whom the paragraph is formed.

It is not at the level of these difficulties in the assured rhetoric of the early Cantos that the modulation of the poem with the writing of the *Pisan Cantos* is engendered. In order to account for this sudden transition, which resumes the poem after a wartime loss of Cantos 72 and 73, it is necessary to consider the changed relation of the writer to social relations, and the collapse of a habitual self-representation following internment. Personal misfortune dislocates the writer from a world of self-evident meaning, and prompts a degree of recorded introspection unprecedented in the poem. This is the area of classic analyses of the *Pisan Cantos*. But whilst it is generally acknowledged that this section infuses a new density of remembrance and affection, the implications of this upon the general course of the poem, and more specifically its retroactive effects on the pre-war Cantos, are seldom considered. These effects are more often deflected in an approval of these Cantos considered separately. Indeed they are the most often anthologized sections of the poem. Clearly the *Pisan Cantos* can stand pre-eminent among poems judged as eloquent expressions of personal feeling, since not only do they constantly display sentiment, but their poignancy is underscored by the extreme and infamous adversity of the circumstances in which they were written.

To adopt such a position, however, is to neglect the continuity of the *Cantos* as an enterprise, even though the dense allusiveness of the *Pisan Cantos* can only find a context in relation to other stages of the poem. The prominent displacement in these Cantos of political and macro-historical issues by a lyricism concerned to stress its discontinuity with the world beyond personal feeling and reminiscence, or beyond the localized and often mythified observations possible from the internment camp, shifts the emphasis of the *Cantos* but does not fracture its founding principles of organization. The domain of the seeing subject, the subject of empiricism situated on an axis of self-possession outside its discourses, is protected from immersion in the manifestly contradictory outside by this dramatized disjunction between an area of unassailable thought and the appropriation by that thought of a world of practice. Moreover, the opportunity of revision in counterpoint is taken up in these Cantos, and has the effect of subsuming the contradiction between the pre-war and post-war modes of writing by establishing a further level of textual organization composed of contrapuntal interest. Disparate modes of writing are then absorbable as juxtapositions constitutive of the ideogrammic method.

The pre-eminence in the *Pisan Cantos* of a new commitment to the self is evident not only in a density of personal allusion, which is necessarily opaque to a reader outside the kind of elucidation provided in Pound's other writings and in the exegetic machinery regularly brought to the *Cantos*, but in occasionally explicit affirmation:

> is not that our delight
> to have friends come from far countries
> is not that pleasure
> nor to care that we are untrumpeted?
> filial, fraternal affection is the root of humaneness
> the root of the process
>
> (74:437)

or:

>   nothing matters but the quality
> of the affection—
> in the end—that has carved the trace in the mind
> (76 : 457)

or again:

>   J'ai eu pitié des autres
> probablement pas assez, and at moments that suited my own con-
>   venience
> (76 : 460)

Several important features of this reconstituted subjectivity are
apparent in these extracts, features which stress a continuity with
the poem's earlier preoccupations, even if at the same time these
features are transposed into the deliberations of an explicit first
person, and disengaged from any claimed penetration of the
world. There is a continuing construction of hierarchical systems
('nothing matters but the quality/of the affection', or 'filial,
fraternal affection . . . the root'); there is the assertion of a
definite extension ('in the end') which pivots on a central and
privileged point (a 'root of the process'); there is a qualitative
disparity between the self and others ('J'ai eu pitié des autres/
probablement pas assez . . .'). These ensure a transformation rather
than a recantation of earlier modes of writing, and in some
measure continue to support the self of rhetoric and of invective
whose consistency has been threatened in a collapse of ideological representations following enforced subjection to an
opposed ideology invested in the institution of American military
jurisprudence.

Consistency is also reaffirmed in the formulation 'amo ergo
sum' repeated throughout the Pisan section. This adaptation of
the Cartesian postulation of a full and self-possessed subject
established in the simple evidence of self-recognition inherits but

modifies its philosophical source. The substitution of 'amo' for 'cogito' serves to emphasize the disinterestedness of personal feeling, and so allows the superimposition on the asserted domain of self-presence of the subject's own produced meanings; the subject's own sensations become both the means and the object of thought. Taking the form of affection, these sensations need suffer no test in terms of social effectivity, communal agreement, or acceptability to convened ethical standards. So at one level the identity of the self shown by the experience of Pisa to be the site of an antagonism with the outside world is restored to a prevailing position of centrality and self-sufficiency by an act of severing the meanings of the self from the meanings for the world.

The assertion of a discontinuity between realms of subjectivity and of practice makes possible an exaltation of contradiction itself, as a pleasurable constituent of a counterpoint which circulates in the stasis of the imagination. Contradiction is in this way disarmed in its threat of struggle or opposition to the domain of subjectivity. Such a displacement of a teleology of practice by a notion of aesthetic gratification in counterpoint is accompanied by a related transformation of paradise from a 'paradiso terrestre' to one of personal sensation:

> Le Paradis n'est pas artificiel
>   but spezzato apparently
> it exists only in fragments unexpected excellent sausage,
>   the smell of mint, for example,
>   (74:438)

Assimilation of fragmentation as an element of paradise overpowers its agitational agency. At another level it also resolves a problem of the composition of the *Cantos*, which may subsequently be considered to be closed in paradise, even if this paradise exists only as a fragment of the projected poem.

The epic tendency to found and celebrate a political dynasty disappears in the *Pisan Cantos*, and is replaced by an elegiac recall of memories and individual associations:

> funge la purezza,
> and that certain images be formed in the mind
> to remain there
> *formato locho*   (74:446)

Here the mind is *'formato locho'*, 'a place already formed or produced', and its contents are immutable and sacrosanct. The effect of counterpoint as an agent of negation or propulsion is dismissed in its assimilation within the area of imagination. Its function there is the pleasurable stimulation of an undisturbable equilibrium:

> . . . and in a dance the renewal
> with two larks in contrappunto
> at sunset   (74:431)

or:

> some minds take pleasure in counterpoint
> pleasure in counterpoint   (79:485)

Liberation of language from its once fiercely defended capacity for correlating with and interpreting the world—a liberation which incidentally makes possible the mythification of the local landscape and installs 'Taishan' and 'Breasts of Helen' as features of the Pisan scene—impels a renewed attention to other aspects of language than referentiality.

But if there is evidence in the Pisan section of a transformation of the writing practices of the early Cantos, there is also an intermittent insistence upon them:

> the mould must hold what is poured into it
> in
> discourse
> what matters is
> to get it across e poi basta   (79:486)

Here the word 'mould' repeats the presumption of a definite perimeter which can enclose meanings, and the words 'e poi basta' —'and then nothing else'—predicate given ends to the production of those meanings. The structure of elucidatory reduction, too, persists as a vestige of Pound's pre-war didacticism:

> for immediate scope
>   things have ends (or scopes) and beginnings.   **To**
> know what precedes   and what follows
>   先   後
>   will assist yr/comprehension of process
>   vide also Epictetus and Syrus   (77 : 465)

Whilst the stabilization of process into sequence is to 'assist yr/ comprehension', such comprehension acknowledges its own condensation in the word 'scopes', which are finite extensions isolated from their context for a specific purpose. Not only does this word 'scopes' reveal in its parenthetical explanation, 'ends', that such isolation serves to make totalities out of open and unmanageable structures, but the sense of 'ends' as defined objectives further suggests a complicity of this reductionism with an already fixed notion of what benefits are to come from comprehension. These reduced certitudes may then be employed in teaching: 'To/know . . . will assist yr/comprehension . . .', 'vide also'. Nevertheless this regathering certainty which sustains the didacticism of the *Cantos* is still tied to a simplified notion of ends and beginnings, precisely what in this episode from Canto 77 a renewed didactic rhetoric attempts to explain.

The Cantos which follow the *Pisan Cantos* are composed of both a gradual resumption of certain of the discursive modes of the pre-war Cantos and a consolidation of this new attention to musicality and counterpoint begun in the parts of the poem written in the D.T.C. They are in this respect a polyphony of diverse kinds of writing whose articulation is no longer sponsored by a pervasive lyrical presence—or the often polemical voice of the Cantos of the 1930s—but which are instead made continuous by an allusiveness which reintroduces elements from earlier stages of the poem in repetition, and in transitions made at the level of the material shapes and forms of language.

The frequency in the course of these later Cantos of shifts prompted by phonic qualities—transitions, that is to say, which are sponsored exclusively at the level of the signifier—makes increasingly difficult those kinds of reading of the poem which rely upon a systematic accretion of signifieds, as themes and so on. Alongside the tortuous opacity of personal allusion maintained from the *Pisan Cantos*, this feature makes difficult material of these later Cantos for an exegetic criticism. The brevity of these allusions and quotations—often calling upon earlier usages within other stages of the poem which are frequently embedded in different and sometimes contradictory modes of discourse—creates an unmanageable number of associative links for attempts to recover a monolithic intended thought which is supposed to underpin an entire section. The almost inevitable conclusion for this kind of criticism is that these later Cantos do not cohere in the way the earlier ones might be made to by interpretation.

The consistently confessional character of the *Drafts and Fragments*, and particularly of Canto 116, suggests that Pound himself considered the developments of his later writing were leading away from coherence. Indeed the termination of the poem with the publication of this section attests that, for whatever reason, the *Cantos* could not be brought to an ordered close, a close both ordered by Pound's earlier prescriptions, and ordered as a coherent cosmological system. However, the valedictory apologia of Canto 116 itself, often praised as personal exposure by the poet and as an admission that he recognizes in increasing age a diminishing power to organize his work successfully, can alternatively be read as an interpenetration of this admission with a final defiance. For theoretical difficulties of the poem inescapable from its very inception are disguised here by a prominence given instead to the limiting effects of the natural process of ageing.

Canto 116 inscribes a struggle between the poem's realization and its incompletion, and the poem's error is claimed to lie in what has not been done rather than in what has, the poem paradoxically right and wrong simultaneously:

a little light
    in great darkness—   (*116* : 795)
But the beauty is not the madness   (*116* : 795)
How came beauty against this blackness,   (*116* : 796)
To confess wrong without losing rightness :   (*116* : 797)

These extracts restate the poem's earliest aspirations towards a completeness to be attained in a notion of transcendence, and the poem closes in a relation to finality identical to its relation at the outset :

        i.e. it coheres all right
            even if my notes do not cohere. (*116* : 797)

These 'notes', like those of the early formulations, are indications of synecdoche, of a totality to be reached only by a faith which can offer the reassurance, 'it coheres all right'. In this absence of a moment when incoherence is rendered coherent, the self-assurance of the subject as an essential unity or identity able to confer meanings upon the world suffers a further interruptive displacement : the subject is shown to be unable to fix a constant position in discourse from which to judge experience, and meanings are shown to proliferate beyond any control which might plan and achieve a coherent end.

Pound makes a partial acknowledgement of this failure to define a set of meanings for the self in the *Cantos* in the recognition in Canto 117, the last of the *Drafts and Fragments* :

        That I lost my center
            fighting the world.   (*117* : 802)

Even in this admission that subjectivity is put into question by language the 'I' escapes, since the 'I' whose centre has been lost is a different 'I' from the reconstituted 'I' who recognizes that loss.[26] Rather than examining what causes this loss of the self in language, the impetus of these last *Drafts and Fragments* is towards the possibility of a transcendent force which might alter that condition :

Out of dark, thou, Father Helios, leadest,
but the mind as Ixion, unstill, ever turning.   (*113* : 790)

It is only in the intervention of a law of 'Father Helios', a paternal law conducted in the form of light and elucidation, that this present unstillness is thought reconcilable in comfortable stasis. Until that intervention stillness and meaningful silence upon a completion of meanings remain bound to the tortuous rack of language. It is the delay in the institution of such a law over language which causes the collapse and failure of the *Cantos*. In the absence of such a law the 'paradiso terrestre' forecast by Pound is unattainable, and the poet is compelled to serve a sentence of interminable signification.

But this decentering of the writer from language is not exclusively confined to the latter stages of the poem, and indeed has already been implicitly acknowledged above in the desire to 'make it new', an effort to resist changing textual effectivities which have escaped the control of their author's intended significations, or of determinate meanings at the instant of their composition or publication. For Pound 'making it new' evidently involves reconstructing a work's founding subjectivity in new social relations, in order as far as possible to reconstitute an imagined relation of text to social relations at the time of composition. This was clearly the emphasis of the poet's epistolary explanations of *Homage to Sextus Propertius*.

Yet the subjectivity which is to be reconstituted is not thought to be entirely deducible from the practices of a text itself, since for Pound the essential reality of the human being is in part obscured by literary decoration. In a letter to W. H. D. Rouse, of February 1935, Pound explains:

I don't see that one *translates* by leaving in unnecessary words; that is, words not necessary to the meaning of the *whole* passage, any whole passage. An author uses a certain number of *blank* words for the timing, the movement, etc., to make his work sound like natural speech. I believe one shd. check up all that verbiage as say 4% *blanks*, to be used where and when wanted in the translation, but perhaps never, or at any rate not usually where the original author has used them.[27]

Not only does this formulation recall the dictum of concision from Imagist poetics, but, like that dictum, is only supportable within the context of a fully constituted subject distinct from the field of language, the source of 'natural speech' and able to determine 'the meaning of the *whole* passage'. The notion of subjectivity which Pound feels to be deducible from a text is thus produced in a selective reading which decides between what conveys meaning and what is merely surplus decoration, or *'blanks'*. Consequently subjectivity is specifically an image produced by a reading whose parameters of selection themselves determine what kind of subjectivity will be discovered. That Pound finds a continuous human essence in the history of culture and exemplified in the present in his own understanding of the world merely demonstrates the extent of imaginary reflection involved in this conception of reading.

Translation, however, presents the *Cantos* with a further problem in its production of materially new texts which occupy a position of adjacency to the text they translate. Repetition in translation establishes a contiguity which diffracts the singularity of textual identity into a multiplicity. Whilst translations are metaphors for the texts they translate, they simultaneously decentralize and undermine definition in founding a play of difference between translated and original versions. Pound is forced to recognize this early in the composition of the *Cantos*, when, following the superimposition of versions of Homer in Canto 1, he querulously complains in Canto 2:

> Hang it all, Robert Browning,
> there can be but the one 'Sordello.'
> But Sordello, and my Sordello?
> Lo Sordels si fo di Mantovana   (2:6)

Yet whilst Pound continues to translate texts into the fabric of the *Cantos* despite this multiplicatory consequence, in the case of his own operetta, still another *Sordello*, he rejects the possibility of translation altogether, suggesting that it produces a different and alien work. Writing to Agnes Bedford, in April 1933, he observes:

- - - - I do NOT want 'Tos Temps' sung in a
translation. The HOLE point of my moozik bein
that the moozik fits the WORDS and not some
OTHER WORDS. . . .
                It is first strophe, purely conventional
meaning. AND NOT TO BE SUNG OR PRINTED
IN ENGLISH.[28]

Whereas a substitutive functioning of translation urges central-
ization and concurrence, the pole of contiguity (the pole stressed
in the specificity of language's musicality for example) promotes
combination and movement.

The composition of the *Cantos* is clearly confirmed in a drive
towards fixity sponsored in a series of recurrences, repetitions and
metaphors which are to gravitate towards a unificatory equivalence.
Yet since that metaphorical pole works by displacing something to
which it is also related metonymically or adjacently, this fundamental compositional drive is inevitably linked to a diametrically
opposed tendency to decentralize and multiply.

Pound's attitude with regard to his operetta *Sordello*—and
indeed his attitude in all questions of the combination and
interrelation of discourses—is a concern to define what relations
may be held to be acceptable, and to prevent all other relations,
or condemn them for obfuscating definition and precision.

Pound's attitude to translation of his own *Sordello* is evidently
scarcely compatible with his project of a cultural reparation to
be made by renewing ancient texts in creative translation. Concern
to reconstitute an original meaning in new versions is clearly
threatened by the production of materially new texts. Over and
above the question of their quality, translations reveal the way
in which the effectivity of a text depends upon its material construction, rather than being traceable to an anthropological origin.

Pound himself, however, circumvents this problem with the
notion of intention, both in his ascription of a 'HOLE point' to
his own work, and in his arrogation of the capability to perceive
intention and authentic meaning in the works of others. The
function he assigns to intention and empirical perception suffice
for Pound to pre-empt investigation of the conditions of the effects
of his own writing. This sacrosanct identity of a poet arbitrating
significances of pieces of writing and supporting an inscrutable

knowledge process needs to be challenged if any advance is to be made in understanding Pound's work beyond simple eulogy or dismissal.

Psychoanalytic theory provides precisely such an opportunity. Lacan has offered a way of conceiving of the human being or subject as developing as an effect of the symbolic processes in which it may be articulated, and is therefore no longer situated, as is Pound's subject, outside its observed structures and discourses in a position of fixed and controlling specularity (maintaining the distinction *percipiens* and *perceptum*), but is rather the effect of a specific production, a history of acts of coming into place from which observations or discourses are possible. The subject is now continually implicated in the field of its own enunciations. Lacan is thus able to deliver a radical critique of forms of assumption of our apparent autonomy, and to reveal the repression of the work of coming into place which alone can support any presumed detachment from the symbolic orders in which we are constituted.

It is the repression of the metonymic implication of metaphor, in all its forms as translation or repetition or whatever, that enables the subject to regulate its discourses, and to figure as an identity confirmed in domination over signification and over meaning. This repression is precisely that of the kinds of continual productivity which inform both a multiplication of meanings in language recusant to any monological interpretation, and the endless chain of structural causality which, including the subject within the structure, precludes the possibility of any empiricist overview or static definition.

Lacan's work will thus make possible an examination of the *Cantos* which is no longer bound to the privileged level of the intending writer, but which, by recognizing the writer's identity as itself an effect of a discursive production, can question the notions of hierarchical or concentric modes of textual organization. Since Lacan argues that language is inextricably bound to questions of sexuality, such an attention to writing will necessarily also have to take into account a sexual organization of the text, where formal and substantive concerns become inseparable.

It may yet appear that the features which make a cohesive completion of the *Cantos* impossible are domesticated by the poet as devices to prevent the disclosure of that impossibility by avowedly deferring the moment of coherence and conclusion. Nevertheless, these features are in that very gesture by-passing the repression by means of which that aspiration is pursued, and so re-emphasizing the very condition of impossibility. Whilst incompleteness is at one level an intermediary condition on the way to completeness, it is also at another level simply incompleteness itself. Repression of the fact of the poem's interminability is thus continually tied to the element it seeks to repress, and the poem from the outset condemned to live out a failure dictated by its own theoretical conditions.

The earlier observation that the poet's recognition of this failure appears during the composition of sections whose discursive continuity is increasingly organized at the level of the signifier in homophonic, and specifically not etymological, transitions directs our attention away from a diachronic order of language and towards a synchronic order of the letter. The redefinition of the linguistic dimension in which the structure of the *Cantos* is enacted militates against any conception—such as Pound's own—of a linguistic conservation which can preserve order and law. It urges instead a form of analysis, such as has been inaugurated by Lacanian psychoanalysis, in which the synchronic linguistic effects of the unconscious, rather than the dispensations of the Logos, may be explored.

Notes

1 For quotation from and commentary upon these early drafts published in *Poetry* in 1917, see Hugh Kenner, *The Pound Era* (Faber, London, 1971), pp. 356–60. For Pound's recollection of his early problems in finding a form which would include everything, see the interview in *Paris Review*, number 28 (1962), p. 23. The interview has been reprinted in *Writers at Work: The Paris Review Interviews* (Penguin Harmondsworth, 1972), pp. 92–113. This particular recollection occurs p. 93.
2 This conversation is described by Kenner, *op.cit.*, p. 354, and by Noel Stock, *Life*, p. 19; *Life* (Penguin), p. 25.
3 *A Lume Spento: and other Early Poems* (Faber, London, 1965), pp. 38–40. Quoted by Noel Stock, *Life*, p. 29; *Life* (Penguin), p. 37.
4 *Letters*, p. 157.
5 Quoted by Noel Stock, *Life*, p. 184; *Life* (Penguin), pp. 230–1.
6 *Pound/Joyce*, p. 103; quoted by Noel Stock, *Life*, p. 289; *Life* (Penguin), p. 367.
7 *Letters*, p. 385.

8 Daniel D. Pearlman remarks that these Cantos 'were written during the war years, and there is conjecture that they have been suppressed because of libellous content concerning politicians who are still alive. According to Mary de Rachewiltz, however, who knows the cantos and was with her father during the years they were composed, they contain nothing libellous.' See *The Barb of Time: On the Unity of Ezra Pound's Cantos* (New York and Oxford University Press, London, 1969), p. 234n. Charles Olson, for his part, records that during meetings with Pound after the war, the poet confided that these Cantos include the narrative of an Italian girl who has been raped leading Canadian soldiers into a minefield, and being praised in the poem as a resistance fighter. See *Charles Olson and Ezra Pound: An Encounter at St Elizabeths*, edited by Catherine Seelye (Viking Press, New York, 1975), p. 69.

9 See Kenner's descriptions of serialization and privately financed publication in *op.cit.*, p. 279 and p. 303.

10 *Letters*, p. 321.

11 *Ibid.* p. 247; and see Olson, *op.cit.*, p. 70.

12 *Letters*, p. 418.

13 *Ibid.* p. 385.

14 Quoted by Noel Stock, *Life*, p. 296; *Life* (Penguin), p. 376.

15 *Literary Essays*, pp. 92–3.

16 Ezra Pound, *Guide to Kulchur* (Faber, London, 1938; reprinted New Directions, New York, and Peter Owen, London, 1952) p. 142.

17 *Literary Essays*, p. 30.

18 *Ibid.* p. 275.

19 The text of Hanno's *Periplus* has been reproduced and translated in *Paideuma*. See, Caroll F. Terell, 'The *Periplus* of Hanno', *Paideuma*, 1, number 2 (1972), pp. 223–8.

20 It is significant, in relation to questions of evolution versus creation and regeneration, that Pound's thoughts on species follow not Darwin, but Darwin's virtual contemporary, and—through intermediary fellow Harvard professor Asa Gray—adversary, Swiss–US natural historian Louis Agassiz. Agassiz was a religious scientist, but deeply out of sympathy with prevailing ecclesiastical forms; he claimed to seek in his *Nomenclator Zoologicus* a classification to resist a Babel of confusion threatening zoology. Largely by way of his theory of homologies and essential patterns with variant forms, Agassiz argued that zoological classification might be a literal and accurate interpreter (in condensed forms) of the overall plan of creation (cf his *Methods of Study in Natural History* (Boston, 1864), esp. pp. 201–32). In alluding to literature in the introduction to his *Outlines of Comparative Physiology* (London, 1851), written with A. A. Gould, Agassiz likens the natural creation to composition, and suggests that it is only by understanding *intention* that we can ever hope to grasp structure.

21 Pound, *ABC of Reading*, p. 29.

22 *Selected Prose*, p. 137; this aspiration is described by Kenner, *op. cit.* p. 475.

23 *Literary Essays*, p. 59.

24 *Letters*, p. 444.

25 *Ibid.* p. 418.

26 Divisions which can appear between two 'I's' of an utterance have been analysed at a linguistic level by Émile Benveniste in a distinction proposed between the *sujet de l'énonciation* and the *sujet de l'énoncé*. Here for example, the 'I' lamenting the loss of a centre is an 'I' reconstituted in the act of enunciation as the *sujet de l'énonciation*, and only the *sujet de*

l'énoncé is constructed in terms of a loss of the self. It might be said that the effect of this division between the two subjects is part of the operations of language which induce this confession by the poet. See Émile Benveniste, *Problems in General Linguistics*, translated by Mary Elizabeth Meek, 1966 (Coral Gables, University of Miami Press, Florida, 1971), part V.

27 *Letters*, pp. 357–8.
28 *Ibid.* p. 328.

Chapter Four

Fenollosa and Pound: the lyric and vision

LACAN has consistently argued that metaphor and metonymy constitute the two great axes of language which regulate the flow of the signifying chain. Working from this affirmation it becomes possible by considering the arrangement of these linguistic tropes to describe insistences within signification, insistences which take the form of repeated points of closure or limits on the positions available to the subject in its discourses. In that such insistences repeat the terms of, or act out, what Lacan has argued is a construction of the subject in language—its accession to an already constituted symbolic system—the relative dispositions of metaphor and metonymy in discourse may be held to inscribe certain modalities of that assumption of language.

If the linguistic system precedes the entry of the subject into the symbolized world, and exists as a pool of signifiers ready and waiting to be used, then the subject's entry or installation within that system is a taking up of certain available possibilities, and a failure to take up certain others. The limits of the subject's experience might be posed as the range of positions it is able to assume in language. In this limited accession is held the subject's individual history, tied to certain signifiers and arrangements of signifiers, and recalled in the constitution of utterances in those breaks where intended meanings are forestalled by another discourse, that of the unconscious.

In order to understand how limits of a discourse are imposed by the dual functioning of metaphor and metonymy, or how these tropes can carry the weight of unconscious operations which have in readings of Freud's work been more usually associated with representations of things and with a content to be exhumed rather than with a constantly mobile surface such as that of the signifying chain, it is necessary to consider briefly how these tropes are

73

developed by Lacan with regard to the subject's constitution in language.

The emphasis of Lacan's work has been to take up and reformulate that area of Freud's discovery of the unconscious in which the infant's entry into the symbolic world as a sexed and articulate individual is laid out. In this return to and re-reading of Freud, accession to language is held to be made possible by a series of separations from the initially total dependence of the infant upon the mother. At first the infant is believed to have no understanding of the functions of its own body beyond an incomprehensible play of sensations which figure as undifferentiated needs such as the need for food. These needs can only be assuaged by the ministration of the mother.

At a stage of infancy called by Lacan the Mirror Phase, the baby who is still incapable of co-ordination of the body recognizes itself as a unity by means of its reflection in a mirror.[1] Yet whilst in this moment of recognition of the body as discontinuous from the world that world is grasped as separate and other from the subject, nevertheless this otherness, following the paradigm of the mirror image, is conceived as being the same as the subject's self, and the world is unbroken by any significant difference. It is because at this stage the subject enjoys a condition of narcissism where anything other is but a reflection of the self that Lacan has referred to this stage as a realm of the Imaginary. But the subject-centred world of the Imaginary is an evanescent and insupportable fiction. Even in the mirror recognition can be confirmed only in a look from the mother, a look which interrupts the otherwise unbroken surface of narcissistic reflection. Moreover, with the intervention of the father into the previously closed dyadic relation of mother and child a third term undercuts this Imaginary unity in a sequence of ways which were formalized by Freud as the Castration Complex. The effect of the third term, and of the complex which it announces, is to force upon the infant a recognition of the world of signifying differences, a realm Lacan has termed the Symbolic, and it is from this realm that the subsequent articulations of the infant may be cut out or selected.

The fact of sexual difference announced by the appearance of the father may be considered to resume the experience of separation already undergone by the infant from the mother's breast and from its own faeces, and serves to focus this notion of separation as the possibility of a loss. At first, on observing the possible presence or absence of the penis, the infant is unable to accept such a difference except as the possibility of the loss of a penis in castration. Moreover, inasmuch as the mother of the previous dyadic bond appears to love the father, her lack of a penis is instantaneously conceived as the cause of her direction of desires towards him. He is, therefore, at this moment, characterized as a fully endowed presence, a terminal point of desire guaranteed in possession of the penile attribute. This provides the possibility for the infant that he or she is loved for this reason, for in some way being the penis, or the token or index of the penis (which Lacan refers to as the phallus) that the mother lacks.

But if the fact of sexual difference makes possible the world of symbolization by setting up oppositions between terms, its puncturing of the Imaginary is also the irruption of what Lacan has been led to call the Real. This is not reality as it may usually appear, and indeed this latter reality is far from, and opposed to the Real. It is rather the implication in the loss of the Imaginary of a residual lack which will forever remain outside the symbolization installed by the emergence of difference. The Real is not the differences themselves, the Symbolic oppositions which will make language possible, but the very condition of difference, in which the unity of the subject has been lost or split. This loss can never be assimilated and may therefore be posed as the possibility of the subject's own death, as a residue, an irreducible outside which cannot be restored for the subject.[2]

It is the unassimilable desire caused by the fact of difference and the subject's existence in the Real which, reaching even possessors of the phallus, displaces the father as the possible terminal point of his desire. Dissolution of the Castration Complex relies upon a renunciation of the father as the image of an assuager of desire, and so a liberation from dependence upon either of the parents. In this way the subject attains cultural and linguistic order only by means of an anxiety about the possibility of genital privation. The Castration Complex, according to Lacan, serves,

the installation in the subject of an unconscious position without which he would be unable to identify himself with the ideal type of his sex, or to respond without grave risk to the needs of his partner in the sexual relation, or even to accept in a satisfactory way the needs of a child who may be produced by this relation.[3]

It is primarily the fact of anatomical variation with its establishment of the possibility of absence which is able to constitute language as a set of oppositions made across what Saussure recognized as a set of absences, rather than as a series of correspondences of words and things.

Whilst at first the baby's needs might find expression in a simple cry, this enunciation, bringing the mother regardless of any specific requirement, establishes itself as a sign in its provision of a difference between the cry and silence, and presence and absence. In *Beyond the Pleasure Principle*, Freud noticed this modulation of presence and absence correlated with the variable sounds 'o' and 'a' in what he called the fort/da game, deriving this name from the two German words 'fort' and 'da' to which the baby's sounds appear to approximate. In this game the infant learns the fact of presence and absence by throwing and retrieving a cotton reel on the end of a piece of string. Experiencing pleasure both in separation from the reel, and in its restitution, the infant repeats the game.[4] To this discovery of the possible articulation of sounds with difference Lacan attributes the infant's admission to the world of language, 'in which the world of things will be arranged'.[5]

Lacan constantly argues beyond this that whilst the cry and the forbearance from crying, or the throwing and recovering of the reel, make possible the arena of language, they simultaneously set up the condition of the unconscious as the locus of all the absences from consciousness which are at any time necessary to support—as constitutive oppositions—the functioning of any enunciated signifier. The unconscious, then, is not a terrible domain existing before the subject, nor indeed a repository for exclusions from a pre-constituted consciousness in repression, but is rather produced in the very construction of the subject *as a subject*. The unconscious is in consequence a necessary constituent of the possibility of signification. It finds its existence from the fact that the constitutive differences of language have to be repressed in order that we may speak at all, since although the entire fabric of the system of language cannot be present in any utterance, it must nevertheless exist elsewhere if it is to be drawn upon. Unconscious desire is the surplus which the constitution of the Symbolic order in these differences establishes. It is without any specific aim or point of satisfaction because it can have no object, being forged as what is left over by, or is excessive to, the symbolic operations through which satisfaction may be attained. In that it is a residual, unreachable undercurrent of symbolicity, it inheres in the signifying chain as a surplus to the effects which establish conscious meanings, and is liable to be made evident in metonymy. 'Desire is situated in dependence on demand' according to Lacan, demand which,

by being articulated in signifiers, leaves a metonymic remainder that runs under it, an element that is both absolute, and unapprehensible, an element necessarily lacking, unsatisfied, impossible, misconstrued (méconnu), an element that is called desire.[6]

In so far as metonymy is liable to induce desire in the signifying chain, and since desire inscribes an inescapable loss in the subject which defines it as fundamentally lacking, metonymy makes manifest in its displacements of the subject a lack-in-being, the loss the subject suffers by being constituted in the Real.[7]

Metaphor, on the other hand, works to establish one signifier in the signifying chain by supplanting another, and achieves its effects by the relationship between the signifier enounced and the signifier or signifiers it has replaced, or occulted, from the signifying chain. For this reason, Lacan postulates that metaphor is the trope constitutive of the repression necessary for language to operate, a repression caused by the fact that as one signifier is enounced, all its paradigmatic and syntagmatic possibilities not immediately implicated in a context are dismissed, and are therefore, though nevertheless existing in the unconscious, absent from discourse.

Whereas metaphor may be seen to sponsor the emergence of signification only in a simultaneous repression, metonymy is proposed as a trope of the interrelation of signifiers outside any appropriation by the subject. As a surplus or overspill, metonymy is irreducible to intended meanings, and indeed is disruptive of them.[8]

But even if metaphor is described here as the linguistic con-

dition of repression, Lacan nevertheless stipulates its incorporation of a metonymic interval, an interval which effectively resists
that repression:

The creative spark of the metaphor does not spring from the presentation of two images, that is, of two signifiers equally actualized. It
flashes between two signifiers one of which has taken the place of the
other in the signifying chain, the occulted signifier remaining present
through its (metonymic) connexion with the rest of the chain.[9]

What Lacan establishes here is that in our discourses metonymy
is inevitably interfused with the function of metaphor by way of
this perpetuated interval, and that both repression and desire
are necessary conditions for the exercise of language. The terms
of this formulation concur with Freud's observations in the essay
'Repression' concerning the formation of symptoms, but significantly re-orientate them.[10] In stressing the radical emphasis of
Freudian theory by elaborating the construction of the subject,
and arguing that the site of this construction is the arena of
language, Lacan has taken up the problematic question in Freud's
formulation of repression of the symptom as a closed or fixed
representation. The emphasis of this intervention is to suggest
that the manifestation of symptoms is not a series of closed
representations such as Freud implies in the notion of the *'outcome'* of a repression, but is a continuous process conducted at the
level of discursive organization, and becomes evident in the
mechanism of metaphor.

   What is important in this first glimpse at several of the crucial
aspects of Lacanian theory is that even the establishment of so
crude a homology between metaphor and repression, and metonymy and desire, calls forth certain questions about the primarily
metaphorical text as committed to a form of repression, and
the primarily metonymic to the evasion of censorship in allow-
ing unconscious desire to speak. A confusion, generated as we
have seen in an interfusion, of the two tropes in the *Cantos*
evidently suggests a collapse of repressive textual practices. The
superimposition of signifiers in metaphor, aligned by Lacan with
what Freud had isolated in *The Interpretation of Dreams* as the
mechanism of condensation, *Verdichtung*, is noted by Lacan,
following Jakobson on this point, as the trope most suited to

poetry, and whose name, itself condensed as Dichtung, gives the term for poetry in German.[11] Pound himself, in the *ABC of Reading*, had noted this felicity of course.[12] But whereas Lacan and Freud discuss metaphor/condensation as simply one of two great poles which operate indivisibly, Pound is concerned to argue a privileged capability for condensation as the prime or exclusive agent of poetry.

In this context it is relevant to consider Pound's enthusiasm for the scholarship of Ernest Fenollosa, in the editing of whose work *The Chinese Written Character as a Medium for Poetry* he encountered a lengthy discussion of the properties of metaphor in relation both to the general desirability of a pictogrammic language, and to the particular suitability of metaphor for the writing of poetry. Pound never tired of recommending Fenollosa's work, claiming it might provide the basis for a resurgence of Western culture reconciled to the wisdoms of the East. Indeed, he introduces his edited text with a prefatory note suggesting it contains 'not a bare philological discussion, but a study of the fundamentals of all aesthetics.'[13] The increasing density of ideograms in the later Cantos suggests that the reading of Fenollosa substantially informs Pound's own writing. Furthermore, since Fenollosa's discussion of metaphor occurs as part of a larger argument concerning the reflection of the mechanics of nature in language, an attention to his observations here and to their adapted use by Pound may provide an account not simply of his conception of this specific trope, but of his more general theoretical notions of language, and how the system of language may be thought to correspond to the world.

The latter stages of *The Chinese Written Character as a Medium for Poetry* concern themselves with the implications of constellations of metaphor, which the author considers to recreate the world's innate 'homologies, sympathies, and identities'.[14] The perception of a set of relations in the natural world, by means of which 'in reading Chinese we do not seem to be juggling mental contours, but to be watching *things* work out their own fate',[15] recommends an accretion of metaphor as 'the revealer of nature . . . the very substance of poetry'.[16] Fenollosa goes on to make clear the metaphysical pretensions of such a perspective :

Yet the Chinese language with its peculiar materials has passed over from the seen to the unseen by exactly the same process which all the ancient races employed. The process is metaphor, the use of material images to suggest immaterial relations.[17]

These relations form a 'bridge whereby to cross from the minor truth of the seen to the major truth of the unseen.'[18] As such they form a network articulated by a constant relation to the hidden continuity which is held to pervade all the various relations, a secret token by way of which they can all be thought to be part of an overall system. However, these various relations of nature are not enacted in a recurrent occultation of one single immanent signifier, such as is conveyed in the notion of the 'unseen', but involve a continual displacement or contagious series of relations which collectively bind all the diverse signifiers into a complex chain of interpermeations. These are sponsored by a constant invasion by any one signifier of adjacent areas which then open up a new complex of possible concatenations. The pattern produced is precisely the inextricable intertwining of metaphorical and metonymic relations set out above, and it is therefore significant that when Fenollosa instances his metaphorical practice of the ideogram, the examples he furnishes are expressly metonymic in character,

in all poetry a word is like a sun, with its corona and chromosphere; words crowd upon words, and enwrap each other in their luminous envelopes until sentences become clear, continuous light-bands.[19]

'Corona' and 'chromosphere' are not substitutions for 'sun' but explicitly contiguities, or 'envelopes'. The verbal formulations 'crowd upon' and 'enwrap' reinforce the contagious rather than imitative potentiality of this practice. Fenollosa in this way demonstrates a fundamental misunderstanding of the two tropes, a misunderstanding whose effect is to breach the irreducible process of language. It is this process (Fenollosa as we shall see has to acknowledge it in a different context) which prevents the conflation of all the available signifiers in any given language into an equivalence.

Processive permutation within the signifying chain in displacement and transformation indicates that a neglect of the metonymic pole of language in favour of the metaphoric, such as is evident in Fenollosa's metaphysics and indeed such as provides the crucial conditions required by Pound's notion of definition, invokes an impossible degree of repression. The static progenitor of all Fenollosa's homologous natural relations is precisely the desire which inheres or insists in signification, and which is called up in the metonymic consequence of successive metaphors. The 'unseen' presence which is thought to lie behind the chain as an immanent order thus appears—and this explains why it must always remain unseen—as an absence, the desire installed by the possibility of a lack described by psychoanalysis as castration.

It is now possible to find a new significance in Fenollosa's comment:

Our ancestors built the accumulation of metaphor into structures of language and into systems of thought. . . . Nature would seem to have become less like a paradise and more like a factory.[20]

This assertion is effectively a lament that the primary presence, the uninterrupted paradise of the Imaginary which the continual superimposition of metaphor is considered to have established in the ancient Chinese language, has been superannuated in the modern linguistic world of difference, where the subject, now only able to create meanings by a work or a struggle in and against the possibilities of language, is involved in a continuous act of production, that of a 'factory'. Cultural renaissance would be exactly a return to birth in the sense that it would seek to regress beyond the apprehension of difference to a natal or infantile Imaginary.

But in order for language to operate we have seen that metonymy and desire are inevitable, and so a vociferous attempt at retrogressive escape from the world of difference and production is an impossible one. Only in conditions in which the divisive fact of difference might be sufficiently repudiated so as to preserve the narcissistic consistency of the world, and yet sufficiently internalized to make the symbolic system of language operable, would such an escape or such a culture be conceivable. It is these conditions which will need to be examined in detail in order to engage the question of Pound's cultural and political aspirations.

There is, too, another fundamental issue raised in Fenollosa's text. This concerns the claim that not only do constellations of metaphor reveal immanent patterns of nature, but that the Chinese language in particular is reflective of nature by way of its mimetic morphology:

But Chinese notation is something much more than arbitrary symbols. It is based upon a vivid shorthand picture of the operations of nature. In the algebraic figure and in the spoken word there is no natural connection between thing and sign: all depends upon sheer convention. But the Chinese method follows natural suggestion.[21]

Meaning is in such a system held to be endorsable by checking the correspondence of an object with its graphic representation, a simple act of looking once more at nature.

The comfortable specularity which lies behind this notion, and in which meaning is produced when 'overtones vibrate against the eye'[22] is precisely a construction of a world of the Imaginary, where difference is dissolved in the elimination of the object of vision as the place of a possible look back at the subject. The subject is thus given as spectator of a world outside productivity, which may be considered in the instance of vision as the distance and angle which construct any particular point of view. The place of the object as the possible site of a look must be eliminated to preserve this relation of specularity since a look from there cannot be assimilated as simply another point of view, but is a radical blindspot in the subject's vision. Specularity replaces the work involved in the point of view with a reassuring certitude of sameness, and the visual intelligibility of the ideogram— Gaudier-Brzeska could, according to Pound, read Chinese quite well by bringing to bear his sculptor's visual sensibility[23]—as indeed of representation in general, attests the extent of our acceptance, our illusion. This effectivity of representation is not put into question by the multiplicity of possible points of view, since what is not embraced by one may be included in another, even if within that range our notions are largely governed by a convention of horizontal elevation, and would be initially confused, for example, by a pictogram for 'man' sketched in a downward vertical plan.

Lacan's examination of Holbein's 'The Ambassadors' in *Le*

Séminaire XI, however, has shown how the introduction of an element of visual intelligibility limited to one constructed viewing position and dispelled from all others breaks up this easy specularity.[24] In the case of this painting the object suspended in anamorphosis is a skull, which can only be seen as such at an oblique angle to the canvas. The intrusion of the skull when viewed in this way forces upon a viewer held in the picture's framed Imaginary the realm of the Symbolic, by demonstrating the necessity of production in the point of view. This optical effect restores the illusion of naturally represented objects to a composition as various marks on the canvas whose differential relations collectively form a picture when viewed in a particular way. By use of this painting Lacan is able to show a fundamental similarity between the organization of the scopic field and that of language, namely as fields established in the order of the Symbolic but functioning in a shift back from this field in a combination with the Imaginary, as representations.

In that what is at stake in such a closing off of the Symbolic to create a point of view is control over a difference which is most forcibly recognized in the fact of genital variation, Lacan refers to the creation of our visual representations in terms of an elusion of castration. Whilst the scopic field is articulated around such a castration by virtue of its composition from a set of differences, our visual mastery is confirmed only in a resistance to that castration. Accordingly, Lacan observes that what Holbein's painting reveals is 'something symbolic of the function of the lack, of the appearance of the phallic ghost',[25] since as the signifier of sexual difference the phallus symbolizes the intrusion into the painting of the lack upon which the organization of the scopic field is founded.

Even in the era of Holbein, Lacan suggests, when an optical science emerged correlative to the first promulgations of the philosophical category of the subject, the constitutive lack in our vision can be seen to subvert the establishment of subjective identity:

Holbein makes visible for us here something that is simply the subject as annihilated—annihilated in the form, that is, strictly speaking, the imaged embodiment of the MINUS-PHI ($-\varphi$) of castration, which for us, centres the whole organization of the desires through the framework of the fundamental drives.[26]

This argument is then enfolded in Lacan's discussion of repetition in its clear enactment of the phallus, the lacking phallus which indicates the castration notated in the Lacanian algebra as $-\varphi$, minus-phi. The skull, whose emergence reveals this lack—and incidentally foreshadows death, which is the only termination of our desire—appears in a frontal view of the painting as a diagonal protuberance.[27]

What is significant in Fenollosa's adoption of vision as the founding condition of a natural language is its initial reliance upon vision itself as natural ('natural suggestion'). Not only is this language fixed against diachronic transformation, which would disrupt any simple equation between representation and meaning and so constrain reading to a conservative archaeology, but the primal moment to which that etymological pursuit might lead can be seen to be itself only a mirage. For such a primal moment is an insupportable presumption about the scopic field, and about the 'naturalness' of what Fenollosa calls 'our forgotten mental processes'.[28]

It is now possible to develop the critique of certain aspects of Pound's thought offered above: in particular, his empiricism and belief in a natural world from which ethics and culture might be derived. These may now be understood in terms of an elimination of the production entailed in sight and in language, an elimination which deceptively suggests a natural world of extraordinarily simple self-evidence, where we need only look at to know. Unquestioning emphasis on such a world can now be grasped as a denial of the castration through which 'the subject is constructed by being cut out from a set of symbolic differences. Appearance as a subject is the effect of a covering for that lack.

But there is another face to Fenollosa's text, a face much less in accordance with Pound's predilection for identity and for stasis, and it is not surprising, therefore, that this face passes without comment from Pound in any of his citations of Fenollosa. Moreover, as we shall see in considering the lyrical sections of the poem, it does not inform the writing practices of the *Cantos*. This aspect of Fenollosa's thought concerns the processive character of nature, which is stressed in Chinese, he claims, in a relative subordination of those parts of language which confer names to those which trace movements and transfers of energy:

A true noun, an isolated thing, does not exist in nature. Things are only the terminal points, or rather the meeting points, of actions, cross-sections cut through actions, snap-shots. Neither can a pure verb, an abstract motion, be possible in nature. The eye sees noun and verb as one : things in motion, motion in things, and so the Chinese conception tends to represent them.[29]

Fenollosa goes to considerable pains to demonstrate, in tracing the verb 'to exist' to 'to stand forth', 'is' to 'to breathe', and 'to be' to 'to grow', that the formulation of a simple ontology is a dilution of earlier, and more energetic, expressions, arguing that static identity is not possible within the natural world.[30] Whilst Fenollosa's observations about nouns and verbs are still reliant finally upon the eye, 'the eye sees . . .', his recognition of perception in continual process relocates the static representation of the ideogram formerly conceived as a discrete and coherent instant, as now a successive play of ideogrammic units, where each constitutive view enjoys an imaginary relation to the object, and where the accretion of representations postulates for itself a summative totality. This clearly resembles Pound's notion of a total structure becoming finally apparent on the completion of the sum of all points of view, and is similarly dependent upon an external full presence.

Yet what Fenollosa proposes is a theoretical interminability to natural process :

And though we may string ever so many clauses into a single compound sentence, motion leaks everywhere, like electricity from an exposed wire. All processes in nature are interrelated; and thus there could be no complete sentence (according to this definition) save one which it would take all time to pronounce.[31]

Whilst a certain hesitancy may be discerned here in the parenthesis which implicitly invites other compatible definitions to reformulate this one, and in the concessive totality 'all time', what Fenollosa commits himself to here is a continual displacement in metonymy, a diffusive leakage. This amounts to a recognition of the metonymic or contagious implication of metaphor, although such a recognition does not provoke, as it should, a requestioning of the selective basis on which certain privileged relations are formed amidst such an infinity, or how out of such

a flux the world may be seen—as Pound would come to see it—
as a set of static proportions. Fenollosa is left in the position of
being unable to give any account of how his 'valid scientific
thought' may be established, that procedure which 'consists in
following as closely as may be the actual and entangled lines of
forces as they pulse through things'.[32] Differentiation of these
forces from those which are not 'actual', and are therefore in-
admissible to science, can only be discerned in an equally 'natural'
relation of observation.

In the lyrical episodes of the *Cantos* these problems of the
Fenollosan epistemology and poetic are only tacitly questioned,
in so far as Pound diverges from the exhortation to stress those
aspects of language, such as verbs, which convey motion and
transfer of energy, and to avoid static nouns. Pound's lyrical,
paradisal sections are regularly characterized by the foregrounding
of unattached nouns, and of parts of the verb most removed from
exchange of energy—passives, infinitives and past participles.
This may be clearly seen in an example from Canto 17, which
intervenes in the course of the poem between discourses pertain-
ing to the First World War and the Russian Revolution in Canto
16, and allusions to armaments dealing and the adventures of
Marco Polo in Canto 18:

> Flat water before me,
> and the trees growing in water,
> Marble trunks out of stillness,
> On past the palazzi,
> in the stillness,
> The light now, not of the sun.
> Chrysophrase,
> And the water green clear, and blue clear;
> On, to the great cliffs of amber.
> Between them,
> Cave of Nerea,
> she like a great shell curved,
> And the boat drawn without sound,
> Without odour of ship-work,
> Nor bird-cry, nor any noise of wave moving,
> Nor splash of porpoise, nor any noise of wave moving,
> Within her cave, Nerea,
> she like a great shell curved

In the suavity of the rock,
                    cliff green-gray in the far,
In the near, the gate-cliffs of amber,
And the wave
                green clear, and blue clear,
And the cave salt-white, and glare-purple,
                    cool, porphyry smooth,
                    the rock sea-worn.
No gull-cry, no sound of porpoise,
Sand as of malachite, and no cold there,
                    the light not of the sun.   (17 : 76–7)

The six verb forms in these twenty-nine lines are all participles, three present, and three past; all are either passive or intransitive, even though two of them, a reiteration of 'moving', imply (paradoxically) a transitive quality enfolded in this latter word's etymology. Clearly these verbal constructions do not trace the transfer of energy from one noun to another in the manner suggested by Fenollosa, but describe a world in which a governing energy insists, either as a completed fact, in past participles whose determination is necessarily passive, or as intransitive present participles in which action is not a transformation through work, but an immanent process.

The stillness which is established by the suppression of production in this world of immanent energy ('out of stillness', 'in the stillness') is accompanied by a preponderance of nouns of negative denomination, a quarter of all the nouns in the passage quoted. These explicit absences then designate verbal effects which must also be non-existent, 'Nor bird-cry, nor any noise of wave moving'. The episode may justifiably be termed 'paradisal' since transcendence is inscribed in a passage through the realm of the linguistic to that of the ineffable, a preternaturality which can only be described in the naming of objects and actions which it is not. It *is* consequently something other than these objects and energies, and can only find its existence in the establishment of a difference from them. What is important in this ineffability as regards a general understanding of language is that the negativization of nouns and their delineation of adjacent areas, for example 'the light, not of the sun', demonstrates precisely a structuration of language in difference rather than in any form of correspondence. What this structure of difference sets up is

D

not the intuition of the unseen, but the conditions of the unconscious, and of desire.

Yet if this passage describes only things which are not, how is
it that we can describe it as a scene, a lyrical presentation, in which
the very term 'presentation' commits us to a notion of presence,
rather than of absence? To answer this question, it is necessary
to reconsider how for Fenollosa language and the world could
be held to order by the sponsorship of vision. For this passage
is constructed explicitly as a pictorial representation, beginning
with the words 'Flat water before me', where this 'before me'
not only determines that what follows is not a play of signifiers
but a record of a perception, but further that this perception is
organized around the perspective of the scopic field. Movement
which cannot be discerned at the level of verbal energy reappears
in prepositional phrases of place, such as 'on past the palazzi',
'between them', or 'in the far . . . in the near', which conduct
a gaze across the field represented. The designation 'now' fixes
the passage in a specific historical instant, and the term 'there' ('no
cold there') locates the viewer outside the area of the viewed,
in an exterior, specular position. In this way the passage constructs its subject as a passive witness to a pre-constituted and
motionless scene, a homogeneous consumer presented outside
the production either of language, which forges a subjectivity
in an otherwise uncontrollable play of signifiers, or of the scopic
field, in which every place is the possibility of the look which
tells castration.

The apparent homogeneity of the subject established in such
a lyrical section is in no way questioned by the interpolation of
the passage between the very different discourses of Canto 16 or
Canto 18. Although contradictions emerge between these discourses, and indeed between the constitutive sections of any single
Canto, yet in so far as discourses maintain individually this
coherent subject position, the constant shifting of the *Cantos*
merely retotalizes the subject in each move. Whilst the poem
may appear discursively discontinuous, it is unified at this level
of organization by the consistency with which it sets up a consumer position for the subject.

But if it is evidently not at the level of the interjection of
lyrical episodes themselves into the course of the poem that this
machinery of fixed subject positions is threatened, it is never-

theless one constitutive aspect of these episodes—their establishment of a restricted set of signifiers which subsequently circulate in the poem as a pool of insistent allusion—which *does* have this effect. Continual reproduction of these signifiers demonstrates how particular meanings may be secured for given signifiers only by specific constructions of the signifying chain. The intra-allusive texture of the poem produces patterns of association which cross and recross their own trails and traces, and this repetition allows new signifieds to graft themselves onto recurrent signifiers according to peculiarities of context in the chain. This cleaves the illusion of a united sign according to which meanings may be held to be determined for any given signifier by an immutable correspondence or definition, and indicates a surplus in the signifier, its capability to produce effects other than those specifiable as a predetermined signified.

The dense counterpoint of particularly the later *Cantos*, which as we have seen Pound considered a major structural agent of the poem, foregrounds a compulsion to repeat in a constant criss-crossing of signifiers. However, the possibility of exact redoubling, which in the fantasy of a language constructed as a series of definitions might reduplicate an original identity unchanged, is precluded by the constitution of language as a set of differences, and consequently repetition serves to differentiate or split any imagined unity.

An example from Canto 110 may illustrate how a plurality of senses can be summoned by an associative complex:

> The harl, feather-white, as a dolphin on sea-brink
>
> I am all for Verkehr without tyranny
>   —wake exultant
>   in carcarole
> Hast'ou seen boat's wake on sea-wall,
>   how crests it?   (*110*:777)

The word 'wake' here clearly at one level refers to the trace of a boat, and indeed this sense is made explicit in its repetition in conjunction with the word 'boat' itself. But the sense of a transition from sleep to waking is also implicated for this first 'wake', since it is implicitly contingent upon a first person subject ('I am all for . . .') and is immediately followed by an expression of feeling ('exultant'). Repetition here establishes a multiplicity of senses for the word 'wake' which can only be arbitrated between according to the specific characteristics of the signifying chain, since there is no etymological or other explanatory link.

What needs to be stressed about these felicities is that they bear no relation either to a theory of the mimetic transcription of nature in language, nor to the possibility of verbal definition, except as transgressions. If it has been seen that the *Cantos* are undermined at the level of their overall organization by a failure to resolve the various discourses in a moment of coherence and in this way to contain meanings within a circumscribing form, it can now be recognized that this foreclosure of such a moment is largely attributable to what Fenollosa recognized as the interminability of a complete sentence which would not have any leaks into further relations and significations. This interminability might be restated as always the possibility of one signifier more, the condition of metonymy and of desire.

The endless prolongation the *Cantos* suffer may be grasped not as the poet's inability to embrace the entirety of world history, though of course this is in another sense true, but as the effect of an ineffectual repression of surplus agencies of language. These assert that language is not a transparent means of communication, but a material to be moulded and worked. And it is this surplus of language, the possibility of a multiplicity of relations to be made at the level of the signifier in homophony and so on, which allows unconscious desire to speak in and across the intended discourses of the poet. Whilst the particular excess meaning chosen above as illustration merely indicates a formalism in which language always says more than we intend, the agencies this example indicates make way for the possibility of considering the text as pervasively traversed by unconscious processes.

In so far as the construction of the subject in language is enacted principally at the level of infantile sexuality, and centrally around the issue of castration, this continual implication of the unconscious in writing amounts to a repetitive inscription of those formative erotic conditions and experiences. Since what is in question in castration is fundamentally the presence or absence of the penis, and so an adoption of a relation to this symbolic penis, the phallus (which Lacan has called a 'simulacrum' of the penis[33]), it will now be seen why an examination of the phallus in the *Cantos* should be both a thematic and a formal affair. Not only can a repudiation of castration's lack by fetishizing the phallus endow a subject with control over difference and so confer a domination over language such as Pound assumes throughout his writing, but the recurrent complexes of association which gravitate together in the *Cantos* find a constant point of return in the male impregnation of the female with seed, and the consequences of this upon growth.

Sexuality appears also at the level of Pound's cultural and political theories of natural fecundity, and is established there in a series of symbolic equations which regulate the associative concatenations of the poem into two loosely grouped areas of circulation, which are invested with opposite values and confront one another. The first of these is the coveted pole of order, verbal definition, truth, light, cleanliness, fertility and paradise, and the second is the force of division and disruption in darkness, chaos, chicanery and hell. Each grouping comes into being by way of a series of alignments and associative exchanges which localize the play in any array of signifiers.

But in order to understand how such thematic insistences relate to the subject's accession to language, and so to the formal constitution of the text, it is necessary to recall Freud's understanding of repetition as a dramatization of psychical conflict. In his clinical experiences dealing with questions surrounding transference and analytic technique, Freud described repetition as occurring when,

the patient does not *remember* anything of what he has forgotten and repressed, but *acts* it out. He reproduces it not as a memory but as an action; he repeats it, without, of course, knowing that he is repeating it.[34]

I will argue that the ubiquitous inscription of the phallus in the *Cantos* and elsewhere in Pound's writing repeats precisely an anxiety about castration. Only a successful resistance to castration might preserve the domination over sight, language and cultural order upon which we have seen Pound's understanding of his own work relies.

That sexuality is in this way for Pound fundamental to the fixing of a law for language and society is announced quite explicitly in a short narrative sequence appended to Canto 22. This describes a trial for rape and blackmail, and is occupied with exactly the attachment of multiple meanings to the signifier. Pound states his own conceptualized position on this multiplication of meanings in relation to the law in a note on style in *A Visiting Card,*

the legal or scientific word . . . must, at the outset, be defined with the greatest possible precision, and never change its meaning.[35]

The determining of linguistic usage in the specific instance of a trial for rape inscribes this implication of sexuality in a juridic context, and in that the trial further concerns a charge of blackmail, incorporates the question of an unjust appropriation of the letter and of language, an appropriation which may be regulated in the court's decision.

The agreed naming of things is important to this sequence in that certain garments of female attire are proscribed, and the girl's recalcitrance to the judge's terminology is precisely a rejection of the set of linguistic equations which make the exercise of the law possible. The judge's admonitions are directed towards her transgression of these sartorial restrictions, and her replies are all linguistically irregular:

> 'Not a veil,' she says, "at's a scarf.'
>
> 'Ermine?' the girl says, 'Not ermine that ain't,
> "At's lattittzo.'
>
> > 'It'z a animal.'   (22 : 105–6)

When held in opposition to the judge's relative elocution, these replies suggest a failing on her part to accept the proper functioning of language. Indeed, this is reinforced by the respectful prefix 'Signori' to the line,

> Signori, *you* go and enforce it.   (22 : 106)

By virtue of this prefix, this comment becomes an unwilling resignation to the breakdown of the law.

Inasmuch as the judge's reproaches about garments concern the decoration of the female body in more than functional clothing, in scarfs or veils, bobbles or buttons and the like, the girl's reluctance can be further understood as a refusal of any complicity in the crime of rape by soliciting it in wearing provocative clothes. The judge's reprimands, continually returning to second person accusations ('Well, anyway, you're not allowed'), cannot in the absence of any reference to other victims or defendants be understood in any way except in the context of the girl as the victim of the crime. Consideration of the obstruction of the law as an effect of her linguistically deviant testimony installs, within the authoritative discourses of the judge, an equation between the undermining of the law and the undermining of the proper operation of male sexuality, which may be restrained from such crimes in the implementation of a law of female clothing. Regulation of the male sexual urge is conceived in terms of a necessity for restrictive impositions upon female conduct, and of restricting expressions of female desire.

The productivity of language, carried in a multiplication of meanings across the various versions of the names for garments which intimately surround the female body, is thus seen to be inimical to any clear functioning of this patriarchal institution of law. In this light it becomes significant that the elements of the text outside the quoted speech of the interlocutors confirm this regulative terminology of the judge:

> And the judge says: That veil is too long.
> And the girl takes off the veil
> That she has stuck onto her hat with a pin,
> 'Not a veil,' she says, "at's a scarf.'   (22 : 105)

In accepting 'veil' rather than 'scarf', the discourse of the poem which articulates these verbal practices—and so claims its access to truth in deciding between them and resolving, as final arbiter, their contradictions in coherence—aligns itself in this discrepancy with the deliberations of the judge. This serves to affirm definition and law over language and sex, and against productivity and desire.

Despite this judgement, the fracture of the signifier and the signified which we have seen to occur throughout the *Cantos*, and indeed to be a general appurtenance of language, suggests a more proper functioning of language in the practices of the girl, who, recognizing the inadequacy of the correspondence of word and thing, initiates discourse to locate the signified:

> And she says: Those ain't buttons, them's bobbles.
> Can't you see there ain't any button-holes?   *(22 : 106)*

Notes

1 This was one of the first interventions made by Lacan in the theory of psychoanalysis, and dates at least from 1936. See the essay 'The Mirror Stage as Formative of the Function of the I as revealed in Psychoanalytic Experience', *Écrits: A Selection*, pp. 1–7; *Écrits*, pp. 93–100.

2 The concept of the Real has been discussed—with detailed commentary on its inevitable difficulty—by Stephen Heath, in 'Anata Mo', *Screen*, 17, number 4, pp. 49–56, and pp. 60–3.

3 *Écrits: A Selection*, p. 281; *Écrits*, p. 685.

4 *Standard Edition*, vol. XVIII, pp. 14–17.

5 *Écrits: A Selection*, p. 65; *Écrits*, p. 276.

6 *Four Fundamental Concepts*, p. 154; *Le Séminaire XI*, p. 141.

7 Lacan refers to this fundamental lack-in-being as a *manque-à-être*. See, *Four Fundamental Concepts*, p. 29; *Le Séminaire XI*, p. 31.

8 Lacan's formulation of these tropes clearly differs from established frameworks of analysis, such as Jakobson's analysis in terms of aphasia, and Christine Broke-Rose's *A Grammar of Metaphor* (Secker & Warburg, London, 1958), which examines how a body of different metaphorical effects may be constructed in various grammatical formations such as the 'genitive link', the verbal relation, or by way of the verb 'to be'. Detailed commentary on existing modes of analysis, and particular examination of distinctions needing to be made between the order of discourse with its constituents paradigm and syntagm and that of 'reference' with metaphor and metonymy, may be found in Christian Metz, *Le Signifiant Imaginaire* (10/18 edition, Paris, 1977), pp. 177–371. Metz's emphasis, however, is not on the definitive contra-distinction of these levels, but on modes of their interrelation.

9 *Écrits: A Selection*, p. 157; *Écrits*, p. 507.

10 *Standard Edition*, vol. XIV, pp. 154–5.

11 For Lacan's remarks on these relationships between the tropes and the unconscious processes, see *Écrits: A Selection*, p. 160; *Écrits*, p. 511. For

Freud's account of condensation, see 'The Interpretation of Dreams', *Standard Edition*, vol. IV, pp. 279–304; for the account of displacement, *ibid.* pp. 305–9. Jakobson's observations on this relationship have already been described in chapter 1, p. 6.

12 Ezra Pound, *ABC of Reading*, p. 36, and see above, chapter 2, p. 25.
13 P. 3. For examples of Pound's exaltation of the work of Fenollosa in the context of a new science upon which to base future civilizations in the West, see 'The Renaissance', *Literary Essays*, p. 219, or 'Immediate Need of Confucius', *Selected Prose*, p. 92.
14 E. Fenollosa, *The Chinese Written Character as a Medium for Poetry* (City Light Books, San Francisco, 1936), p. 22.
15 *Ibid.* p. 9.
16 *Ibid.* p. 23.
17 *Ibid.* p. 22.
18 *Ibid.* pp. 22–3.
19 *Ibid.* p. 32.
20 *Ibid.* p. 24.
21 *Ibid.* p. 8.
22 *Ibid.* p. 32.
23 *Ibid.* p. 30n.
24 *Four Fundamental Concepts*, pp. 79–90; *Le Séminaire XI*, pp. 75–84.
25 *Four Fundamental Concepts*, p. 88; *Le Séminaire XI*, p. 82.
26 *Four Fundamental Concepts*, pp. 88–9; *Le Séminaire XI*, p. 83.
27 Lacan locates the 'tuché' in which the subject is approached in this picture by the Real in the look installed by the eyes of the skull, and remarks upon the use of the mask in painting—especially the paintings of Goya—which also has this effect. But the emergence of castration in the painting—the demonstration of what Lacan refers to as his 'soft watch', alluding to paintings by Salvador Dali—relates to a structure of vision, not to the representation of a content. Hence Lacan's small enthusiasm for Dali's own paintings in this passage, *Four Fundamental Concepts*, pp. 87–90, *Le Séminaire XI*, pp. 82–4. For discussion of the geometry of vision in relation both to sexuality, and to representation and theatricality, see Roland Barthes, 'Diderot, Brecht, Eisenstein', in *Image-Music-Text*, essays selected and translated by Stephen Heath (Fontana, London, 1977).
28 Fenollosa, *op.cit.*, p. 21.
29 *Ibid.* p. 10.
30 *Ibid.* p. 15.
31 *Ibid.* p. 11.
32 *Ibid.* p. 12.
33 See *Écrits: A Selection*, p. 285; *Écrits*, p. 690.
34 In 'Remembering, Repeating, and Working Through', *Standard Edition*, vol. XII, p. 150.
35 *Selected Prose*, p. 291.

Chapter Five

Dissimulating authority: Gourmont, the haves and the have-nots, Fascism

IN order, then, to demonstrate how sexuality emerges in the argumentative content of the *Cantos*, it is necessary to lay out at least some of the symbolic equations which gradually insist upon certain privileged relations between signifiers in the poem's patterns of association. These equations also bar relations between other signifiers, until certain complexes evince a degree of synonymy or equivalence, whereas others are polarized into antithetical opposition. The accumulation of this practice, working with a limited range of signifiers frequently reduplicated, establishes a code of exchange and interchangeability, and fuses various paths of association until the presentation of one signifier implies the possibilities of signification of other signifiers which are not in that instance manifest. This practice works within a finite extension marked out by the opposing investments of other patterns including other complexes of signifiers.

The importance of isolating this recurrent nucleus of association is that it underpins cultural and historical hypotheses made at other levels of the poem, and so contributes to the formation of inscribed meanings. An analysis of how these meanings are constructed, and what is deficient or ineffectual in that construction must be made if prevalent interpretations of the poem which operate by consuming those inscribed meanings are to be shown to be misguided, and so dislodged.

Canto 39 opens with a sexual encounter 'in the ingle of Circe':

> When I lay in the ingle of Circe
> I heard a song of that kind.
>   Fat panther lay by me

Girls talked there of fucking, beasts talked there of eating,
All heavy with sleep, fucked girls and fat leopards,

(39:193)

Diffusing through discourses which recount the finding of Hathor
afloat in a box, the Canto closes in a celebration of reproduction:

> Beaten from flesh into light
> Hath swallowed the fire-ball
> A traverso le foglie
> His rod hath made god in my belly
>   Sic loquitur nupta
>   Cantat sic nupta
>
> Dark shoulders have stirred the lightning
> A girl's arms have nested the fire,
> Not I but the handmaid kindled
>   Cantat sic nupta
> I have eaten the flame.

(39:196)

Several important and recurrent chains of association in the
Cantos circulate here, ones which as we shall see are fundamental
to erecting the power of the phallus. 'Beaten from flesh into
light' recalls the 'beat of the measure' (39:195) fifteen lines
before, the rhythmic pattern of both sexual intercourse and
poetic discourse. The passive construction 'beaten' reflects a passivity of women in all Pound's formulations of coition, 'hath
swallowed', 'his rod hath made god', 'I have eaten', or the earlier
'fucked girls'. Indeed, this passivity may be seen to order at the
level of the diathetic disposition of the verb the respective roles
of male and female in the short poem ' ἱμέρρω ',[1] where on the
other hand the male desire for Atthis is exclusively represented
in active verbs.

Significantly, the girl of Canto 39 whose 'dark shoulders have
stirred the lightning', is thus transformed into light and a conception of divine offspring. Not only does this initial darkness
invoke the dark continually ascribed in the *Cantos* to women,
inscribed largely in the nocturnal wiles of Circe and the more

directly infernal occupations of Proserpine, but her corporeality
('beaten from flesh') alludes to a section of Canto 29 where this
bodily constitution is further elaborated:

> She is a submarine, she is an octopus, she is
> A biological process,
>
> (*29* : 145)

This corporeality—in Canto 39 opposed to ethereal knowledge—
is refound here in the word 'biological', and the general comment
about the female, 'Chiefest of these the second, the female'
(*29* : 144) now forges further links whereby this subordinate
creature woman becomes related to the sea ('she is a submarine'),
and to polyvalency (she is 'an octopus').

In Canto 113, for example, a reference to the sea can by a
smooth transition introduce the uncertain disposition of the
female:

> Sea, over roofs, but still the sea and the headland.
> And in every woman, somewhere in the snarl is a tenderness,
>
> (*113* : 789)

Not only does this formulation allude to the teeth of Scilla
mentioned in Canto 47 (*47* : 236 and 238), but reflects back upon
the rhythm of sex and poetry by way of its continuation in Canto
90 as a situation of the spring consecrated to the Muses, Castalia,
directly over the sea:

> Castalia is the name of that fount in the hill's fold,
>   the sea below,
>   narrow beach.
>
> (*90* : 605)

This suggestion is itself extended in Canto 94—just as Pound's
theory of poetry is also one of ethics—to the notion of the law
of Antoninus which can rule over the sea:

'Law rules the sea'
meaning lex Rhodi
(94 : 639)

The light into which the girl of the sexual encounter in Canto 39 is transformed further anticipates that of Father Helios, who at the end of Canto 113 leads out of darkness and away from the mind's confusion. Accordingly, the girl's sexual accession to light is to be understood as specifically a mental clarification. It is this light which 'has entered the cave' (47 : 238) in that section of Canto 47 which precipitates, as in the 'Ver novum!' (39 : 193 and 195) of this Canto, the coming of spring's fecundity: 'Fruit cometh after—' (47 : 238). The transfer of this light, conducted in the flame or lightning which is swallowed by the female, is in this way precisely the ejaculation which invests the female with knowledge.

The beginning of Canto 95 not only endorses this equation between loving and lightning, but the longevity of its progeny indicates a cultural ordination which accompanies vegetable growth:

LOVE, gone as lightning,
enduring 5000 years.
(95 : 643)

Indeed these cultural implications of 'amor' are further ramified in a diagram in *A Visiting Card*: [2]

```
R O M A
O       M
M       O
A M O R
```

A similar relation is established in the poem 'Tenzone' in *Lustra*, where reluctance to accept Pound's early collection is made analogous to the flight of a 'timorous wench from a centaur/

(or a centurion)', the felicity of the shared syllable 'cent-' installing a link between the equine lust of mythological centaurs, the publication of verse, and the power of Roman military order.[3]

In Canto 47 the light entering the cave is drawn explicitly on the model of the sexual interrelation of male and female:

> So light is thy weight on Tellus
> Thy notch no deeper indented
> Thy weight less than a shadow
> Yet hast thou gnawed through the mountain,
>   Scylla's white teeth less sharp.
> Hast thou found a nest softer than cunnus
> Or hast thou found better rest
> Hast'ou a deeper planting, doth thy death year
> Bring swifter shoot?
> Hast thou entered more deeply the mountain?
>
> The light has entered the cave. Io! Io!
>
>   (47 : 238)

The accumulation of these correspondences confirms the penis as the organ governing stability and order, and whose emissions, coming as the culmination of the poetic and sexual measure, invest the female, the reader, and the earth with knowledge, law and light.

Woman is the receiver of the phallic transmission, the 'handmaid' of Canto 39 who has 'nested the fire'. In Canto 47, it is significantly 'cunnus' which is the 'nest' chosen and beloved above all others. The subordination of woman suggested in the formulation 'handmaid' is corroborated in Canto 29:

> Chiefest of these the second, the female
> Is an element, the female
> Is a chaos
> An octopus
> A biological process
>   and we seek to fulfill ...
> TAN AOIDAN, our desire, drift ...
>
>   (29 : 144)

A rather longer example from Canto 99 may show how the phallus makes an explicit appearance in these associative concatenations:

> Unsifted hot words, at first merely to flatter
> as an animal his eye eating light
>   or run to rat holes
> Laws must be for the general good,
>   for the people's uprightness,
>   their moral uprightness.
> Ch'ung² venerate
> Black out the eroders, hsieh²
>   venerate honest men
> The great balance is not made in a day
>   nor for one holiday only.
> The business of relatives is filiality,
>   a gentleman's job is his sincerity.
>
>   (99:697)

> Wang: that man's phallic heart is from heaven
>   a clear spring of rightness,
> Greed turns it awry,
> Bright, gleaming, ming
> kuang¹ in traverse
> need you go so far to burn incense?
> VIII. Let the laws be made clear,
>   Illumine the words of procedure,
>   (99:697-8)

> But their First Classic: that the heart shd/be straight,
> The phallos perceive its aim.
>   (99:702)

> Soldiers also have bodies,
>   take care of the body as implement,
> It is useful,
> To shield you from floods and rascality.
>   (99:706)

Here Wang's observation that 'man's phallic heart is from heaven/ a clear spring of rightness' not only brings together the penis

and the heart, and thus amor ('the heart shd/be straight'), but
further, by way of the epithet 'clear', addresses itself to light and
flame as emblems of knowledge and law as well as of male dis-
semination. The 'spring' to which this clarity is attributed resumes
the association of the Castalian fount, as a source of fluid presiding
over inspiration and art.

That this fluid should be one of 'rightness' also engages conceptions of the law, which needs to be illumined to be made
'clear'. Laws which are required for the people's 'uprightness' are
those which sift 'hot words', and so reproductive seed assumes
the function of ordering language as well as of controlling public
order. In Canto 106 a relation is forged between this notion of a
public law and the fecundity of nature:

> That the goddess turn crystal within her
> This is grain right
>
> (*106* : 753)

This action now becomes intelligible as an incorporation of the
crystal, whose hardness recalls the opposition of 'phallic' and
'macerations' in *Hugh Selwyn Mauberley*.[4] By turning the crystal
within her, the goddess can reflect the light inherent in the
phallus, her internalization of the gem recasting the notion of
eating the flame. The female of the later Cantos can be a reflection
of phallic light both as an image—a virtual mirror reflection of
that male consistency—and as a figure of secondary importance,
a disciple who simply absorbs the creativity which emanates
from the male genital, her 'deep waters', again in Canto 106,
'reflecting all fire' (*106* : 753).

This configuration in which 'hot words' are restrained by law
prompts a tenacious insistence upon civilizations being upheld by
their ability to define the word, and by their adoption of the
related principle of a natural increase spreading from the prov-
enance of the phallus and implemented in the distribution or
transmission of seed. Over-production, on the other hand, operating in excess of the regulation of the phallus as a kind of unbridled productivity, disrupts all Pound's economic and linguistic
systems.

In 'Immediate Need of Confucius' Pound writes:

The kind of thought which distinguishes good from evil, down into the details of commerce, rises into the quality of line in paintings and into the clear definition of the written word.[5]

Here clarity becomes the arbiter of good and evil as well as being the principle of artistic creation, and a continuity is postulated between law, economics, painting and writing. In the *ABC of Economics* Jefferson's politics are understood in luminous terms, 'By the light of his intelligence American economics improved from the time of the revolution till the confusion of the U.S. civil war.'[6] Clarity becomes equatable with intelligence, and is held in opposition to confusion.

In 'National Culture—A Manifesto 1938', this polarization of law and order, clarity, definition, and men of genius, as against chaos and confusion, is further extended to include the opposition of clean and dirty (in the word 'befouling'), an opposition which we shall see in the next chapter is central to Pound's vituperation against Jewry:

The befouling of terminology should be put an end to. It is a time for clear definition of terms. . . . It is not a revolution of the word but a castigation of the word. And that castigation must precede any reform.

An administration that can not or dare not define money, credit, debt, property, capital, is unlikely to provide a durable solution of national chaos or evolve a durable system of national order.

In aiming this manifesto at a few dozen just men I am trying. . . .[7]

The nation, like the female, is chaos until administered by men capable of definition, order and castigation.

But the associations of the quoted episode from Canto 99 have by no means been exhausted by this elaboration. The formulation of the business of relatives being 'filiality', for example, enacts the revivification of law in descent of generations, so that the aim of the 'phallos', that 'First Classic', should not be lost, but rather supported for posterity. The protection of this first law, which it becomes the office of succeeding generations to uphold, requires defence against those elements which seek to submerge it. Accordingly, the 'soldiers' of the nation are exhorted to take care of their bodies, to shield themselves from 'floods and rascality'. This specification of a protection of the body becomes important in the recognition, enforced in earlier extracts, that it is woman who is conveyed as the sea, the flood, and now 'rascality'. In 'For a New Paideuma' Pound argues, 'Any man who thinks in our time . . . ought to start sorting out the confusions. Against which sea there is no dyke save a clear terminology',[8] and admonishes E. E. Cummings, in a letter of 18 January 1941, 'If nobuddy ever stick finger in hole in dyke, water flood etc.'[9]

From this last series of associations it becomes possible to seize still another significance of Pound's selection of the voyage of Odysseus as the central motif of the *Cantos*. For not only is Odysseus the lone sailor who can navigate over dangerous seas, escaping the snares of women such as Scilla or Circe on his way, but it is specifically this encounter with Circe, who during sex in her darkened island bedroom tells Odysseus that he has to pass through hell on his voyage, there to be made wise before gaining his proper home, which focuses the borrowing from Homer's narrative. The implication of Circe in darkness, the knowledge she offers Odysseus in his experience of her body which causes him a hell which will separate him from his former identity, and her duplicit involvement in his heroic quest for knowledge are all profusely inscribed in the poem. So are his navigation over sea, his authority, his urge to find his own nation and proper identity, and his bravery.

And if it remains doubted that such a dominance of the phallus organizes the *Cantos* at this level, this cannot be ascribed to any negligence on Pound's part in promulgating its operation, either within the poem in this dense pattern of insistences, or elsewhere in careful theorization. So it is perhaps initially surprising that Pound's translation of Rémy de Gourmont's *Physique naturelle de l'amour: essai sur l'instinct sexuel*, rendered as *The Natural Philosophy of Love*, should have received little critical attention. What is more surprising still is that this oversight has largely extended also to the substantial postface of 1921 written by Pound himself, which lays out, in agreeing with and going beyond certain positions of de Gourmont, a view of the physiological sexual functions set in relation to mental operations. It is difficult to account for this scant attention in critiques sympathetic to Pound's work in any other way than as defensive concealment, since undoubtedly the postface offers a major contribution to the poet's theoretical commitment to the derivation of philosophy and politics from nature.[10]

Pound's translation, from an original French of 1904, was published by the Casanova Society in 1926, and sold with a notice urging discretion in resale and distribution, the particular suitability of its publisher becoming evident on even a cursory glance at the postface, where Pound is led to affirm:

It is more than likely that the brain itself is, in origin and development, only a sort of great clot of genital fluid held in suspense or reserve.[11]

This genital fluid is subsequently specified as male when Pound postulates an 'intimate connection between his sperm and his cerebration'.[12] In this view:

The mind is an up-spurt of sperm, no, let me alter that; trying to watch the process: the sperm, the form-creator, the substance which compels the ovule to evolve in a given pattern.[13]

Such a connection forged between the reproductive organs and the brain, in which the sperm originates ideas and patterns which 'compel' the ovule, is also reflected—and this reveals the extent of the interrelation between the theory advanced here and the concerns of the *Cantos*—in a metaphor of light. For light is,

a projection from the luminous fluid, from the energy that is in the brain, down along the nerve cords which receive certain vibrations in the eye.[14]

Artistic activity and intelligence are similarly derived from this phallic progenitor:

Creative thought is an act like fecundation, like the male cast of the human seed.[15]

The artist is consequently considered to be,

really the phallus or spermatozoid charging, head-on, the female chaos. . . . Even oneself has felt it, driving any new idea into the great passive vulva of London, a sensation analogous to the male feeling in copulation.[16]

Not only does this formulation reiterate the description of the female as a 'chaos', as in Canto 29, and so emphasize a relevance of these discourses to the construction of the *Cantos* of an unusual proportion to have been missed by a tradition of Pound criticism animated by a zealous exegetic attention to supplementary material, but also anticipates later definitions. These include that of 'greatness' in *Guide to Kulchur* as 'an unusual energy coupled with straightness, the direct shooting mind'.[17]

But if cerebration is a squirt of sperm, how is female thought to be described? In considering the 'female chaos', Pound is led to return to the insect world:

In insect life a female predominance . . . the need of heat being present, the insect chooses to solve the problem by hibernation, i.e. a sort of negation of action.[18]

Woman's social function is accordingly given as not necessarily to think, but to reflect and support man:

Without any digression of feminism . . . one offers woman as the accumulation of hereditary aptitudes, better than man in the 'useful gestures', the perfections; but to man, given what we have of history, the 'inventions', the new gestures, the extravagance, the wild shots, the impractical, merely because in him occurs the new up-jut, the new bathing of the cerebral tissues in the residuum, in *la mousse* of the life sap.[19]

Woman, injected with these new perceptions and connections, is to receive and nourish them, and to follow their creator:

Woman, the conservator, the inheritor of past gestures, clever, practical, as Gourmont says, not inventive, always the best disciple of any inventor.[20]

Here female characteristics are not only generalized, but de-historicized, and the whole issue of a transformation of sexual positions by political struggle foreclosed by a knowledge of 'what we have of history', and by her natural, physical lack of the phallus. It is not by accident that Pound as one of the editors should have participated in the alteration of the magazine title

The New Freewoman to the *Egoist* at the beginning of 1914.[21]
In such an alteration the challenge of political liberation for
women is replaced by the assurance of the ego's self-possession.

It is from this conception of woman that she can be called
'ductile' in the poem 'Condolence',[22] and the claim made in 'I
gather the limbs of Osiris' :

It is not until poetry lives again 'close to the thing' that it will be a
vital part of contemporary life. As long as the poet says not what he, at
the very crux of a clarified conception, means, but is content to say
something ornate and approximate, just so long will serious people,
intently alive, consider poetry as balderdash—a sort of embroidery for
dilettantes and women.[23]

Even from so short an extract it is evident that the associations
which pervade the *Cantos* overlap with those of Pound's prose:
meaning is a function of the mind 'at the very crux of a clarified
conception', where not only does the metaphor of light insist
in the word 'clarified', but its genital derivation is conveyed in
the sense of 'conception', another metaphor accredited for Pound
following his readings of Fenollosa.

Moreover, the male organ, the source of meaning and poetry,
intrudes in this quotation in a repetition as the 'vital part', and
the link between dilettantes and women finds some explanation
in the assertion in 'The Serious Artist' that 'the dilettante has
no axe to grind for himself'.[24] A similar repetition to this of the
'vital part' is to be found in an early 'Envoi' dating from Pound's
graduation as Master of Arts in 1906:

> Go little verse . . .
>   But prithee tell
>   To the bards in hell
> Who live on nothing a year
>   That a Master of Arts
>   And a man of parts
> Is trying the same thing here.[25]

The dispensation of thought and creative activity as a sudden
rush of sperm makes developmental reasoning unnecessary, since

the single impulse of the genital 'up-jut' is invested with absolute authority. Reasoning only intervenes, there is only argument or discussion, when the surge of fluid for some reason fails, resulting in an 'approximate' rather than a 'clarified' conception:

There is only reasoning where there is initial error, i.e. weakness of the spurt, wandering search.[26]

Meaning is characterized as an immediate prerogative of the phallus, undermined only in its failed operation, or by those forces which subvert its authority.

It is in this context, where both in Pound's prose and in the *Cantos* themselves the phallus is exalted as absolute guarantor of meaning in constant repetitions, that an attention to the construction of the subject in its accession to language in terms of the unfinished Oedipal structure known as fetishism needs to be undertaken. That Pound recognized in the investigation of the Freudian field a certain threat to this assurance in possession of the phallus is indicated in his almost exclusively deprecatory references to the analyst, of the kind 'the grey epoch of Freud', in a letter to Laurence Binyon of 30 August 1934,[27] or his cursory dismissal of the Oedipus story itself as 'a darn silly lot of buncombe—used as a peg for some very magnificent phrases' in a letter to Iris Barry, of 29 August 1916.[28] Vilification of Freud, of course, has never been uncommon. What is peculiar to Pound's objections is that they centre on a repudiation of analyses of the unconscious and sexuality specifically at the level of language (the magnificent phrases of the play are held to displace the force of the Oedipus discovery), and indeed address language for a final dismissal of Freud's theories. In a letter to C. K. Ogden, of 28 January 1935, for example, Pound speaks of inventing a language to deny the unconscious, 'a real licherary and mule-drivin' language, capable of blowin' Freud to hell.'[29] And it is exactly the denial of the unconscious that his fetishized language of communication does seek.

The account of the dissolution of the castration complex advanced above turned on the emergence of the desire to the father, which annuls the faith invested in him by the child as the terminal point of his own desires. Inasmuch as the existence of the father's desire has to be understood as a lack, a shortcoming even in possession of the phallus, the child can no longer see in the father the transcendence of the lack first detected in the fact of the mother's apparently absent genital. In modulating an exaltation of the father as triumphant over lack into a recognition of desire, the child cannot escape the symbolic castration which, in the work of Lacan, makes possible the accession to the world of difference and of language.

Upon first experience of the fact of anatomical difference, either on observing another child's differing genital endowment, or on witnessing in the form of the parental bodies this possible variation in another generation, the child is, according to Freudian theory, unable to grasp this play of presence and absence in any other way than as the possibility of privation, and is consequently affected with a sudden terror of castration. No doubt this partly arises from the earlier recognition of the self as a discrete unit paradigmatic of the otherness of the world, and it is indeed in terms of an inability to conceive of difference in a being otherwise so like the infant's self that Freud has suggested this terror is announced.[30]

In his 1927 essay 'Fetishism', Freud outlined a modality of a child's possible reaction to this discovery, almost without exception encountered only in male children:

What happened, therefore, was that the boy refused to take cognizance of the fact of his having perceived that a woman does not possess a penis. No, that could not be true: for if a woman had been castrated, then his own possession of a penis was in danger; and against that there rose in rebellion the portion of his narcissism which Nature has, as a precaution, attached to that particular organ.[31]

Fear of the possibility of castration cannot allow the phallus as signifier of difference, a signifier which may then confirm decisively those earlier separations from the breast and from the faeces, but rather at the very instant of this recognition instigates a fixation upon the presence of this organ. More usually in the general structure of fetishism, the fixation is to a displaced representative, the fetish objects such as the shoe, the corset, fur, mackintoshes and so on, which in consequence become a necessary precondition of libidinal satisfaction. What Freud stresses in this essay is that the objects serve without exception as substitute forms for the penis whose assumed presence was put in jeopardy.[32] The various object choices of the fetishist follow unanimously the prototype of the male organ itself, consecrating it with undoubted authority.

If for the fetishist the function of the phallus as signifier is fundamentally misconceived, nevertheless whilst the assumed presence of the genital remains what Freud has termed 'a token of triumph over the threat of castration and a protection against it',[33] this triumph has even so been purchased at cost of demoting the signifier to rank of perpetual signified. Since the female genital has already been seen this presence has to be signified on the female body also. The fetishist is obliged to indulge a further misrecognition of the female by replacing the organ she has been empirically known not to have:

It is not true that, after the child has made his observation of the woman, he has preserved unaltered his belief that women have a phallus. He has retained that belief, but he has also given it up. In the conflict between the weight of the unwelcome perception and the force of his counter-wish, a compromise has been reached, as is only possible under the dominance of the unconscious laws of thought—the primary processes. Yes, in his mind the woman *has* got a penis, in spite of everything; but this penis is no longer the same as it was before. Something else has taken its place, has been appointed its substitute, as it were, and now inherits the interest which was formerly directed to its predecessor. But this interest suffers an extraordinary increase as well, because the horror of castration has set up a memorial to itself in the creation of this substitute. Furthermore, an aversion, which is never absent in any fetishist, to the real female genitals remains a *stigma indelebile* of the repression that has taken place.[34]

Thus the complex structure of the fetish, which Freud points out in returning to the question in 1938 is motivated by a concern for the defence of the ego, involves both a repression of difference and a partial recognition of it, a recognition which infuses desire.[35] This form of response Freud designates a *Verleugnung*, a simultaneous taking of two courses, a recognition and a disavowal of the female genital.[36] Freud suggests this is not at all an uncomfortable condition for the fetishist, and indeed can be held a positive advantage in the prosecution of libidinal drives.[37]

The relevance of this to the analysis of discourse is that since language is constituted in differences, a total repudiation of difference by the subject in its construction would rule out the possibility of speaking or writing. The condition of the fetishist is a partial allowance of difference—sufficient to create the conditions of representation and to set up desire—but also a mastery over that difference in its closure or recovery as consistency and sameness. Fetishism may in this way be held to describe a condition of discourse in which desire and difference can be controlled by their effacement whenever the certitude of identity is willed. Oscillating between repression and recognition, the fetishist is able to control desire and suppress it at caprice, and so enjoys a comfortable mastery over language.

Yet this comfort is constituted as an oscillation between the neurotic's worry and repression, and the guilt installed with the advent of desire and the acknowledgement of castration. Accordingly, Lacan and Wladimir Granoff in their commentary on Sandor Lorand's analysis of Little Harry suggest that fetishism is established on the axis of anxiety and guilt.[38]

If there is conflict in attitude to castration for the fetishist, there is necessarily also a related conflict at the level of the function of the father. On the one hand, the neurotically anxious defence against the return of the repressed truth of the female genital addresses itself to an Ideal Father, described by Lacan as the phantasy of a figure who would close his eyes to desire, and stand firm beyond the mother who is unable to assuage hers.[39] Of this father Moustafa Safouan observes, stressing the reliance by the subject on the uncompromised patron authority of this figure, 'the subject has only one priority, to put him back on his pedestal . . . in order for himself to stay there.'[40] On the other hand there is the Symbolic Father, whose incursion into the closed relationship of mother and child and subsequent proscription of the mother in the Oedipus Complex subject the infant to the fact of difference by way of the fear of castration. This Father arouses an undying enmity from the child, an enmity whose recognition, Freud argues, leads to the guilt installed by the superego. What is crucial here is that the fetishist's disavowal enables both the possibility of a recognition and a negation of sexual difference to be retained. The fetishist finds a pleasure in vacillation between two attitudes, recognition and denial, desire and identity, separation and mastery, enjoying separation with the continual and necessary proviso that the loss can always be restored, the lack covered over.

It is this partial regression which allows consideration of fetishism as an instance *par excellence* of *suture*.[41] Its inversion of the phallic lack as phallic presence sets the subject in position to bestride the realms of symbolic and imaginary, infusing and extinguishing desire with authority. It is exactly the filling-in of phallic lack which confers the power over discourse which is the crucial feature of a representational conception of language. Whilst for representation to be possible there also has to be the possibility of desire, identifications are constructed by super-imposition upon an initial but retracted admission of lack. Accordingly, Lacan and Granoff point out that the study of fetishism is central to an understanding of the ego.[42] And it is, incidentally, this instatement of the ego against the fact of sexual difference which most clearly indicates what is entailed in a titular alteration from *The New Freewoman* to the *Egoist*.

It is now possible to propose certain necessarily tentative relations between the world of language supported by the fetishist, that is, a world grasped by the fetishist in despite of language, and psychogenic elements of particular social structures, insofar as these rely upon determinate forms of authority. An intro-jection originates in the establishment of a law over discourse and of the father, but takes on such public forms as, for example, the 'Throne and Altar' of Freud's 'Fetishism' essay, any danger to which arouses an analogous anxiety to that over the cruel possi-bility of castration.[43]

Since the power of communication is guaranteed only in the unequivocal possession of the phallus, men, as at one level pre-suming this in their endowment with a penis, may consider them-selves invested with special privilege, even special responsibility, for establishing and maintaining meaning and culture. This pre-sumption, which is founded in a sustenance of phallic endowment against the reality of difference and castration, makes its contri-bution to the formation of patriarchy. Whilst a reinstatement of the penis in women makes them possible objects of libidinal attraction for the fetishist, nevertheless the continuation of a residual absence co-existing with this inlaying of the penis is sufficient to exclude them from meaningful exchanges of dis-course. Although the threat of castration latent in women's attested absence of a penis is largely disarmed in the replacement of that organ, nevertheless the persistence of a trace of a lack beneath this restored presence necessitates her continual control, a resistance to her desire whose emergence can only lead to anxiety.

The resistance to a difference indicating desire which is necessary for the support of patriarchy also contributes to the confirmation of notions of nation and state, reliant as these are upon a conception of homogeneity and coherence. These social structures are produced in a set of representations of an imaginary unity, and invoke a condition of interests being best served in social cohesion. Since to threaten the assurance of representation is to put into question the very notion of identity which underpins these social formations, it is not surprising that any threat to social coherence should be greeted with violently defensive responses, capable of assuming the various possible forms of the reaction to the fear of castration.

Returning to Pound's texts it is possible to see a variety of ways in which this construction of linguistic and political orders insinuates itself in both prose and poetical writings, as well as in certain memories of childhood recalled by the poet in interviews late in life. In an article in *Tel Quel*, Marcelin Pleynet has begun a study of these memories by isolating those which centre on Homer Pound's occupation as Assistant Assayer at the United States Mint, demonstrating how such memories explore the Oedipal relation of the young poet to his father.[44]

Given particular attention by Pleynet is the memory, related to Donald Hall in 1962 but concerning the year 1893, in which Pound recalls seeing coins shovelled into counting machines in the mint vault by men stripped to the waist beneath the light of gas flares. Pleynet suggests:

It is the Name-of-the-Father, properly *weighed*, which as a screen will have to be defended from the nudity ('to the waist') which in the shadow of the vaults treats this name as if it were manure (litter).[45]

This associative node focuses the threat posed by darkness, the naked body and an abuse of gold coinage, which, epitomized in the degradation of that coinage as the ungovernable productivity of the anus—as manure—transgresses the law over money, over the pound sterling and Pound the son, established by Homer in his capacity as assayer and father. Such law needs to be upheld by the light of the gas flares against those who transgress authority by showing disrespect to the fixed value of money.

Indeed, a monetary subversion of paternal authority is inscribed in another of Pound's prominent memories from this period. This describes Homer's receiving at the mint lead bricks covered with a layer of gold used during the days of the gold rush, according to Pound's recollection, to dupe pioneers. Since these were the days of free coining, the authority of the mint and its assayer, where these false ingots invariably ended up, could be understood to be undermined by such a malpractice.[46] That Pound's economic theories of later years are in part traceable to such memories, and to their erection of a law, is attested by the relation of this particular personal memory as part of the argument of the essay 'Economic Nature of the United States'.[47] Such an irruption of unconscious determinants in the formation of theories conceived as empirical reveals at what risk the certitudes of experimental judgement and the revelations of the luminous detail are forged.

Another memory again, also recorded by Pleynet, remarks a link between the weighing of money and that of words, and so establishes at the level of an infantile recollection bound to the fixing of the law a co-determination in Pound's subsequent economic and literary theories. This reminiscence concerns the ability of Homer to weigh a man's name on his visiting card. Language and the very identity of person may be submitted to paternal arbitration, and the memory binds together various strands of the poet's name, Pound the name itself, pound the unit of money and of weight.[48] In the *ABC of Reading*, for example, Pound collocates name and financial reference:

You do not accept a stranger's cheques without reference. In writing, a man's 'name' is his reference. He has, after a time, credit. . . . The verbal manifestation on any bank cheque is very much like that on any other.[49]

In commenting to James Laughlin about allegedly offensive language in Cantos 52–71, he charges:

Certain evil habits of language etc. must be weighed, and probably will be found wanting.[50]

Here deficiency in weight, the 'evil', comes back precisely upon a lack coupled with a desire inscribed in the word 'wanting'.

If proper weight is the guarantee of value, it is not surprising that to abolish weight should be an erosion or deconstruction less imaginable even than surpassing in judgement and power Buddha or Christ; thus in Canto 28:

> 'Je suis . . .
> (Across the bare planks of a diningroom in the Pyrenees)
>   . . . plus fort que . .
>   . . . le Boud-hah!'
> (No contradiction)
> 'Je suis . . .
>   . . . plus fort que le . . .
>   . . . Christ!'
> (No contradiction)
> 'J'aurais . . .
>   aboli . . .
>   le poids!'
> (Silence, somewhat unconvinced.)
> And in his waste house, detritus,
> As it were the cast buttons of splendours,
>
>   (28:137)

In the Chinese Cantos a connection between the office of the arbiter of currency and the transmission of that authority and responsibility to a son is forged. At least initially, moreover, the son is resistant to this paternal delegation of succession, which is established in terms of regal lineage:

> Silk, gold, piled mountain high.
>   Take it before Prince Tçin gets there.
> Thus Ouang Yeou to the Khitan of Apaoki
>   whose son was lost in the mulberry forest
>
>   (55:292-3)

The invasion of this sense of a son lost to the monetary law of the father, unmistakable in the convergence of piles of gold, of a Prince heir to national authority, and a lost son, traverses any historical specificity of narrative, and suggests that the recording of what we have of history is not in any way so simple a transcription as Pound's discourses claim. The very practice of enunciation here invites a revelation of subjective history quite removed from events in tenth-century China.[51]

In Canto 56, regal responsibility is stressed precisely in terms of weight or gravity:

> Aidez mon petit-fils à soutemir
> La dignité de cest pouvoir
> le poids de son office
> Et comme au Prince . . .   (56 : 310)

Circulating in this quotation are money, weight, name, the intervention of a law and a succession of the son.

But if the value of money and of language is to be upheld and sustained in succeeding generations by preservation, how is that value to be defended against supercession and erosion? It is here that the function of the son becomes more than simply to repeat an internalized law, but to go beyond it and replace it. The law which has to be defended against the son himself calls upon him to remake and restore it, and it is here that Pound's campaign to 'make it new' is pitched, a veneration and yet a replacement, to establish just authority over and beyond precedent, and untransgressable. Accordingly, in 'The Wisdom of Poetry', the poet's task is to cast new currency in Homer's mint, to renew it as it suffers attrition:

Thought is perhaps important to the race, and language, the medium of thought's preservation, is constantly wearing out. It has been the function of poets to new-mint the speech.[52]

In shifting attention from the name 'Pound' itself to the poet's forename 'Ezra', Pleynet has suggested that it is the similarity Ezra and Usura—used regularly in preference to the English 'usury' —which not only prompts Pound's early endeavours to alter the name into such forms as X-Ray and Ra, but which is further a token of a perversity of the son, Ez(u)ra, to the law of the father.[53] In this light, the poet's selection of Usura as the single most important iniquity to be arraigned insistently throughout the *Cantos* constitutes a continual inscription of a resistance to established law. The promulgation of the poem's own system of order in its exaltation of a truth of personal definition, and in its temporary espousal of Fascism, serve to replace the paternal phallus with an even greater and more potent phallus.[54]

It is not by accident that in the essay 'Translators of Greek: Early Translators of Homer', Pound delights in a phallic affinity of his name, significantly described in an essay concerning renewals of Homer, the father both of poetry and of the poet:

The phonetic translation of my name into the Japanese tongue is so indecorous that I am seriously advised not to use it, lest it do me harm in Nippon. (Rendered back *ad verbum* into our maternal speech it gives for its meaning, 'This picture of a phallus costs ten yen'. There is no surety in shifting personal names from one idiom to another.)[55]

Not only is the archly assumed surety of a shifting from one language to another not to be concealed here by brackets (and after all the bilingual pun is a recurrent artifice of Pound's poetic), but the latent castration threat to such a phallus is clearly enacted in the advice not to use it for fear of harm 'in Nippon', in the female's bite, in Scilla's sharp teeth. It is also significant that the phallus is here again intimately bound to finance, in costing 'ten yen', and to visual representation, to the possibility of a 'picture'.

There are other associations of the name Ezra, too, which locate it in this node or knot of money, law and filial succession. The poet's early exposure to Christianity could not have left him ignorant—despite his later rejections of that religion—of the properties of the Biblical Ezra, the scribe in the law of Moses, the prophet and the law giver who weighs out gold to the priests.[56] Marcelin Pleynet also notes the density of the 'r' sound in Pound's writing, which he claims phoneticians suggest is the sound of the phallus, a sound appearing in 'Ezra' itself, in 'Usura' and in 'contra naturam'.[57]

Indeed, Pound's affection for Gaudier-Brzeska's 'Hieratic Head of Ezra Pound', which the poet adopted as the heading of his note-paper and which he moved to the Albergo Rapallo in 1932, may be accounted for at one level—a level quite apart from the friendship interrupted by Gaudier-Brzeska's untimely death during the First World War—by its adoption of these nominal associations.[58] The designation 'Hieratic' embraces an element of priestliness and prophecy, as well as of hieroglyphics, exalted by Pound by way of his work on Fenollosa. Formally the sculpture presents an erectile elongation, described by Wyndham Lewis as 'Ezra in the form of a marble phallus'.[59] Yet on seeing the sculpture's shape on Pound's notepaper, Arnold Leese, one of the poet's English anti-Semitic correspondents, could only see in this form a Hebrew derivation also discernible in the name Ezra itself, and was only to be relieved of his anxieties upon receiving from Pound a detailed genealogy.[60] And Pound's pleasure in the phallus finds still another outlet in his suggestion to Joyce, refuted by the latter, that the Blarney Stone is nothing more or less than a phallic source of delight and enlightenment for ladies.[61]

Such a glimpse of the suggestive consequences of an introjection of paternal law to be maintained in a succession of that name (even if against a resistance manifest in the name of the son, Ezra, whose Jewish derivation encourages its mutation into the Jewish evil, Usura) prompts consideration of Pound's larger theoretical arguments concerning social organization and policy. The poet's economics now appears in terms of a central opposition between those forces which set up, define and enforce fiscal law, and those which are held to subvert this law for private gain.

The returning proposal of Pound's economic commitments, beyond the various allegiances to Gesell or Major Douglas, is the substitution of a gold standard by a more stable order of paper money backed by the authority of the State. This replaces a standard which can be undermined by usurocracy's manipulation of gold value by one which remains totally impervious. Accordingly, where such a gold standard has either precipitated or continues to collude with private banks, Pound prescribes the acquisition by the State of the right to issue its own money, arguing that the perpetuation of a gold—and to a lesser degree silver—standard, supported by international banks outside the control of national government, allows a monopolization of that commodity by a small, privileged sector of any community. This sector, the usurocracy, are able to manipulate for private gain the rate of currency exchange and interest, and hence the value of money.

In quelling such an appropriation of the population's working power by an act of assuming the right to issue its own money, the State can eliminate external or international interests. The value of money may be fixed by the State's own power to enforce it, fixing currency and credit levels and the level of production by constraining the work force to a reduced working day.

In Pound's economic system the State must also determine what is to be usefully produced:

The issue of credit (or money) must be just, i.e. neither too much or too little.
Against every hour's work (human or kilowatt hour), an hour's certificate. That can be the first step. That can be scientific. Ultimately it must be scientific.
But it will not get you out of the necessity of using intelligence *re—* what and how much you produce.
What? can be answered by 'Everything useful or desirable'.[62]

This is how in the *ABC of Economics* Pound suggests that the Just Price should be established, claiming a scientificity in the enumeration of labour hours. But this act of counting loses any basis of scientificity in the subsequent concepts 'Everything useful or desirable'. These concepts can only be established as reflections of the inclination of whatever dominant faction regulates State authority. The criterion of scientificity and of justness is executive power.

Yet Pound insists that this Just Price, which he calls in an article for the Mosleyite journal *Action* 'the ROOT of economic science',[63] is the opening condition or premise of economic debate, rather than a produced effect. What constitutes the Just Price lies outside discussion, Pound arguing that such a law of price is to be assumed anterior to the debatable questions of economic science:

Starting with that, the minor problems, or the parts of the total problem, fall into place.[64]

By implementing the Just Price, the 'economic truth, which several honest men and groups approach (I mean in under-standing)' of Pound's letter to Edwin Muir, 25 March 1937, may be achieved.[65]

E

Whereas in the ideal State this truth might be democratically convened, since only 'several honest men' approach it in understanding, the immediate effectuality of such economics resides in the responsible action of those who, in possession of the truth, implement it for the best interest of the population at large. In 'What is Money For?', Pound is led to chastise Douglas for failing in this responsibility:

Both the Douglas Social Creditors and modern Catholics POSTULATE the JUST PRICE as a necessary part of their systems. The valid complaint against Douglas is that he didn't invent and set up machinery for ENFORCING the just price. . . .
Only the STATE can effectively fix the JUST PRICE of any commodity by means of state-controlled pools of raw products and the restoration of guild organisation in industry.[66]

Not only does the notion of a requisite appendage, the 'necessary part' of Douglasite systems, here infiltrate Pound's formulation, but his suggestion of a restoration of guildism is elsewhere explained as reliant upon a similar informing plenitude, a central administrative power of the state. In *Action* again, Pound writes:

Guildism without a centre means mere war between towns and barons.[67]

The problem of centralized enforcement negating individual choice perplexes Pound only in so far as somehow long-term education must come to vindicate present policies. His criticisms of Fascist Italy in *Guide to Kulchur* are not anxious over any excess of State intervention and regulation:

In Italy the trouble is not too much statal authority but too little.[68]

Whilst disagreeing with the contention that only force can restrain human greed and competition, and replacing this force with a marginal note on 'education' in his copy of Henry Adams's text *The Degradation of the Democratic Dogma*,[69] Pound insists, in a letter to E. E. Cummings of 18 January 1941, that this process of education should pivot on endorsing his own and compatible perceptions:

The Institute should stand for continual curiosity as to the nature of MAXIMA standards of excellence in all the arts.

To that end, the members including the worst should be placed in prison until they have read at least the main demands of my published criticism, let alone other critical demands of at least equal critical merit.[70]

In its evaluative selection and exclusiveness such a formula anticipates the Fascist imperative, related by Pound to Charles Norman in 1939 in conversation, that freedom of thought should extend only to those who are qualified to hold it, a maxim later prefixed to Pound's broadcasts for Rome Radio.[71]

This maxim is clearly a recipe for censorship, and in the article 'The Liberal, Request for an Effective Burial of Him', in *Action* in August 1938, Pound urges,

some regulation of the Press to prevent the lowest and worst type of monopolists and exploiters from systematically misleading the nations.[72]

Since thought, language and truth are not productions but rather dispensations of nature, it is to a science of nature, in biology, that recourse needs be made to trace their possible disorders. In the article 'Race', Pound observes:

The creators of darkness and obfuscators of the Press can be damned or shot without any bitterness between one race and another. But to suppose that a difference of policy is due to a mere ideology or to mere reason, when it has roots in blood, bone and endocrines, is to take a very superficial view of society, humanity and human co-ordinations.[73]

But what, apart from implicitly different essential characteristics of various races, constitutes the biological root which underlies reason and ideology and can lead to shooting?

We have already seen that only 'several honest men' approach in understanding economic truth. Discussing privilege in the *ABC of Economics*, Pound suggests:

Any new governing class is bound to be composed of exceptional men, or at any rate of men having more energy and being therefore more fit (apt) to govern than their fellows.[74]

It is not simply a binding likelihood that authority is to be held by men ('bound to be composed of men'), but further that the endowment of these men for public service inheres in their energy, which makes them first biologically 'fit' or capable, and then only parenthetically suitable '(apt)' for the task. Women, whose inclination to hibernate Pound remarks in the Gourmont postface, are therefore lacking in the necessary 'energy' for such enterprises.

That the intersexual relations of Pound's discourses inscribe rather a history of symbolic production across and against castration is suggested in the emphasized protection of administration against the threat of desire in the essay 'Kublai Khan and his Currency'. Kublai's foresight is praised for defending transmission of meaning from woman's effects on man, her subversion:

As for administrative efficiency, the ages have gained little. Kublai's post-riders with their coats buttoned behind and *sealed* with official seals so that there should be no question of their having dallied by the wayside, or reclined upon alien couches, are sufficient memorial to his insight into man's character.[75]

The attraction of this insight—valued as an index of 'administrative efficiency' over and above other indices such as geographical social distribution or level of technological achievement —prompts its reiteration in Canto 18:

> And his postmen go sewed up and sealed up,
> Their coats buttoned behind and then sealed,
> In this way from the voyage's one end to its other.
>
> (*18*:80)

Significantly the context of this instance in Canto 18 is that of a voyage for the sake of knowledge, a voyage undertaken by a man across the female sea of lack and desire.

In protecting the law from desire, Kublai becomes one of the many male leaders enlightened beyond the general tenor of their times who have been able to found what Pound considers firm social orders. In the *Cantos* appear Sigismundo, Kung, Jefferson, Adams, Mussolini and others, all men of enough presence to overcome the ignorance of their age and replace it

with enlightenment and order. That such a political affiliation
to the establishment of total male order extends to the consideration of literature is suggested in *The Spirit of Romance*
as the belief that 'the study of literature is hero-worship'.[76] In
the essay 'The Serious Artist' the aspiration is expressed 'to write
a poetry that can be carried as a communication between intelligent men'.[77]

Beyond this assignation of authority to men on account of their
allegedly natural endowment, appendages of power further
dramatize that power's enactment of the fetishized penis. It is
not a question of there existing an order for which men incidentally find themselves suitable, and can therefore function well in,
but of an order historically produced by the specific determinations
of a male construction grounded in the effects of the ego's
defence against the fear of castration. Here again the long-
standing public consecration of these symbols tends to obscure
their suggestiveness. Mussolini, who is in the essay 'Date Line'
affirmed a 'male of the species',[78] resurrects the ancient Roman
fasces. But Pound makes a distinction between these pretorial
sticks and the Duce's intelligence:

Mussolini as intelligent man is more interesting than Mussolini as the
Big Stick. The Duce's aphorisms and perceptions can be studied apart
from his means of getting them into action.[79]

Yet this assertion in the *ABC of Economics* cannot be sustained
in conjunction with certain of Pound's other pronouncements. If
the mind, intelligence itself, is merely a clot of genital fluid, then
what is at issue in Mussolini's intelligence is precisely the Big
Stick. The distinction between perception and implementation
of ideas cannot hold against Pound's assertion in *A Visiting
Card* that any idea which does not go into action 'is a truncated
idea. It lacks an essential part', where again it is a phallic stake.[80]

It becomes increasingly clear that these two concepts, mind
as sperm and inactive thought as impotent sperm, are linked in
Pound's writing in repeated assertions of a lamentable lack. In
Guide to Kulchur ideas which do not go into action fail 'because
of some inherent defect in the idea',[81] and in the article 'Race',
'Adams' personal limitations and lack of timing are ample explanation as to why his idea did not go into action.'[82] Kung, who

in Canto 13 'raised his cane against Yuan Jang' (13:58) thus becomes the 'Master Kung' of the essay 'Immediate Need of Confucius', where a need can only be understood as a lack:

Let me try to get this as clear as possible. A 'need' implies a lack, a sick man has 'need'. Something he has not. Kung as medicine?[83]

So, too, the sick man of the *Pisan Cantos*, the fragmented poet ('I am Noman'), invokes the reunited and so no longer deficient 'tally stick' to recover fixed, undivided identity:

> Very potent, can they again put one together
> as the two halves of a seal, or a tally stick?
>
> (77:467)

And in the *ABC of Reading*, the critical requirement is of 'measuring rods'.[84]

These asseverations of the necessary appendage of power have largely focused upon its anxious defence against the possibility of a lack. But also inherent in the oscillation between a recognition and a disavowal of castration is a possible gravitation towards a disavowal which breaks to a larger extent with the constraints of the reality principle, and so establishes a reality sponsored by an unequivocal manifestation of what is pleasurable. In this case what is pleasurable is a condition of unimpeachable order conferred by self-possession in the phallus.

This is the area of an account of Pound's allegiance to representations of Fascism which operate at a visceral level, and therefore cannot be reduced to economistic analysis. A continuity is established in Pound's writings between an order of discourse dependent on the fetishized phallus, the assurance of the ego this installs, and declarations of allegiance to Italian Fascism in the 1930s and early 1940s. The operation of a centre, axis, or pivot provided by the phallus appears in Pound's recollections of Italy on his return after the years at St Elizabeths:

Europe was a shock. The shock of no longer feeling oneself in the center of something is probably part of it.[85]

The continuity between Pound's enthusiasm for Fascism, and his concerns in the *Cantos* and in his other writings is clearly evident in the celebration of 'Fascio' in *A Visiting Card* :

A thousand candles together blaze with intense brightness. No one candle's light damages another's. So is the liberty of the individual in the ideal and fascist state.

THE STATE

In August, 1942, the following elucidatory statement was heard on the Berlin radio : the power of the state, whether it be Nazi, Fascist, or Democratic, is always the same, that is—absolute. . . . In the beginning was the word, and the word has been betrayed. The introduction of any ordered discourse is composed of conscious or unconscious quotations. . . . The Master Kung collected the Odes and the historical documents of the ancient kings, which he considered instruments worthy of preservation.

We find two forces in history : one that divides, shatters, and kills, and one that contemplates the unity of the mystery.

'The arrow hath not two points'.

There is the force that falsifies, the force that destroys every clearly delineated symbol, dragging man into a maze of abstract arguments, destroying not one but every religion.

But the images of the gods, or Byzantine mosaics, move the soul to contemplation and preserve the tradition of the undivided light.[86]

The associative patterns and emphases of the *Cantos* reappear here : the deduction of 'elucidation' from 'blazing light', the protection or betrayal of word and meaning, an unproblematic functionalism of preserved historical documents, and the subversion of man in a bewildering 'maze of abstract arguments'. The division of the subject in the symbolic enforced by the fact of castration is also pervasively resisted in an anaphora of 'one', the coherence and unity of the arrow with its one point. It is this division or splitting of the subject in its accession to language by way of castration which shatters truth, destroys the possibility of religion, and bespeaks an unacceptable difference.

Notes

1 *Collected Shorter Poems*, p. 123.
2 *Selected Prose*, p. 297 and p. 304.

3 *Collected Shorter Poems*, p. 91.
4 *Ibid.* p. 206.
5 *Selected Prose*, p. 90.
6 *Ibid.* p. 226.
7 *Ibid.* p. 132.
8 *Ibid.* p. 258.
9 *Life*, p. 385; *Life* (Penguin), p. 492.
10 In this respect it is significant that when in 1958 New Directions reprinted the postface as part of *Pavannes and Divagations*, the back cover of this edition advertises 'a representative collection in the master's lighter vein'. Not so for Donald Davie, who finds a cultural importance in metaphorical derivations from sexual intercourse and its effects: 'so long in fact as we want to hold by the ancient claim for artistic creation that it reveres the Natural Creation by emulating it—it is clear that the arts are directly menaced by every piece of propaganda for family planning or voluntary sterilization', *Pound* (Fontana, London, 1975), p. 110.
11 R. de Gourmont, *The Natural Philosophy of Love*, translated with a post-script by Ezra Pound (Casanova Society, London, 1926), p. 169.
12 *Ibid.* p. 180.
13 *Ibid.* pp. 172–3.
14 *Ibid.* p. 176.
15 *Ibid.* p. 173.
16 *Ibid.* p. 170.
17 Ezra Pound, *Guide to Kulchur* (Faber, London, 1938, reprinted New Directions, New York & Peter Owen, London, 1952), p. 106.
18 de Gourmont, *op.cit.*, p. 171.
19 *Ibid.* p. 170.
20 *Ibid.* p. 179.
21 See *Life*, p. 140 and p. 146; *Life* (Penguin), p. 176 and p. 184.
22 *Collected Shorter Poems*, p. 91.
23 *Selected Prose*, p. 41.
24 *Literary Essays*, p. 55.
25 *Life*, p. 28; *Life* (Penguin), p. 36.
26 de Gourmont, *op.cit.*, p. 179.
27 *Letters*, p. 347.
28 *Ibid.* p. 147.
29 *Ibid.* p. 354.
30 See, for example, Freud's comments on his analysis of Little Hans, in 'Analysis of a Phobia in a Five-Year-Old Boy' ('Little Hans'), *Standard Edition*, vol. X, p. 106.
31 *Ibid.* vol. XXI, p. 153. This is not to say, however, that there cannot be cases of fetishism in subjects who are biologically of female sex. See, for example, M. Wulff, 'Fetishism and Object Choice in Early Childhood', *Psychoanalytic Quarterly*, 15 (1946), pp. 450–71. The case concerns a girl with a fetishistic attachment to her mother's stockings turned inside out, and to a 'magic blanket' employed as a substitute for the coverlet of the parental bed.
32 *Standard Edition*, vol. XXI, p. 152.
33 *Ibid.* p. 154.
34 *Ibid.*
35 See 'Splitting of the Ego in the Process of Self Defence', *ibid.* vol. XXIII, pp. 275–8.
36 *Ibid.* vol. XXI, p. 153.

37 *Ibid.* p. 152.

38 J. Lacan and W. Granoff, 'Fetishism: The Symbolic, the Imaginary and the Real', in *Perversions, Psychodynamics, and Therapy*, edited by Sandor Lorand, associate editor M. Balint (London, 1965), pp. 265–76 (p. 273).

39 *Écrits: A Selection*, p. 321; *Écrits*, p. 824.

40 'Le sujet n'a qu'une seule hâte, le remettre sur son piédestal . . . pour lui-même y rester.' M. Safouan, *Études sur l'Oedipe* (Seuil, Paris, 1974), p. 45.

41 'Suture' is a term borrowed by psychoanalysis from surgery, where it refers to a closing or stitching over of a wound which remains open and unhealed beneath the surface. See Lacan's comments in *Four Fundamental Concepts*, pp. 117–18; *Le Séminaire XI*, pp. 107–8. A detailed examination of this concept, describing both its analytic importance and its uses in the study of film, may be found in *Screen*, 18, number 4 (1977/8), pp. 23–76. This dossier comprises articles by Jacques-Alain Miller, Jean-Pierre Oudart and Stephen Heath.

42 Lacan and Granoff, *op. cit.*, p. 266.

43 *Standard Edition*, vol. XXI, p. 153.

44 Marcelin Pleynet, 'La compromission poétique', *Tel Quel*, 70 (1977), pp. 11–26, esp. pp. 22–5.

45 'c'est le nom du père, qui tout bien *pesé*, en tant qu'écran devra être défendu de cette nudité ("jusqu'à la ceinture") qui dans l'ombre des souterrains traite ce nom comme si c'était du fumier (litter),' *ibid.* p. 22. This memory is described by Noel Stock, *Life*, p. 7; *Life* (Penguin), p. 9, and related to Donald Hall in *Paris Review*, 28 (1962), p. 40.

46 *Life*, p. 7; *Life* (Penguin), p. 9.

47 *Selected Prose*, p. 141.

48 *Life*, pp. 7–8; *Life* (Penguin), p. 8. *Tel Quel*, 70, p. 22.

49 Ezra Pound, *ABC of Reading*, p. 25.

50 Quoted *Life*, p. 376; *Life* (Penguin), p. 480.

51 This is how the passage is glossed in the *Annotated Index to the Cantos of Ezra Pound* under the relevant entries.

52 *Selected Prose*, p. 331.

53 *Tel Quel*, 70, p. 25. It is significant that when Safouan outlines four stages in the development of a psychoanalysis, he proposes both a recognition and symbolization of the issue of castration, and a realization of a number of the subject's desires often bound to his or her relation to a personal name. See Moustafa Safouan, *op.cit.*, pp. 38–40.

54 This wish to displace the paternal phallus with one of fabulous potency is clearly illustrated in Dugmore Hunter's case of a teacher of literature wanting to castrate the literary fathers such as Shakespeare whose work he teaches, and become himself omnipotent. See 'Object-Relation Changes in the Analysis of a Fetishist', *International Journal of Psychoanalysis*, 35 (1954), pp. 302–12.

55 *Literary Essays*, p. 259.

56 Ezra 7, 8, 9.

57 *Tel Quel*, 70, p. 25. Pleynet cites as his authority for this equation drawn from phonetics an article by Ivan Fonagy, 'Les bases pulsionelles de la phonation', *Revue française de psychanalyse*, January (1970). The article in its turn refers to work by I. Hoolos.

58 *Life*, p. 308; *Life* (Penguin), p. 391.

59 Quoted in Hugh Kenner, *The Pound Era* (Faber, London, 1971), p. 256.

60 *Life*, p. 343; *Life* (Penguin), p. 437.

61 *Pound/Joyce*, pp. 241–4.
62 *Selected Prose*, p. 222.
63 *Action*, 13 August 1938, p. 9.
64 *Ibid*. p. 9.
65 *Life*, p. 343; *Life* (Penguin), p. 436.
66 *Selected Prose*, p. 263.
67 *Action*, 13 August 1938, p. 9.
68 Pound, *Guide to Kulchur*, p. 254.
69 *Life*, p. 382; *Life* (Penguin), p. 488.
70 *Life*, p. 386; *Life* (Penguin), p. 493.
71 This comment to Charles Norman is quoted *Life*, p. 364; *Life* (Penguin), p. 465. The announcement for Rome Radio is cited *Life*, p. 393; *Life* (Penguin), p. 502.
72 Ezra Pound, 'The Liberal, Request for an effective Burial of Him', *Action*, 27 August 1938 p. 13.
73 Ezra Pound 'Race', *New English Weekly*, 15 October 1936, p. 12.
74 *Selected Prose*, p. 217.
75 *Ibid*. p. 176.
76 Ezra Pound, *The Spirit of Romance* (J. H. Dent, London, 1910; revised edition New Directions, New York, & Peter Owen, London, 1960), p. 7.
77 *Literary Essays*, p. 55.
78 *Ibid*. p. 83.
79 *Selected Prose*, p. 231.
80 *Ibid*. p. 304.
81 Pound, *Guide to Kulchur*, p. 189.
82 Ezra Pound, 'Race', *New English Weekly*, 15 October 1936, p. 12.
83 *Selected Prose*, p. 93.
84 Pound, *ABC of Reading*, p. 30.
85 *Paris Review*, 28, p. 50.
86 *Selected Prose*, pp. 276–7.

Chapter Six

Identity and the other face

THE above presentation of a resistance to castration centred on the disavowal of a genital difference empirically witnessed on the body of the parents or of fellow siblings. This description, however, was not without its own elision of certain complexities of the castration complex, complexities which arise largely in the pre-existence in psychoanalytic theory of lack to the observation of bodily variation. These need to be examined both in order to provide a more accurate account of Lacan's theory of the causation of the subject, and to account for certain significant features of Pound's writing which relate to a specifically non-genital erogenization of the body.

Problems surrounding the location and generality of castration were alluded to above in a consideration of the production of the scopic field. This field exists in the order of the symbolic, but is only experienced in given conjunctions of that field with that of the imaginary, the latter predominating to the point where, for example, Lacan asserts that this field is the one whose drive 'most completely eludes the term castration'.[1] The significance of such scopic organization is that castration as evidenced in the empirical fact of differing genital endowment is customarily discerned by way of vision, the young child looking to the difference, which act is itself already a production in the scopic field. Seeing sexual difference, then, as the central moment of a turn from the imaginary to the symbolic, is an immersion in the fact of castration encountered by way of an anterior produced relation to a lack or castration in the structuration of the scopic field.

Rebuttal of genital privation by replacement of the penile appendage in women can enable the fetishist to renounce the fact of anatomical difference, and so partially forestall the field of the symbolic by superimposing this continued defensive captation of the ego upon a previous visual suppression. Yet the possibility of a full recognition of difference in this genital scenario can only be understood as some kind of metaphor or summary of an already established lacking condition in the subject. Castration is not simply the presence or absence of the penis—and from this site the installation of a relation to the question of the phallus—but is rather the most prominent term of a more general fact of loss and absence, whose recognition is in Lacan's work fundamental to the construction of the subject.

The importance of this for Lacanian theory is that whilst the phallus becomes the privileged signifier of difference, it does so specifically as a resumption of various earlier constitutive separations. Just as the Mirror Stage became decisive confirmation of a gradually emerging unity of the subject's body even before the baby might co-ordinate that body in controlled movement, castration functions to impose at the genital level the possibility of a loss already incipiently apprised by those earlier separations.

The importance of this dispersion of the scene of castration upon consideration of Pound's writing is that since difference cannot be with total effectivity discountenanced at the level of the penis, constructions of discourse grounded in the presence of that organ cannot so simply circumvent the intrinsic shortcoming of the subject. The absence and desire they corroborate as the condition of language will remain nevertheless a pervasive feature of any text, promoting such moments of collapse of controlled discourse as those in the *Cantos*, and sponsoring the kind of emergence of desire in the text's multiplication of meanings indicated above.

Since the conditions of representation and the category of empirical truth already shown to be central to Pound's work necessarily involve a resistance to difference which must now be taken as preceding the castration complex itself, any understanding of these texts calls for an examination of pregenital moments in the construction on the subject. These have regularly been formalized as the oral and the anal stages, which focus diffuse erotogenic bodily sensations in the functioning of the drives.[2] From this investigation it will become possible to consider Pound's repetitions of a resistance to pregenital lack at the level of those continual insistences of the *Cantos* which consist in an invective against submission to bodily discourses described in sexual permutations which in any way confiscate the establishment of meaning and culture by the phallus. These insistences underpin a constant vilification of Jewry, of eunuchs, and of both erotic and defecatory anal practices. Dramatized in this vilification is a disavowal of castration which takes the form of reviling those orifices—and here a relation to the presentation of women in the *Cantos* becomes immediately evident—which inscribe a lack, and of designating all practices and persons held to have suffered any loss or submission to difference in terms adopted from the functioning of those organs.

In considering pre-Oedipal sexuality one crucial emphasis of Lacan's teaching has been to deconstruct any representation of the pregenital stages as following a kind of subjective evolution. Lacan displaces such a notion with the idea of repeated division. The subject is born divided, and is subsequently redivided in its construction. In answering F. Dolto's question at the close of the first section ('The Unconscious and Repetition') of the seminars published in English with the title *The Four Fundamental Concepts of Psycho-analysis*, a question concerning the requirement of a conceptual isolation of the stages, Lacan is led to reproach such consideration of these as evolutionary:

The description of the stages, *which go to form the libido*, must not be referred to some natural process of pseudo-maturation, which always remains opaque. The stages are organized around the fear of castration. . . . The fear of castration is like a thread that perforates all the stages of development. It orientates the relations that are anterior to its actual appearance—weaning, toilet training, etc.[3]

Here the stages relate to a castration which only becomes 'actual' on its 'appearance', that is to say, when it is seen, but which is nevertheless omnipresent already as an absence or lack. Whilst the most obvious situation of castration is the installation of the phallus as signifier of difference (thus elevated to primacy among these important moments of the accession to symbolicity) its origin as an absence is to be traced even further back than the migration of the libido in the oral and anal stages. These are punctured by the fact that underlying any immediate gratification of the drive is a residue installed by the divisive constitution of that gratification according to a modulation of presence and absence. The subject is constructed not in a sequence of natural graduations, but in a series of overlapping losses or splits which are articulated not in some mysteriously developmental provision of nature, but in produced relations.

Against any notion of the assuaging of a specific demand in the drive, Lacan frequently insists that the immediate aim of the drive is immaterial.[4] Rather its quest is the partial closure of an original lack, tabulated as, though not originating in, the *objet petit a:*

The *objet petit a* is not the origin of the oral drive. It is not introduced as the original food, it is introduced from the fact that no food will ever satisfy the oral drive, except by circumventing the eternally lacking object.[5]

The division or splitting of the subject is in this way situated before what is here its reappearance as a functioning of the drive. It must for Lacan therefore be theorized in terms of some originally lost complement of the body, a counterpart to what is already absent at the time of birth. To this lost bodily attribute Lacan assigns the name *lamella*, and describes its activities in terms of a history of a subject born as *l'hommelette*, both little man and dispersed egg whose membranes are broken, spreading haphazardly.[6] The lamella is described by Lacan as an organ 'whose characteristic is not to exist, but which is nevertheless an organ.'[7]

The subject distinguishes itself gradually according to excitation in various erotogenic zones, where the drives operate to attempt closure of the sense of loss of this anatomical complement already non-existent at birth. The lamella is accordingly based on a lack traceable to the cycle of sexed reproduction, and to the partition of the species into two sexes. The subject is implicated in a loss which is its fundamental condition, and the manifestation of that loss in desire is clearly not to be glazed over by any mere disavowal of sexual difference.

It is not a question here of a specifically different relation to sexed reproduction for men and women, but of a necessarily deficient relation of any subject to sex, and hence, from this individual insufficiency for continuance of life, an implication in death.

The subject is in consequence always caught short, its imper-
fections inscribed everywhere *en route* from *l'hommelette* to
subject. The $-\varphi$ (minus phi) which in the Lacanian algebra
represents the phallus as signifier of castration—it being no
accident that the shorthand 'phi' is in phonetic anticipation of
that signifier—may also be utilized as description of the *objet a,*
in any of its various representatives. When considering the gaze
for example, Lacan instances the eye:

It is in this way that the eye may function as *objet a,* that is to say, at
the level of the lack $(-\varphi)$.[8]

The central lack of desire is 'always indicated in a univocal way
by the algorithm $(-\varphi)$'.[9] Clearly this lack, in all its forms whether
at the level of the drives, of the dislocation of the scopic field,
or at the level of the phallus itself, threatens that opposite function, the Φ, which is the traditionally held masculine relation
to the phallus. In his discussion of female sexuality in *Le
Séminaire XX: Encore*, Lacan renders this relation algebraically:

Let us take to begin with those things on the side where every x is a
function of Φx, that is to say, from the side where the man is situated.[10]

The threat posed to this relation by the $-\varphi$ reveals on how flimsy
a surface this Φ is created over all the various representatives of
the *objet a* which accompany being from the very instant of
birth.

Clearly this psychoanalytic account of the subject's causation is
radically opposed to Pound's insistent reiterations of subjectivity
as autonomous identity outside signification, capable and controlling source of its own meanings. If it has already been argued
that the appearance of this consistency may be achieved only in
the disavowal of the lack which is revealed in the genital scenario
of the castration complex, it is now equally important to show
how pervasive is the threat levelled at this closing over of lacks
by their frequent return. This return becomes manifest in the
subject's discourses in the violence of their resistance to any
subversion of a presumed self-possession, a resistance also to the
emergence of unconscious desire. In order to reveal the short-

comings of Pound's understanding of properties of discourse—on which his notion of cultural order relies—it is necessary to show how despite all protestations as to the terminability of meaning and the effectuality of precision and definition, these proclaimed features of discourse are inevitably toppled by the irrepressible desire of the Other.

The relation between the fetishization of the male penis and certain patterns of discursive organization has already bordered on a series of symbolic equations whose investment circulates around a disavowal of castration. In so far as a continuity can be established between these defences against genital difference and against other lacks traversing the subject, the scene of castration may be read back into the subject's pregenital sexual organization as indeed a perforating thread. At the level of symbolic equations a continuity appears in the inscription within the chain of association around genital deficiency of further equations which recount a failure of control at other erotogenic sites also crucial to the psychical economy.

Pre-eminent among the nodes of association describing genital inadequacy are those presenting figures of feminity as subversive of the dominant meanings of the male. Genital loss in castration is also represented by Pound in the form of eunuchs, in such instances as the choice offered in *Hugh Selwyn Mauberley* between rule by either a Pisistratus, or by a 'knave' or a 'eunuch'.[11] This construction not only insists that a ruler's shortcoming is to be traced to a genital deficiency, but in propinquity to the formulation 'knave', links that defect to an analogous lack caused if not by clinical deprivation, then by an insufficient maturation. This latter sense then absorbs its further implication of a youthful naughtiness or deviance, functions which are superseded in the full flowering of manhood.

It is entirely consistent, then, that the Chinese Cantos should continually describe the threat to order as an infiltration by eunuchs into the elect domain of the leader, epitomized as we have seen by Mussolini, 'a male of the species'.[12] Sigismundo, too, is according to *Guide to Kulchur* 'an entire man'.[13] In Canto 54 learning and scholarship as the agents of transmission of order and cultural meaning are threatened with liquidation by a eunuch conspiracy:

And some grandees formed an academy
and the eunuchs disliked the academy
     but they never got rid of the eunuchs

HAN HUON was run by eunuchs
HAN LING was governed by eunuchs
     wars, murder and crime news
HAN sank and there were three kingdoms
     and booze in the bamboo grove
where they sang: emptiness is the beginning of all things.
                                   (54 : 281)

In addition to the explicit infringement of order here felt as the eunuchs' alignment with 'wars, murder and crime news' (this last term linking the state of cultural meanings with that of linguistic meanings and their availability), there is a further veiled castration in the song of these lacking abrogators of order, 'emptiness is the beginning of all things'. This emptiness concerns the absence or loss which is fundamental to the Lacanian conception of the subject, and which is totally inimical to the imaginary plenitude continually invoked in the *Cantos* as a moment of original paradisal presence.

In Canto 55 eunuchs appear as perpetrators of trickery and deceit, and are linked to the recurrent representation of women:

'Men are the basis of empire', said our lord HIEN-TSONG
     yet he died of the elixir,
fooled by the eunuchs, . .
                                (55 : 291)

Since not only is the empire upheld by its men but also perpetuated in a succession of phallic possession, eunuchs disrupt the transmission of cultural order in their murdering of son and **heir**:

MOU's first son was strangled by eunuchs,
                                (55 : 291)

These transgressions by the eunuchs are constantly invaded by their fundamental sexual transgression against the procreative operation of the penis:

> And yet he was had by the eunuchs,
>
> (55:291)

And,

> yet he also was had by the eunuchs after 15 years reign.
>
> (55:291)

The threat such an obstruction poses to penile sexuality and in particular to phallic discourse is held in the formulation 'squabbles', a linguistic confusion and inadequacy of definition and precision analogous to that ascribed to women:

> Squabbles of governors, eunuchs
> Sun Te put out the Eunuchs
> and got himself murdered (55:292)

Soon following these appearances of the transgressive force of genital inadequacy emerges in Canto 56 a pattern of association which rebinds this function of the eunuchs to the associative clusters outlined above, and significantly infuses a further nexus which diverges from this genital specificity:

> YAO, CHUN, YU controller of waters
> Bridge builders, contrivers of roads
> gave grain to the people
> kept down the taxes
> Hochang, eunuchs, taoists and ballets
> night-clubs, gimcracks, debauchery
> Down, down! Han is down
> Sung is down

Hochang, eunuchs, and taozers
empresses' relatives, came then a founder
saying nothing superfluous
cleared out the taozers and grafters, gave grain
            opened the mountains
Came taozers, hochang and debauchery
And litterati fought fiercer than other men to keep out the
                                                    mogul
drifting dung-dust from the North.
Hochang southward like rabbits
        half a million in one province only
                                            (56:302)

Several threads previously encountered converge here. In as much as female sexuality has been aligned in the *Cantos* with water, with the sea and with flooding, the presentation of these leaders as 'bridge builders' serves to trace in this episode the male's construction of a route across female confusion. The latter is brought into line with other subversive forces, 'hochang, eunuchs, taoists', all purveyors of an ungoverned sexuality conveyed in the term 'debauchery'. The cultural repercussions of this controlling of the waters are an ability to provide food for the population from agriculture and to restrain taxation successfully.

Prominent on the other hand among subversive agencies—and important below in the context of anti-Semitism—is the bond of maternal relation, the 'empresses' relatives' who take on both genealogical and covetous senses of the word 'grafters'. The displacement of a father-son identification and succession of order in an introduction of a female lineage which proliferates lack allows an unbridled multiplication. This, then, characterizes the hochang's southward journey, their 'half a million in one province only'. Indeed, the hochang are likened to 'rabbits' in respect of this ungoverned reproduction. But the founder whose linguistic practices re-introduce order by 'saying nothing superfluous' opens the mountains, and in so doing alludes to the explicitly copulatory section of Canto 47 which asks 'Hast thou entered more deeply the mountain?' (47:238). He is in this manner maintained by the full panoply of phallic association in re-establishing order and prosperity.

What is important in this passage from the point of view of an

interrelation of genital and non-genital sexual organizations is the
formulation 'drifting dung-dust from the North'. The threat to
social order is posed here not by a deficient genital endowment,
but in the produce of the anus. That this is not an isolated
instance may be indicated in an example from Pound's letter
to F. V. Morley, of 9 May 1937, where he observes:

Kulchur occurs in or above the stinking manure heap, and can not be
honestly defined without recognition of the dung-heap.[14]

In these terms Pound explains the libellous language of the
Cantos. The definition of culture is to be its contra-distinction
from this anal produce. What sponsors this rejection of anality
in favour of the fetishization of the penis (which as we have
seen creates culture) is that although erotic pleasure in the anal
stages of infancy may be controlled by a retention which prolongs
excitation of the sphincters, in general the anus locates a bodily
efflux or discourse which is a constantly repeated losing. Anality
bespeaks a submission to these discharges or discourses of the
body, and is a falling short or lack in the subject which transgresses any assumption of autonomy at the genital level.

Vituperation throughout the *Cantos* is constructed in terms of
such erotic irregularity, where the standard of regularity is the
controlling operation of the penis, and its assignation to those
who presume its unequivocal presence of a power of meaning and
order. This agency is clearly undermined by all functions which
are not totally controllable and are therefore considered, within
the terms of the poem's recurrent associations, as perversions.
Beside the precipitations of the anus appear other transgressions
of the penis including contraception, which interrupts the moment
of coition, and all forms of genital disease.

In so far as a desire for financial gain in the form of usury
takes the place of desire for sexual gratification whose outcome
is natural production, usury itself enters this nexus. And since
certain sects of the Christian Church have levelled a prohibition
against expressions of copulatory inclination, they too figure in
this pattern of association and are weighed against the consecration of coition by other cults, exemplified for Pound in the
Eleusinian mysteries.

In *Guide to Kulchur* Pound accordingly proposes a direct continuity between codes governing sexuality and cultural ordination:

Putting usury on a pedestal, in order to set avarice on high, the protestant centuries twised all morality out of shape. 'Moral' was narrowed down to application to carnal relations.[15]

Confining morality to carnal relations is for Pound exactly a failure to acknowledge the derivation of public order from these carnal relations, and he writes in the same work:

The puritan is a pervert, the whole of his sense of mental corruption is squirted down a single groove of sex. The scale and proportion of evil, as delimited in Dante's hell (or the catholic hell) was obliterated by the Calvinist and Lutheran churches. I don't mean to say that these heretics cut off their ideas of damnation all at once, suddenly or consciously, I mean that the effect of Protestantism has been semiticly to obliterate values, to efface grades and graduations.
    Pius' last encyclical (against communism) is on the track of this. The term corporate has some significance.[16]

Several new threads of insistence are inscribed here, particularly concerning the threats posed by Communism and Semitic races. These will be discussed shortly. Explicit formulations install the notion of castration (the heretics who 'cut off their ideas') as well as alluding to the body in the sudden insertion, without any explanation, 'the term corporate has some significance'. In *Polite Essays* Pound describes this term as emerging at the time of Fenollosa as an ideal, the beginning of a new means of thought concerned for unification and the appearance of completeness.[17] That this term refers directly to the body is of course no accident.
    In the celebrated Usury Canto, number 45, usury is a 'sin against nature', is 'CONTRA NATURAM', and indeed this Canto ends in a series of images of interrupted procreation: usury 'stayeth the young man's courting', and 'lyeth/between the young bride and her bridegroom' (45:230). It 'blunteth the needle in the maid's hand/and stoppeth the spinner's cunning' (45:229), where this 'cunning' anticipates the 'cunnus' of Canto 47, the 'nest softer than cunnus' (47:238). In Canto 116 this 'cunnus' is again implied in the diminutive 'cuniculi' (116:795), whose Latin sense as an underground passage or tunnel, a mine,

or a rabbit introduces a variety of possibilities, all of which converge upon Pound's representation of the female genital, infernal,
internal, reproductive beyond reason, and full of despised gold,
the 'gold her grandmother carried under her/skirts for Jeff
Davis' which 'drowned her when she slipped from the landing
boat' (77:471).

Usury's obstruction of insemination embroils the domain of
art and language, the virgin disabled by usura from receiving
her 'message' (45:229) (an annunciation of a particularly phallic
commission), and 'clear demarcation' (45:229) obfuscated. The
'gnawing' of usury in this Canto, 'it gnaweth the thread in the
loom' (45:230), emerges as castration in the less restrained
formulation of a war-time speech,

the kikes have sucked out your vitals. A mild penetration, for a hundred
years they have bootlicked your nobility and now where is your nobility?
You had at least the semblance of control.[18]

Here 'control', tantamount to 'nobility', is subverted by this act
of gnawing away at the 'vitals'. The result of that castration is
explicitly 'a mild penetration'. And this gnawing into is
reiterated—also juxtaposed to anti-Semitism—in the essay 'What
is Money For?':

This tendency 'to gnaw into' has been recognised and stigmatised from
the time of the laws of Moses and he called it *neschek*.[19]

Although usury is here affirmed as a sin condemned by the Jewish
race, its proper name and its earliest recognition are both encountered in that race, functions which within Pound's scheme
of a mimetic language can only establish for it a firm ethnic
foundation. And in the essay 'Gold and Work 1944', too, the
'hidden work of interest . . . is everywhere gnawing away,
corroding'.[20] Indeed, Hugh Kenner notes that Pound's very last
poem, a version of Horace, *Odes* III, 30, includes the lines:

This monument will outlast metal and I made it
More durable than the king's seat, higher than pyramids.
Gnaw of the wind and rain?
                    Impotent
The flow of the years to break it, however many.[21]

Corrosion of phallic authority is nowhere more clearly enacted than in genital disease. In a letter of 11 May 1940 Pound suggests of usury's damaging effects:

Roman Empire flopped because of low price of grain, egyptian dumping etc. Usury buggared that empire, but low price of grain was basic part of usury syphilis.[22]

'Buggary' and 'syphilis' have in common that they both interrupt the fecundity of seed. In a letter to Carlo Izzo, 8 January 1938, explaining features of the Usury Canto, Pound terms the Quattrocento a 'morally clean era' because 'usury and buggary were on a par', the two implicitly opposed to coition:

As you see, the moral bearing is very high, and the degradation of the sacrament (which is the coition and *not* going to a fatbuttocked priest or registrary office) has been completely debased.[23]

Dante, according to Pound in 'Economic Nature of the United States' lived in an era when usury was 'damned to the same circle of Hell as the sodomites, both acting against the potential abundance of nature.'[24] Similarly Cromwell's time was an era when 'by great wisdom sodomy and usury were seen coupled together', a formulation which dramatizes sexual conjunction in its own adopted metaphor.[25]

In the weight of Dante's alignment of hell, sodomy and usury, and of the assertion that English and American finance 'has made printing a midden, a filth, a mere smear. . . . There is no mediaeval description of hell which exceeds the inner filth of these mentalities',[26] it becomes unsurprising that Pound's own delineated hell in Cantos 14 and 15 should be traversed by images of interrupted sex and defecation. Immediately in Canto 14 appears:

> The stench of wet coal, politicians
>   . . .
> Standing bare bum,
> Faces smeared on their rumps,
>   wide eye on flat buttock,
> Bush hanging for beard,
>   Addressing crowds through their arse-holes,
>
> (*14*:61)

This smearing of the faces on the rumps introduces, by way of its phonic play on 'faces' and 'faeces', another tangential chain of association in the poem, the privileged relation of face and anus. In Canto 16:

> 'Was it? it was
> Lord Byron
> Dead drunk, with the face of an A y n . . . . .
> He pulled it out long, like that:
>   the face of an a y n . . . . gel.'
>   *(16 : 71)*

Not only does this phonic elision inject an accrued enmity to anal functions, but in its hesitant movement towards the word 'angel' takes up the interfusion of Christianity in the defecatory nexus. The transition which then follows introducing 'that son of a bitch,/Franz Josef of Austria', sets up the terms of a further node in Canto 50:

> in hell's bog, in the slough of Vienna, in
>   the midden of Europe in the black hole of all
> mental vileness, in the privvy that stank Franz Josef,
> in Metternich's merdery in the absolute rottenness,
> among embasterdized cross-breeds,
>   *(50 : 247)*

These infernal and defecatory variations are then pursued throughout this latter Canto.

Also in the extract from Canto 16 Lord Byron's being 'dead drunk' resumes an association of a loss of control in inebriation with lack, the eunuchs' and hochang's 'booze in the bamboo grove' related in Canto 54 to an originary absence *(54 : 281)*. It might be said, too, that this 'grove', a pleasant shade afforded significantly by trees, but also related phonically to the 'groove' or furrow of the female sex to be ploughed, repetitively requires in the *Cantos* the erection of the pillar. In Cantos 78 *(78 : 481)* and 79 *(79 : 492)* this requirement is expressed as the Latin 'aram nemus vult' or 'aram vult nemus', and in Canto 90 as 'Grove hath its altar' (*90* : 607), where what is erected is also sanctified. That this elevation over a natural declivity institutes culture is indicated in *A Visiting Card*:

Italy has lived more fully than other nations because she has kept up the habit of placing statues in gardens. The grove calls for the column. *Nemus aram vult.*[27]

What is erected here is the source of civilization and art.

The politicians of Canto 14, 'addressing the crowds through their arse-holes', their profiteering achieved in 'drinking blood sweetened with sh-t' (*14* : 61), are 'betrayers of language' in as much as their discourses, tainted by this anal submission, defect from the phallic standard of control. In doing so they become,

> the perverts, the perverters of language,
>   the perverts, who have set money-lust
> Before the pleasures of the senses;
>
>   (*14* : 61)

Their discourses are held to be a confusion,

> howling, as of a hen-yard in a printing house,
>   the clatter of presses,
> the blowing of dry dust and stray paper,
> foetor, sweat, the stench of stale oranges,
> dung, last cess-pool of the universe,
>
>   (*14* : 61–2)

This formulation of a communicative confusion returns as always to the female in its analogy to a 'hen-yard'. For 'hen' refers not merely to the apparent aimlessness of the movements of poultry, but also to that face of the metaphorization of foul sexuality which makes 'hen' a general term of female exclusiveness.

Pound's hell is further characterized, in its geographical local-ization as London (which in turn assumes sodomite associations by being called in *Guide to Kulchur* 'Gomorrah on Thames'[28]), as following the topography of the anal organ itself,

> the great arse-hole,
>   broken with piles,
> hanging stalactities,
>   greasy as sky over Westminster,
> the invisible, many English,
>   the place lacking in interest,
> last squalor, utter decrepitude,
> the vice-crusaders, fahrting through silk,
>   waving the Christian symbols,
> . . . .   frigging a tin penny whistle,
> Flies carrying news, harpies dripping sh-t through the air,
>
> (*14*: 62–3)

In this extract the 'stalactities' of the anus, its piles, invert the erection of that stalagmite the penis, and so repeat the extreme investment the opposition of the two sustains in the metaphorical economy of the *Cantos*.

The erotic functioning of the phallus is further obstructed in this hell by the 'condom full of black beetles' which interrupts not just semen but knowledge:

> . . . . .m Episcopus, waving a condom full of black-beetles,
> monopolists, obstructors of knowledge,
>   obstructors of distribution.
>
> (*14*: 63)

Christianity again participates in this obstruction with its 'clerical jock strap hanging back over the navel' (*15*: 64), as does unsuitability for coition, 'sadic mothers driving their daughters to bed with decrepitude' (*14*: 62), and disease, 'infinite pus flakes, scabs of a lasting pox' (*15*: 65).

A reflection on what happens when the reproductive distribution of labour in sex is re-arranged prompts both the story of the Honest Sailor in Canto 12, and the lyric appended by Pound to a letter to T. S. Eliot, of 24 December 1921, in which he praises his own 'Caesarian operation' on *The Waste Land*. The lyric begins:

> These are the poems of Eliot
> By the Uranian muse begot;
> A man their Mother was,
> A muse their Sire.[29]

The associative complex at the end of this lyric, drawing together its previous occupation with art as conceived and delivered on the model of sexual reproduction, argues a respective value for phallic and anal, and takes up certain homosexual implications of the story of the Honest Sailor. In that narrative the father's death-bed confession of homosexuality laments an inadequate preparation of the son 'to take over the bisness' (12:56). This maternal father's imminent death can only confirm the lacking function of an absent father already demonstrable in the form of the 'rich merchant in Stambouli' (12:57).

In the epistolary lyric, on the other hand, the deficient-because-absent father of the immaculate conception is re-established in the form of that divinity's resurrection as prophet, Pound the poet who assumes the authority of the paternal law:

> He writes of A.B.C.s
> And flaxeed poultices,
> Observing fate's hard decrees
>   Sans satisfaction;
> Breeding of animals,
> Humans and cannibals,
> But above all else of smells
>   Without attraction
> Vates cum fistula.[30]

Whilst at one level 'flaxeed poultices' are emollients made from dampened linseed and applied to the skin, the pronunciation 'flae-ksied' introduces the further senses of the word 'flaccid', also 'flae-ksied', suggesting limp, flabby and feeble. It is these latter senses which are then taken up in 'fate's hard decrees', 'sans satisfaction', and 'breeding'. Indeed the 'smells/Without attraction' are precisely the emissions of the anus which confront the elected power of the phallus. Finally, 'vates cum fistula', the 'soothsayer with a pitch or pan pipe', exposes the significance of this association, conferring the power of prophecy on those who possess the pipe. This is the same musical pipe—and Pound's interrelation of poetry and music is conveyed not only in the project of his operetta *Sordello* but also in the 'beat of the measure' in Canto 39 (*39*:195)—which as a flute in Canto 25 lies by Sulpicia's thigh. But in this instance the fluid is spilt on the grass:

> Lay there, the long soft grass,
>   and the flute lay there by her thigh,
> Sulpicia, the fauns, twig-strong,
>   gathered about her;
> The fluid, over the grass
> Zephyrus, passing through her,
>   'deus nec laedit amantes.'
>   (*25*:118)

Since here penetration fails, and the fluid of creation is spilt, an immediate modulation into mental barrenness follows:

> And from the stone pits, the heavy voices,
> Heavy sound:
>   'Sero, sero . . .
> 'Nothing we made, we set nothing in order,
>   . . .
> 'And what we thought had been thought for too long;
>   (*25*:118)

Not only is this flute by Sulpicia's thigh travestied in the anal register in 'a tin penny whistle' in Canto 14 (*14*:63), but immediately preceding Pound's lyric of the letter to Eliot, he writes precisely of failed genital delivery. This takes the form of his own 'cogitating an excuse for always exuding my deformative secretions in my own stuff, and never getting an outline'. This chastisement is intelligible in terms of the low energy of the verb 'to exude', or to 'allow to ooze out'. Failure of creativity is accounted for—as in that other writing of the same year 1921, the postscript to *The Natural Philosophy of Love*—as the weakness of the genital spurt which cannot make things clear or definite, which cannot get 'an outline'.

Creativity can only be refound in the achieved copulation of man and a female nature which receives his imprint. In Canto 82 Pound remembers this and terms it 'connubium terrae', the experience of lying in fluid:

> Kipling suspected it
> to the height of ten inches or over
> man, earth : two halves of the tally   (82 : 526)

Whilst in a letter to William Carlos Williams, of 21 October 1908, Pound disclaims that his own dislike of the pagan custom in which 'men loved men' is 'materia poetica', clearly at one level this is not the case.[31] That dislike is repetitively inscribed in the *Cantos*, both as an enmity to any discursive practice recognizing the fact of castration and desire, and also in a constant abrasion of anality within the poem's insistent patterns of association.

It is, moreover, on this question of textual organization around a suppression or recognition of lack and desire encountered most fundamentally at the level of sexuality that a debate between Pound and James Joyce took place, before the experience of *Finnegan's Wake* had rendered Joyce's writing practices totally opaque to Pound. That this divergence of writing practices is engendered at the level of sexuality is evident in the terms of exchange between the two writers, namely of respective phallic and cloacal obsessions. In a letter of 10 June 1919 Pound writes to Joyce of a disappointment with the Sirens episode of *Ulysses*. The issues at stake in this letter are especially crucial for the two writers owing to their common choice to work from Homer's *The Odyssey*. The novel, according to Pound, has 'gone down as far as the lector most bloody benevolens can be expected to respire'.[32] Pound admonishes Joyce: 'Fahrt yes, but not as climax of chapter=not really the final resolution of fugue', and 'One can fahrt with less pomp & circumstance'.[33]

Beyond the many parodic allusions to anality which Pound inserts, 'I don't arsk . . .', 'constatation (no p. for second t.)', 'rest lightly upon this editor/for he rested lightly upon thee',[34] the emphasis of this rejection is claimed to be against the public disclosure of personal obsessions,

obsessions arseore-ial, cloacal, deist, aesthetic as opposed to arsethetic, any obsession or tic shd. be very carefully considered before being turned loose.[35]

As well as reiterating once again an interconnection which binds together deism and anality—itself an obsessive pre-occupation— this condemnation is closely accompanied by Pound's own favoured attachment,

gallic preference for Phallus—purely personal—know mittel europa humour runs to the other orifice.—But don't think you will strengthen your impact by that particular.

Mass effect of any work depends on conviction of author's sanity.[36]

Here again, an allusion to the other orifice incites a mention of Christianity in the words 'Mass effect'. In the shift from anality to a natural religion (one which resists contraception and buggary) by way of their intersection in deism, the deficiencies of 'mittel europa humour' are displaced by 'sanity'.

There is, however, a further important relation which underpins Pound's aversion to anality. Whilst the functioning of the anus is organized around a separation from the faeces, and so related to a later recognition of the possible loss of the penis in castration, the surrendering of the faeces to a parent in infancy proclaims that object as the first unit of exchange, the first gift. This Freud indicates in his paper 'On Transformations of Instinct as Exemplified in Anal Erotism'.[37] He further suggests in this paper, as in his earlier 'Character and Anal Erotism',[38] that from this prototype of the gift an unconscious relation is forged between money and specifically gold, and faeces, a relation which may take over from anal erotism as a character trait in later life. This anal gift, and its later substitute gold, cannot be perfectly controlled for increased auto-erotic pleasure, but has instead to be given up on demand. So a defiance by the ego to that surrender, significantly a resistance to the loss of excrement which prefigures a loss entailed in castration, may be further seen as a resistance to what is uncontrollable, and therefore unacceptable, in gold.

It is the privileged relation between a defence of the ego against castration in fetishism, vilification of anality, and a concomitant rejection of gold which enters most vigorously Jews and usurers in the patterns of condemnatory association in the *Cantos*. The mitteleuropean disposition 'to the other orifice' of Pound's letter to Joyce is precisely such an inclusion of Jews within the domain of anality. This is not an isolated instance. In 'Bureaucracy, the Flail of Jehovah', the first sentence is 'Bureaucrats are a pox',[39] which in taking up the Hebrew allusion of its title intricates anality within the terms of an obstructed genitality. In the essay 'History and Ignorance', Pound's thesis that wars are created by usury and its defensive shroud of ignorance of economics is related back to defecation:

History that omits economics will not eternally be accepted as anything but a farce or a fake. The gross cloacal ignorance of professors, of reporters who offer chronicles with no economic analysis, can not forever pass as enlightenment.[40]

It is not just in the term 'cloacal ignorance' that anality emerges here, significant though the interrelation of these terms is as regards the recurrent representation of the female. The anus is also evident in the rejection of history without economics as 'a farce or a fake', where a phonic displacement reveals the privileged relation between 'face' and 'arse', apparent as the 'c' of 'farce' softens the 'k' of 'fake'.

Politicians, alias in *Guide to Kulchur* servants of 'an usuriocracy, that is foetor',[41] emerge in this same circulation in the note 'Definitions', in *Der Querschnitt* in January 1925:

4. Politicians: fahrts of the multitude.[42]

In the essay 'Gold and Work 1944' ignorance and usury are convened in the section 'The Enemy':

The enemy is ignorance (our own).[43]

This passage then diffuses through a citation of financial dealings by Rothschilds and Sassoons.

When in the *ABC of Economics* Pound refers to 'economic mess' this term 'mess' clearly has a double edge, leading one way into a notion of disorder and disarray (so transgressing the structural prerogative of the phallus) and another into dirtiness.[44] In *Guide to Kulchur* the nineteenth century is described simultaneously as the 'age of usury' and 'mainly mess'.[45] Indeed, Pound later in the same work returns to 'the foetor of the first half of the XIXth century'.[46] In *A Visiting Card*, too, usurers are a 'mess', although Pound here opines:

Fortunately these messes have no sense of proportion, or the world would already be entirely under their racial domination.[47]

In 'Gold and Work 1944' gombeen-men, whether they be exotic or indigenous, are considered the 'most stinking dregs of humanity'.[48] From being exotic they become indigenous by immigration, and in *Action* Pound describes 'an immigration of largely undesirable dregs'.[49]

In the *ABC of Economics* disorder in America is described as a condition in which 'Their dung has covered their heads',[50] and in 'National Culture, A Manifesto 1938' the usurers find themselves in 'filthy and damnable control of the Union'.[51] In a letter to Harriet Monroe, of 16 July 1922, Pound's dislike of Hebrew scripture erupts:

Damn remnants in you of Jew religion, that bitch Moses and the rest of the tribal barbarians. Even you do still try at least to leave the reader in ignorance of the fact that I do NOT accept the current dung, and official opinions about the dregs of the Xtn superstition, the infancy of American laws etc.[52]

There is an unhesitating flow here from 'that bitch Moses', a law giver ascribed not a paternal but a female identification, 'tribal barbarians', 'ignorance of the fact', 'dung', 'dregs', and 'infancy of . . . laws'. In another letter to Henry Swabey, of 9 May 1940, the Bible as text of the Hebrew religion is considered:

Black superstition and general filth. . . . Whole thing a perversion. . . .
All the Jew part of the Bible is black evil.[53]

It is further related in *A Visiting Card* once more to a specifically
Hebrew usury:

The usurers, in their obscene and pitch-dark century, created this
satanic transubstantiation, their Black Mass of money.[54]

In 'Gold and Work 1944' this usuriocratic, Hebrew-Christian,
perverted and infernal blend is intertwined, by way of the nineteenth century's designation as an era of usury, with Marxian
economics, 'a species of monetary Black Mass'.[55]

In the imagined Italian 'Republic of Utopia' on the other hand
where contentment is held to be 'due both to their laws and to the
teaching they received from their earliest schooldays'—that teaching installing a thought which 'hinges upon the definitions of
words'—the inhabitants 'do not worship money as a god, they
do not lick the boots of bloated financiers or syphilitics of the
market-place'.[56] Their social paradise opposes 'the disgusting
messes served up periodically by *The Times* or *Nouvelle Revue
Française*', interest in which gradually disappears 'from the
drawing-rooms of the more empty-headed young ladies—of both
sexes' as they become better acquainted with 'the best books'.[57]
These 'messes' are delivered 'periodically', either in a journal
or periodical, or in an implicit menstruation, 'periodically' an-
ticipating the 'young ladies' later in the quotation. This allusion
to the menstrual flood, or what Pound calls in his postface to *The
Natural Philosophy of Love* 'an ovular bath', describes a submission to the discharges or discourses of the body which is an
abdication of total personal autonomy. Pound claims, also in the
Gourmont postface, that 'where one woman appears to benefit by
an alluvial clarifying, ten dozen appear to be swamped'.[58] It is
significant, too, that this allusion introduces alongside these
'young ladies' more 'empty-headed' persons, young ladies of male
sex who submit to castration and so fall short of the fullness of
masculinity.

A lacking relation to the phallus is immediately counterposed
in the following paragraph of 'Gold and Work 1944', from

F

which these extracts come, to agricultural prowess, tested in 'ploughing contests to see who can drive the straightest furrow'.[59] This contest alludes quite plainly to the sense in Canto 47 in which ploughing, as the agrarian practice by means of which seed penetrates the soil, assumes the force of male insertion in copulation. Then in the next section of this essay, a section entitled 'Particulars of the Crime', in which the crime is examined in terms of its component 'parts', the twentieth century's estrangement from the paradisal world of Utopia is explained as resulting from usury, barbarism and ignorance. The importance of particulars is given as follows:

It is no use assembling a machine if a part is missing or defective. One must have all the essential parts.[60]

Whilst in the first phrase it is explicitly the machine which must be complete, the second phrase instantly forges an important ambiguity between three senses: one must have all the parts of the machine; one machine must have all its own parts; and one must have all one's own parts of oneself.

On this necessity of having a full complement of parts hinge certain of Pound's observations in *Guide to Kulchur* concerning animal reproduction. In distinguishing between the 'process of lower animals which breed by scission' and 'the process of the schismatics', Pound is led in this work to praise the practice of the former.[61] Yet his praise on this point runs against a condemnation expressed in Canto 15:

> This sort breeds by scission,
> This is the fourmillionth tumour.
> In this *bolge* bores are gathered,   (15:65)

Here 'bores' are not simply tiresome persons but the various orifices of the body, and Pound's condemnation is again established in terms of a bodily lack. In *Guide to Kulchur* Pound argues that in reproduction by scission 'the detaching segment has in it all the necessary elements for its life and its own operations'. The schismatic's constitution is on the other hand by division and lack:

The schismatic is a splinterer, his process is an emphasis on something fragmentary and a rejection of the totality. He does not want an organism containing all faith, or the constructive urges of all.

He therefore creates, as opposed to a small totality,

the possibly larger fragment which has not in itself the sum of the potentials.[62]

Moreover, Pound has earlier in this work reviled the need for food coupled with a separation from that food in the moving animal:

Obviously the need of nutriment indicates incompleteness in the moving animal. It is not self-sustaining, it is not completely autonomous.[63]

Failure of autonomy, aligned with a lack characteristic of Pound's descriptions of female sexuality and anality, and reminiscent of the splintering forces threatening Fascio's light, is considered less desirable than the condition of trees. In gripping the earth trees have their own direct and unimpeachable access to nutrition, which inheres in the abundance of nature and the plenitude of the maternal soil. The moving animal has suffered a constitutive separation from this soil.

To be forged as fundamentally inadequate or lacking is simultaneously to fall short of fixed, definite truth. Pound includes within the patterns of invective of his writing those kinds of politics which do not recognize a definite totality, and which unlike Fascio's contemplation of the undivided light have recourse to argumentation to establish positions, rather than appealing to faith and to self-evident facts. In propounding dialectics, Marxism (and what appear from constant juxtapositions and exchanges its equivalents for Pound: Bolshevism, Communism, Socialism and the Left) recommends itself pre-eminently for circulating in associations fixated on bodily lack.

These political forces of socialism are the most bitter enemies

of Fascism, existing for Pound as forces which 'divide, shatter
and kill', and which are opposed in principle to the 'corporate'
ideal, in any of its senses. Their call for dialectics is rejected
against the certitude of a definitive truth even if that truth has
to be invoked rather than demonstrated:

I mean or imply that certain truth exists. . . . Truth is not untrue'd
by reason of our failing to fix it on paper.[64]

Communism is 'merely barbarous and Hebrew'.[65] Bolsheviks, like
Protestants, have in *A Visiting Card* 'wiped the consciousness of
the greatest mystery out of the mind of Europe'. Their 'argumentation' displaces 'faith', and their 'sterility' replaces 'fecundity':

Latin is sacred, grain is sacred. Who destroyed the mystery of fecundity,
bringing in the cult of sterility?[66]

In a series of disjointed intrusions Communists, Hebrews and
barbarians all enter *Guide to Kulchur* as soon as the threat of a
lack arises:

The Greeks, being *maqueros* (happy men) with no moral fervour, left
a hole or a sense of lack, and into that hole there poured a lot of crass
zeal.[67]

In the 1939 essay 'Integrity of the Word', the section entitled
'Corrosion' begins not with usury or 'kikes' as above but 'the
Left claim. . . .'[68] In *A Visiting Card*, Pound further includes as
a 'falsification of the word' Marx's notion (and J. S. Mill's
according to Pound) of commodities as materialized labour. This
notion Pound believes has the effect of 'denying both God and
nature', since it closes off from the process of production the
necessary part played by the world we are given, nature. Moreover, this natural wealth Pound argues is augmented by our social
credit, our inheritance of accumulated inventions and ideas which
reduce the amount of labour necessary to production, and so contribute to the *means* of production. His conclusion is that Marxist
economics is misguided in the belief he ascribes to it that labour
is the exclusive source of wealth. Rejecting Marx, Pound pursues
his economic researches in Social Credit theories. Marx, however,

argues energetically against such simplifications of his position, attributing to such reductions definite political assumptions and interests. For Marx it is the *appropriation of nature* by certain sectors of the community which creates the conditions of labour and the tyranny of exchange value.[69]

Pound's concern is consistently to condemn political forms related to Marxism; in significantly 'A Note on Race', Socialism is described:

Socialism as seen in England shows all the worst features of German stupidity. All the lacks which made the average German the butt of the Great Frederick's sarcasm.[70]

Here the trace of suggestion moves from 'race' through 'Socialism', 'stupidity', and 'lacks' to the implicit anal register of 'butt'.

In replying by letter to Nancy Cunard's circular enquiring as to writers' positions relative to the Spanish Civil War, Pound, whose own contribution to the Left Review's publication *Authors Take Sides on the Spanish War* was grouped in the section entitled 'Neutral?', describes the editor and signatories as follows: 'Your gang are all diarrhoea'.[71] The article itself is exemplary of how obsessional patterns of vilification take over in Pound's discourses, and it is quoted in full:

Questionnaire an escape mechanism for young fools who are too cowardly to think; too lazy to investigate the nature of money, its mode of issue, the control of such issue by the Banque de France and the Stank of England. You are all had. Spain is an emotional luxury to a gang of sap-headed dilettantes.[72]

In Canto 35 a cameo of Jewish life is constructed in terms pivoting on an inadequacy inscribed in the body's openings or fissures,

> this is Mitteleuropa
>   and Tsievitz
> has explained to me the warmth of affections,
> the intramural, the almost intravaginal warmth of
> hebrew affections, in the family, and nearly everything else. . . .
> pointing out that Mr Lewinesholme has suffered by deprivation

of same and exposure to American snobbery . . . 'I am a product,'
said the young lady, 'of Mitteleuropa,'
but she seemed to have been able to mobilize
and the fine thing was that the family did not
wire about papa's death for fear of disturbing the concert
which might seem to contradict the general indefinite wobble.
It must be rather like some internal organ,
some communal life of the pancreas. . . . sensitivity
without direction . . . this is . . .
Oh yes, there are nobles, still interested in polo
said the whoring countess of course there were nobles.

(35:172–3)

The family is denigrated explicitly according to an identification
with the mother, that quality traced to an 'intravaginal warmth',
to the maternal genital.[73]

That this maternal genital, like the 'empresses' relatives' in
Canto 56 (56:302) accentuates a lack destructive of the phallus
and the father is suggested further in the early poem 'Commission':

Oh how hideous it is
To see three generations of one house gathered together!
It is like an old tree with shoots,
And with some branches rotted and falling.[74]

For in this extract the growth of the tree, whose relation to the
importance of a 'root' and to inseparability from the earth has
already been commented upon (as has the importance of 'shoots'
and 'shooting') is impeded by its surplus of ailing appendages.
The effect of strangulation of the tree by these relations is to
make some of its branches or protruding limbs fall off.

The family resembles 'some internal organ', held in opposition to some external organ, and is consequently sensitive and
liable to excitation, but without 'direction'. The maternal relation
is linked to a loss of control in the young lady's admission ' "I am
a product . . ." '. It becomes in consequence a contradiction to
'the general indefinite wobble' that art should be able to con-

tinue undisturbed even after 'papa's death'. This is contradictory because if art is, as in *The Spirit of Romance*, 'a fluid moving above or over the minds of men'[75] then it might be expected that art would collapse on the demise of the father.

Whilst Mr Lewinesholme's 'deprivation' is grammatically one from affection, the separation of this 'deprivation' from 'of same' across the end of an unusually long line suggests a disjunction of this loss from its object. This suggestion is consolidated in both the distant remove of the pronoun 'same' from its antecedent (seventeen words and a notated lacuna) and the apparent contradiction this lack of affection establishes with the previous assertion of a 'warmth . . . of hebrew affections'. In this way the endowment of the Jewish man is put into question, making way for the 'general indefinite wobble'. Finally, in this extract 'nobility', which has been recurrently linked in Pound's writing to control, is held to persist in the Mitteleuropean community only in the form of a 'whoring countess', her sexuality bound up in a rapacious desire for money.

Such a usurpation of sexual desire by a perverted desire for money—in this case in the form of a levy upon the expression of male sexual desire—is termed in the essay 'Gold and Work 1944' *'pecuniolatry'*, or the elevation of money into a god. Such idolization, according to Pound,

was due to a process of denaturalisation, by which our money has been given false attributes and powers that it should never have possessed.

Gold is durable, but does not reproduce itself—not even if you put two bits together, one shaped like a cock, the other like a hen.[76]

What is wrong with money for Pound is that it has assumed attributes which confer power, and to which it is not entitled. By the psychical equation of excrement and gold, and by a recognition in anal oblation of a later genital castration which establishes the stool as an anticipatory representative of the penis, money has appropriated all the various facets of genital sexuality. But whilst for the anal erotic there can be pleasure in retention, the anus more regularly is the site of a constant losing. Gold for Pound needs to be displaced as a unit of exchange since it cannot be properly controlled. Like the passing of faeces it transgresses the law of his father and of his phallus. The adoption of gold

as a unit of currency levied on male sexual desire by woman constitutes a displacement of her dependence for gratification upon
the male phallus by elevating a rival against it. It is on this account
that Pound's criticism of *'pecuniolatry'* attends immediately to
genital organization around reproduction in his illustration of the
cock and the hen, implicitly to the centrality of *the* phallus in
that process.

Since Pound's representations of Jewish men have imposed a
constant divergence from this authoritative phallic organization
of sexuality around coition, a particular form of *'pecuniolatry'*
is manifest in them:

> 'How do you get inspiration?
> 'Now my friend Hall Caine told me he came on a case
> 'a very sad case of a girl in the East End of London
> 'and it gave him an inspiration. The only
> 'way I get inspiration is occasionally from a girl, I
> 'mean sometimes sitting in a restaurant and
>   looking at a pretty girl I
> 'get an i-de-a, I-mean-a biz-nis i-de-a?'
>   dixit sic felix Elias?
>
>   (35:173–4)

Sexual anticipation on seeing a girl is harnessed to propagation
and fecundity in the regime of the fetishized phallus, with its
concomitant elusion of scopic castration mastering the field of
vision and holding off the difference which is woman. For Pound
this standard of vision is subverted by its appropriation to financial
inspiration. Transgression of the phallic inseminating urge by
'pecuniolatry' is effected in a reorientation of the libidinal investment of vision towards a new object. In describing 'pecuniolatry'
as the perversion of a normal erotic standard of pleasure constituted in sexual appetite, Pound reveals again how crucial to his
politics of nature is the continued mastery of the phallus in all
its representative forms—as a controller of women, of vision, of
law and of language. For the Jewish man, the displaced desire for
gold is thought to support a drive for profit opposed to the proper
function of the libido, which is to strive for culture by means of
coition.

It is significant, then, that in the much later Addendum for Canto 100, published with the *Drafts and Fragments*, a transgression of mastery in the field of vision should appear within the circulation of the poem's vitriol, entered there as 'envy':

> Here is the core of evil, the burning hell without let-up,
> The canker corrupting all things, Fafnir the worm,
> Syphilis of the State, of all kingdoms,
> Wart of the common-weal,
> Wenn-maker, corrupter of all things.
> Darkness the defiler,
> Twin evil of envy,
> Snake of the seven heads, Hydra, entering all things,
> Passing the doors of temples, defiling the Grove of Paphos,
> *neschek*, the crawling evil,
>   slime, the corrupter of all things,
> Poisoner of the fount,
>   of all fountains, *neschek*,
> The serpent, evil against Nature's increase,
>   Against beauty   (Add. *100* : 798)

The regular features of acrimony are here: usury once again implicated in darkness, the inferno, a poison against procreation, disease and particularly syphilis, all operating to corrupt and undermine the well-being of society, poisoning its fountain. Hydra the seven-headed snake alludes to the polyvalency of the octopus, and of the cephalopodic female of Canto 29 and again of Canto 114:

> Their dichotomies (feminine) present in heaven and hell.
>   Tenthrils trailing
>   caught in rocks under wave.
> Gems sunned as mirrors, alternate.   (*114* : 791–2)

The labyrinthine polymorphism of this creature is to be escaped only in enlightenment,

			pure Light, we beseech thee
		Crystal, we beseech thee
	Clarity, we beseech thee
				from the labyrinth
					(Add. *100*: 799)

This formulation of the labyrinth is also to be found in Canto
93, in a parallelism with hell,

		to enter the presence at sunrise
		up out of hell, from the labyrinth
		the path wide as a hair
					(*93*: 632)

Here the octopus of multiple protrusions is replaced with an
entry which is a losing. But the threat offered by woman is maintained in her being 'present in heaven and hell' (*114*: 791), both
erotic object and yet inevitable apprisal of the fact of castration.
The Hebrew tradition of the snake is also evident 'Fafnir the
worm', the 'crawling evil' aligned with usury. In Canto 52 usury
is also a snake, 'neschek is against this, the serpent' (*52*: 257).
	But beyond these insistent associations an unprecedented in-
clusion illustrates a further threat to any imaginary, in this case
in the construction of the scopic field. This threat is contained
in 'envy', the 'twin evil' of darkness, and which is related to usury
by the shared term greed. Lacan has traced the etymology of
this 'envy' to the Latin 'invidia' and has postulated of it the
voracious functioning of the evil eye. This eye operates by means
of its,

fatal function of being in itself endowed—if you will allow me to play
on several registers at once—with a power to separate.[77]

This look has the effect of poison, that same operation Pound here
attributes to usury.
	In giving an account of this *invidia,* which derives not from

a jealousy of things needed or wanted but from envy of things of no use to the subject, Lacan argues:

Such is true envy—the envy that makes the subject pale before the image of a completeness closed upon itself, before the idea that the *petit a*, the separated *a* from which he is hanging, may be for another the possession that gives satisfaction, *Befriedigung*.[78]

In suspension from the *petit a* of its own desire, the subject confronts what it sees as a circumvention of that loss, a completeness of satisfaction. The evil eye has a virulent capacity to separate that completeness by introducing a rift or flaw there, the look that is radically subversive of the scopic field. Since the advent of desire is also that of the fact of individual death, to inflict this separation is also to inflict death.

In this way the evil eye of *invidia* can be the poison which alongside all the other instances inscribed in this passage of invective threaten self-satisfied possession. In terms of the associative chains of the *Cantos*, the menacing eye demonstrates how ubiquitous is the threat of something missing to the subject, even to the visualized world made certain for empirical truth and representation. The extent of this threat draws the *Cantos* ever tighter into the knot at the level of content which repeats the need of the essential organ, and acrimoniously attempts to stave off lack wherever, as holes in the dyke, it threatens castration.

At another level of the construction of the *Cantos*, however, castration reappears in the intervals of signification, in moments of disruption of intended meanings when the seemingly homogeneous surface of language is broken into a tissue of signifiers which have to be worked to be read. That this kind of castration may be linked to effects at the level of content was demonstrated by Freud in the early days of dream analysis, access given to this relation by way of the aperture condition of the female organs. In a section of *The Interpretation of Dreams* when Freud considers means of representation and, in alluding to an exchange between his categories of dream form and dream content, recounts the fact of gaps in the dream dramatizing the female genitals, this can be understood to signify, in its acceptance of difference, the introduction of desire.

Particularly important in Freud's account is that the 'gaps in

the dream', the 'there's something missing' come as the climax of
a man's dream narrating the bedtime undressing of an elderly
lady and her two daughters. Freud comments:

The 'gaps' were the genital apertures of the women who were going
to bed; and 'there's something missing' decribed the principal feature
of the female genitalia. When he was young he had had a consuming
curiosity to see a woman's genitals and had been inclined to hold to the
infantile sexual theory according to which women have male organs.[79]

So Freud cites textual intermittences in the context of penis
fetishism as betokening a re-emergence of desire inscribed at the
level of a repetition as female organs.[80]

Lacan's reconstruction of psychoanalysis as more thoroughly a
work on language as it operates across the body has been able
to advance this fundamental insight. Lacan has postulated that
language precedes the subject, and that the subject is created as
an effect of language, a speaking. Yet the subject appears as the
source rather than the effect of meanings. This dissimulation is
a resistance to language in the form of a closing over, a parrying
of the field of the Other in order to bind together symbolic and
imaginary. In this delicate position the subject's signification
emerges.

Extreme entrenchment in a presumed authority over language
involves an increased repression of the system of differences of
which language consists. Nevertheless, these discourses are invaded with unintended slips and mistakes, and in this way
reclaimed from their appropriation by the subject. Discourse
authorized by a control over language made possible in the
condition of fetishism most vigorously endeavours to suppress
difference, covering it with fixed and resolute identity, and the
myth of a language completely in the service of a speaker or
writer. But since this self-possession disavows or seeks to close
off an initial division in language and in sexuality, even extreme
repression of constitutive differences and separations is beset by
unexpected irruptions.

Here various lacunae in the composition of the *Cantos* take on
a fresh importance, in so far as the intervals they introduce between the poem's various discourses install an uncontrollable
element of desire. Further gaps beyond the control of the writer

contribute to this effect, including the libellous omissions and the missing Cantos 72 and 73. These have the effect of deconstructing a consistent subject position outside language where the reader can preside in simple judgement on the text, and incipiently implicate the reader in a relation of interrogation. The act of reading becomes one of producing relations to the text rather than merely consuming an already formed inherent meaning. In this way the poem's gaps have the capacity of the evil eye to separate and forestall any complete satisfaction.

This separation threatens at a structural level the very paradise of possession that is defended from an analogous castration at the level of content. The definition of words accumulated in the ideogrammic method as the forcefields of nature and the indelible inscription of perfect control which makes good art are vaporized by the trace of desire. In these various instances where desire for all its acrimonious suppression in the *Cantos* reappears, the simple effectivity of Pound's desired precise language breaks down. Its fixing of meaning across and against difference is subverted precisely by the desire of the Other.

Notes

1 *Four Fundamental Concepts*, p. 78; *Le Séminaire XI*, p. 74.
2 For a description of Freud's notion of the stages including reference to Lacan's conceptualization of the drives, see Juliet Mitchell, *Psychoanalysis and Feminism* (Penguin, Harmondsworth, 1974, reprinted 1976), pp. 26–9.
3 *Four Fundamental Concepts*, p. 64; *Le Séminaire XI*, p. 62.
4 Passim; see, for example, *Four Fundamental Concepts*, p. 168; *Le Séminaire XI*, p. 153.
5 *Four Fundamental Concepts*, p. 180; *Le Séminaire XI*, pp. 164.
6 See *Four Fundamental Concepts*, pp. 197–8; *Le Séminaire XI*, pp. 179–80.
7 *Loc.cit.*
8 *Four Fundamental Concepts*, p. 104; *Le Séminaire XI*, p. 96.
9 *Four Fundamental Concepts*, p. 105; *Le Séminaire XI*, p. 97.
10 'Prenons d'abord les choses du côté où tout x est fonction de Φx, c'est-à-dire du côté où se range l'homme.' J. Lacan *Le Séminaire XX: Encore* (Seuil, Paris, 1975), p. 67.
11 *Collected Shorter Poems*, p. 207.
12 See above, chapter 5, p. 123.
13 Ezra Pound, *Guide to Kulchur* (Faber, London, 1938; reprinted New Directions, New York, & Peter Owen, London, 1952), p. 94.

14 *Letters*, p. 386.
15 Pound, *op.cit.*, p. 256.
16 *Ibid.* p. 185.
17 In 'We Have Had no Battles but We Have all joined in and Made Roads', *Polite Essays* (Faber, London, 1937), pp. 49–56. The 'corporate ideal' is described pp. 50–1.
18 *'Ezra Pound Speaking': Radio Speeches of World War II*, edited by Leonard W. Doob (Westport, Connecticut and London, 1978), p. 61.
19 *Selected Prose*, p. 268.
20 *Ibid.* p. 321.
21 Quoted by Hugh Kenner, *The Pound Era* (Faber, London, 1971), p. 548.
22 *Life*, p. 382; *Life* (Penguin), p. 488.
23 *Letters*, p. 397.
24 *Selected Prose*, p. 146.
25 Ezra Pound, *Impact: Essays on Ignorance and the Decline of American Civilization*, edited with an introduction by Noel Stock (Chicago, 1960), p. 233.
26 Pound, *Guide to Kulchur*, p. 184.
27 *Selected Prose*, p. 302.
28 Pound, *Guide to Kulchur*, p. 228.
29 *Letters*, pp. 234–5.
30 *Loc.cit.*
31 *Ibid.* pp. 37–8.
32 *Pound/Joyce*, p. 157. The extreme antithesis between Pound's fetishized phallus and Joyce's 'cloacal obsession' has been pointed out by Colin Mac-Cabe, *op.cit.*, p. 170n. MacCabe also indicates here the musical metaphors these respective predilections can assume, Pound's horn and Joyce's wind section, and suggests that Joyce at least was aware of the far-reaching consequences of this disagreement. An intrication of musical metaphor in the circulation of the *Cantos* is clear in Canto 79 'can that be the papal major sweatin' it out to the bumm drum?/what castrum romanum . . .' (79 : 485).
33 *Pound/Joyce*, p. 158.
34 *Ibid.* pp. 157–9.
35 *Ibid.* p. 158
36 *Loc.cit.*
37 *Standard Edition*, vol. XVII.
38 *Ibid.* vol. IX.
39 *Selected Prose*, p. 187.
40 *Ibid.* p. 237.
41 Pound, *Guide to Kulchur*, p. 132.
42 *Selected Prose*, p. 183.
43 *Ibid.* p. 314.
44 *Ibid.* p. 216.
45 Pound, *Guide to Kulchur*, p. 26 and p. 183.
46 *Ibid.* p. 258.
47 *Selected Prose*, p. 283.
48 *Ibid.* pp. 315–16.
49 *Action*, 20 August 1938, p. 13.
50 *Selected Prose*, p. 216.
51 *Ibid.* p. 131.
52 *Letters*, p. 250.
53 *Ibid.* pp. 444–5.

54 *Selected Prose*, p. 277.
55 *Ibid.* p. 316.
56 *Ibid.* pp. 306–7.
57 *Ibid.* p. 307.
58 Rémy de Gourmont, *The Natural Philosophy of Love*, translated with a postscript by Ezra Pound (Casanova Society, London, 1926), p. 171.
59 *Selected Prose*, p. 307.
60 *Loc.cit.*
61 Pound, *Guide to Kulchur*, p. 332.
62 *Loc.cit.*
63 *Ibid.* p. 243.
64 *Ibid.* p. 295.
65 *Life*, p. 355; *Life* (Penguin), p. 453.
66 *Selected Prose*, p. 287.
67 Pound, *Guide to Kulchur*, p. 330.
68 Pound, *Impact*, p. 96.
69 *Selected Prose*, p. 277. A clear rejection by Marx of the thesis that labour alone generates wealth may be found in his marginal notes to the *Programme of the German Workers' Party*, where he reproaches Lasalle and his followers for precisely such a simplification : 'Labour is *not the source* of all wealth. Nature is just as much the source of use-values (and in point of fact material wealth consists of such!) as labour, which is itself only the manifestation of one natural force, human labour-power. . . . The bourgeoise has very good grounds for attributing a *supernatural creative power* to labour; since it follows directly from the fact that labour is conditioned by Nature, that the man who possesses no other property than his labour-power must in all systems of society and at every level of culture be the slave of other men who have made themselves the owners of the material conditions of labour. He can only labour with their permission and hence only live by their permission.' *Critique of the Gotha Programme*, with appendices by F. Engels and V. I. Lenin, edition authorized by the Marx-Engels-Lenin Institute, Moscow (Martin Lawrence, London, 1933), pp. 21–2.
70 Pound, *Impact*, p. 247.
71 *Life*, p. 345; *Life* (Penguin), p. 440.
72 Ezra Pound, 'Neutral?' in *Authors Take Sides on the Spanish War* (Left Books, 1941), p. 29.
73 Christine Brooke-Rose describes this Canto not as a depiction of Jewish life in particular but as one of 'the European middle-class and its cultural chaos', *ZBC of Ezra Pound* (Faber, London, 1971), p. 175. There is a great danger here of minimizing Pound's anti-Semitism, particularly with regard to the war-time speeches. Claims can be made, for example, that the contents of these would not have been treasonable if uttered in America where freedom of speech reigns (cf. *ibid.* pp. 243–4). But when current editions of the *Cantos* are still censored, and when much of Pound's writing is for some reason still not publicly available, this can lead to a much diluted characterization.
74 *Collected Shorter Poems*, p. 98.
75 Ezra Pound, *The Spirit of Romance* (J. M. Dent, London, 1910; revised edition New Directions, New York, & Peter Owen, London, 1960), p. 7.
76 *Selected Prose*, p. 318.
77 *Four Fundamental Concepts*, p. 115; *Le Séminaire XI*, p. 105.
78 *Four Fundamental Concepts*, p. 116; *Le Séminaire XI*, p. 106.

79 *Standard Edition*, vol. IV, p. 333.
80 Textual intermittences, in the form of omission in selection, are also described by Pound in these terms. In 'How to Read', he refers to 'Eliot's castrated edition of my poems', *Literary Essays*, p. 18.

Chapter Seven

Conclusion: knowledge at sea

THE emphasis of the arguments offered above has been that the termination of the *Cantos* in admissions of defeat and failure is not traceable simply to features of biography, but is the inevitable effect of a fundamental misconception of the operation of language; implicit in that misconception I have argued is a misunderstanding of the place of the subject in signification. Such a view is clearly quite opposed to Pound's own celebrated lament:

The plain fact is that my head just doesn't WORK. Stretches when it just doesn't work.[1]

The foregoing account of Pound's writing suggests a demonstrable inadequacy in his various theorizations when confronted with and traced in the specific practices of his texts. Such an attention is able to point out the potentiality of those texts whose opposition to Pound's conceptualizations most emphatically calls for their recasting or displacement. Whereas simply to concur in the poet's above recognition of a 'plain fact' of diminishing power is implicitly to accept other 'stretches' when his head does work, when his intentions *do* flow through into the poetry, to trace the failure of his understanding of language in his own writing practices is to put those general theories into question, and so to entreat a much more radical rethinking of poetry.

Within the framework of these arguments the *Cantos* were considered as a quest, at one level grounded in the search of Odysseus for a lost home and an identity. This quest intermittently punctuates the text with its endeavour to recover an original, lost meaning, in language a coincidence of word and thing where the subject can rest in comfortable certainty, and in terms of social structure, a fixed and unchallengeable political order. An eclipse of this domination over linguistic and social meanings, and of the subject's identity, was held to be first discernible in the constant foiling of controlled discourses which are to purvey meanings, and in the appearance in those discourses of an uncontrollable desire.

The weight of these perceptions is to replace the notion of an intention to be communicated with an understanding of the text as an area of possible meanings constrained not by an intraducible authorial seal, but by determinate practices of discursive organization. These may be examined in terms of the positions they make available for the subject. The replacement of an understanding of reading as consumption of a single essential meaning ('essential' both as possessed of a core or essence, as well as compulsory and not to be exchanged for any other) will necessarily include in its terms both the construction of the subject who reads and the historical instant of the act of reading. Any fixed or trans-historical effectivity of writing becomes in this light unsustainable. It is impossible to encounter language outside either a subjective history latent in any utterance or a larger social history which situates the linguistic act.

The poem consequently cannot be argued to contain fixed meanings nor to enfold a coherent, monological hypothesis of its own, which is held in transcribed documentation, for example. It must rather be read as a production of relations across language, and so must be thought to invite a certain multiplicity of engagements. To recognize this plurality of meaning in the text is not merely an invitation to all kinds of voluntaristic appropriation, but rather makes way for a tissue of relations hinged always on the given conditions of the text's organization. Its multiple effects are in the service of the matter of language those interminable modes of intelligibility traverse. Since such consideration of the text calls upon the accession to symbolicity as a crucial turn of subjective history—and one reiterated in each enunciation—it cannot be described without an address to a psychoanalysis which attempts to account for the subject's relation to the signifier.

Central to the intervention of desire in discourses of the subject otherwise controlled by the fetishized penis was seen to be, within the register of the eye, an introduction of the look into vision as transgression of the scopic field, with its particular produced conjunction of symbolic and imaginary which locates the specular, the world of assured vision. In this intervention a relation between the eye and the 'I' became conspicuously apparent, in as much as the delusion of an identity for the subject depends on a resistance to castration, the eye being the organ most capable of that resistance. So it is in the register of vision that the subject appears most assured of itself, the effectivity of sight seeming to be supported by all kinds of neurological co-ordination and motivity.

It is from such domination that the model of empiricism is founded, a truth of experience as it is registered to the eye. Such truth conferred upon sense impressions by their elusion of castration was seen to characterize in vital respects Pound's notion of the functioning of the word and the world, the eye giving substance to the 'I', the identity of the self. In this context it is significant that Pound's childhood attempts to alter his forename away from the associations of 'Ezra' should consistently address themselves to perspicacity or luminosity, to 'X-ray', or to 'Ra', pronounced 'ray'.[2]

Much later Pound writes in *Polite Essays*:

Men are good or bad in the year 1935 in proportion as they will LOOK at the facts, new facts, any facts.[3]

Here any impression may become a fact by its simple designation as such, although the liberalism of Pound's exhortation to scrutinize 'any facts' is elsewhere restricted by an evaluation which distinguishes between sense impressions to be retained and those to be rejected. To this effect Pound avers in a letter to Dr Joseph Brewer, of 6 May 1938:

Certain facts are facts and certain lies are lies. This is a different distinction from that between one theory and another, or between one policy and/or expediency and another.[4]

Since truth and sight inter-penetrate, to transgress truth in a lie is for some reason to fail to see.

In the *ABC of Economics* Pound laments the opacity in which experience is often held, wishing to replace that with a trans-

parency of vision capable of rendering experience unequivocal
and simple:

People are so little used, or shall we say the readers of books and
papers are so little used to using their eyes, or so little travelled as
never to have seen simple phenomena.

Has the reader ever seen women at a well curb, or at a public spigot
or pump?[5]

'Simple phenomena' may be construed to remain simple only
so long as the look is excluded from the use of the eyes, so long
as castration is eluded and the work of intelligibility displaced
by the revelation of truth.

The assurance of those parts of the *Cantos* founded in such
an appropriation of the scopic field can persist only so long as
representation and specularity can be held in place, the poem
made desperate by the threat of castration, hence its ubiquitous
condemnation. The specific construction of this position of specularity against the fact of sexual difference, the look to be over-
looked only by a glazing over of that difference, is intimated in
the above quotation in the selected instance of a gaze upon
women. In this gaze the difference posed by the female is fixed
and mastered.

That such a resistance to difference repeats what is in the genital
scenario the fetishization of the male penis is inscribed here in the
explicit disposition of women around the public 'spigot', that
annular projection regulating liquor flow which fits a corresponding depression or socket in an adjacent piece. The phallus makes
its appearance as central occupation of the female in the field from
which its function as signifier is most vigorously excluded. That
this corking of the female is at stake in the establishment of
'plain facts' is clear in a letter from Pound to Louis Dudek
written during the poet's incarceration. Pound laments: 'The
younger generation does NOT plug much for factual history.'[6]

In addition to this empiricism the *Cantos* affirm a further
epistemological mode, a contemplation of mysterious, transcendental unity. Such contemplation has already been encountered
in Fascism's asseverations of the undivided light, and can be
seen to rely upon Pound's recurrent postulation of an unquestioned, original plenitude. In *Guide to Kulchur* Pound even

proposes that the efficacy of this contemplative mode can itself be verified empirically. This suggests a continuity between the two epistemological structures which of necessity still relies upon another quarter for its veridical support, upon the guaranteeing full presence of the subject.

Writing against the syllogism, Pound takes up Richard St Victor's observation of three modes of thought:

There are three modes of thought, cogitation, meditation and contemplation. In the first the mind flits aimlessly about the object, in the second it circles about it in a methodical manner, in the third it is unified with the object.

That is something a man can check up on. It is a knowledge to be verified by experience.[7]

In presuming that there is a world of potential objects of discourse awaiting mental apprehension, Pound claims the value of contemplation to be that it merges with the object, and seizes its reality. The effect of syllogistic discourse is conversely to lose reality, and Pound prefaces his citation from Richard St Victor:

The syllogism, time and again, loses grip on reality. Richard St Victor had hold of something: sic. . . .[8]

The necessary condition for mastering reality is to have something that can be kept hold of. Contemplation unifies in so far as its solitary exclusion from contradiction and its protraction of the gaze eliminate all the divisive contingencies of argumentation (Fascism eliminates such contingencies in its own way). It is therefore held to elude all the lacks implicit in the subject and discourse, those lacks summarized in the intervening look of another. Accordingly, contemplation is able to elevate empirical truths to the domain of a transcendental truth where the congruence of mind, eye and object which is the reposeful condition of the contemplative gaze may be held to partake of an unbounded metaphysical presence.

In the *Cantos* there emerges a tightening counterpoint concerned with the interrelation of amor, the eye, and the flame or crystal. In this mergence of the perceptible and the divine the poem's paradise is created. In a letter to Homer Pound, of 11

April 1927, Pound describes this emergence of the divine in the worldly:

The 'magic moment' or moment of metamorphosis, bust thru from the quotidien into 'divine or permanent world'. Gods, etc.[9]

And in Canto 94 this purview is expressed as a vertical chain rising into the heavens:

> Beyond civic order:
> l'AMOR.
> Was it Frate Egidio—'per la mente'
> looking down and reproving
> 'who shd/mistake the eye for the mind'.
> Above prana, the light,
> past light, the crystal.
> Above crystal, the jade!
>
> (94:634)

The light, gems and love converge upon the theosophical breath of life, the 'prana', and are merged, even though possessed of their internal hierarchy, in these encircling textures of 'Gods, etc.'. Canto 91 urges,

> that the body of light come forth
> from the body of fire
> And that your eyes come to the surface
> from the deep wherein they were sunken,
>
> (91:610)

The 'return' from being 'sunken' of the eyes refinds that surfacing within the area of the poem's associations embodying castration, in as much as here sight, identity and order are to emerge from a metaphorical sea.

Earlier, in Canto 90, occurs the repeated and capitalized line 'UBI AMOR IBI OCULUS EST' (90:609), the inescapable conjunction of the eye and love, and its pattern of fecundity based in possession of the phallus:

Trees die & the dream remains
>Not love but that love flows from it
>ex animo
>& cannot ergo delight in itself
>but only in the love flowing from it.
>>(*90* : 609)

This convergence in the later *Cantos* absorbs the principle of
order and selection, the 'What thou lovest well remains/the rest
is dross' (*81* : 520–1), as well as the primacy of specularity, the
'First came the seen' (*81* : 521). It links them in a divine perception conceived in an apotheosis of the phallus, the 'God's eye
art'ou' of Canto 106 (*106* : 755). These various instances enact
a resistance to castration whose polyphonic and pervasive presence
is woven in this final network of association centering on the
flame, the eye, the crystal, and in gemmology, the close of the
poem in paradise.

Within such a perspective of truth conferred by the eye and
the 'I' it appears initially paradoxical that the *Cantos* should
return, in the figure of Tiresias, to an instance of blindness, a
deprivation of the sight which confers truth not in terms of an
indictment of inadequacy, but as an affirmation beyond the loss
of ocular powers of oracular ones. If blindness is to be understood as a castration, then the introduction of Tiresias in Canto
1 is particularly problematic, being offered there as specifically
an antidote to infernal impotence:[10]

>I sat to keep off the impetuous impotent dead,
>Till I should hear Tiresias.   (*1* : 4)

When subsequently in Canto 47 the prophetic functioning of
Tiresias is described, that functioning is revealed as a sustenance
of the mind 'entire' even in the adversity of blindness and death
(*47* : 236).

It is, too, this completeness which is reiterated in Canto 80,

where Tiresias 'still hath his mind entire' (80 : 494). The ability
of Tiresias to prophesy a return home to Ithaca is conferred by
preservation of mental powers 'entire', not lacking, even in the
overlapping of the two lacks of subjugation to blindness and to
individual death. From hell, already characterized as locus of
castration in multiple forms, Tiresias indicates an exit, a way to
find the knowledge that must in Canto 47, and significantly, be
'sailed after' ('Yet must thou sail after knowledge/Knowing
less than drugged beasts' (47 : 236)). Even in the suggestion from
the seer of a way to have truth revealed, the formulation of that
quest as a navigation returns upon the poem's overdetermination
of castration anxiety in the requirement that truth must be found
beyond castration's life-quenching grasp.

That the question of Tiresias as the blind seer is bound up
with sexuality is made further apparent in certain aspects of the
classical myth which inform, by way of the Homeric poem, its
adoption in the *Cantos*. Tiresias's blindness is attributable in all
extant variants of classical mythology to a specifically sexual
determination. In several authors this takes the form of a
deliberation of more pleasure in sex for women made by Tiresias
in a debate between Jupiter and Juno, the mortal judging from
personal experience of both sexes, and receiving blindness in
retribution for his decision from a disagreeing and disgruntled
Juno. Indeed, the earlier change of sex which offers Tiresias
the possibility of making his judgement derives from a seeing and
separating of serpents in copulation. In other writers Tiresias's
blindness has its origin in a viewing of Minerva bathing. In both
cases what is crucial is a sexual curiosity assumed beyond the
proper condition of men in Tiresias's use of his eyes, a knowledge of sexual difference derived from the serpents or from the
seeing of the female body. Both experiences result in the castration
of blindness.

In the essay 'The Psychoanalytic View of a Psychogenic Distur-
bance of Vision' Freud has accounted for such an infliction of
blindness in terms of a talion punishment of sexual scopophilia,
and, in describing the myth of Lady Godiva, has presented a
closely analogous case.[11] Freud suggests in this paper that whilst
clearly not all disorders of vision lie within the domain of
psychogenesis, nevertheless numerous myths might be susceptible
of analysis in terms of neurotic disorder. More specifically, in

the essay 'The Uncanny', in returning to the question to comment on the unavoidable 'substitutive relation between the eye and the male organ which is seen to exist in dreams and myths and phantasies', Freud makes it clear that blindness is within this construction of talion punishment not some randomly chosen affliction, but exactly a castration.[12] This castration is inflicted when the eye is no longer able to elude it by fixing its representations, by holding off difference in a domination which is the fundamental condition of specularity. It is also inflicted by the superficially opposite condition when a libidinal appropriation of vision impinges too greatly upon the more general functions of the eye. In that condition the psyche takes its revenge upon usurpation by causing a failure of any operation of the eye, in blindness.

Tiresias, however, is not the only example of a central and exalted figure in the *Cantos* who is blind. Pound returns several times to the myth according to which Homer is held to have been blind, both in the *Cantos* themselves and in the prose writings. Canto 2 has the lines:

> And poor old Homer, blind, blind, as a bat,
> Ear, ear for the sea-surge, murmur of old men's voices:
>
> (2 : 6)

This assertion is re-affirmed in Canto 7 (7 : 24). In the essay 'I Gather the Limbs of Osiris', Pound writes:

Homer of the Odyssey, man conscious of the world outside him: and if we accept the tradition of Homer's blindness, we may find in that blindness the significant cause of his power; for him the outer world would have a place of mystery, of uncertainty . . . his work, therefore, a work of imagination and not of observation.[13]

Whilst this latter formulation explicitly opposes the emphasis of a poetry of empirical evidence (such as Pound repeatedly suggests) and focuses instead on the mysterious, this apparent contradiction loops back upon itself in the continuity established elsewhere between the function of the eye and that of imaginative contemplation.

The effect of that continuity is to bind together the initial implication of the eye in the world of practice, in its work towards a 'paradiso terrestre', with a subsequent disjunction from the world in a shift towards the indestructible paradise of the mind, and of the eye looking inwards. In so far as these higher truths of inner contemplation and imagination are directly super-imposed upon the same progenitor as that of the light, amor, and so on (even to the point where light in Canto 91 inscribes its indispensable power of penetration, '*compenetrans* of the spirits' (*91* : 611), Homer's capabilities in blindness must, like those of Tiresias, be considered a restitution beyond castration.

The wisdom in blindness in which the spirit is liberated from the world is the optimism of the later *Cantos*, and a counter-current to their acknowledgements of failure. The eye no longer looks to the facts, but is a repetition of God's eye, an eye not to be plucked out. A resistance of this eye to any extinction appears in Canto 81 :

> To have gathered from the air a live tradition
> or from a fine old eye the unconquered flame
> This is not vanity.
> Here error is all in the not done,
> all in the diffidence that faltered . . .   (*81* : 522)

But vanity or self-regard *is* precisely the character of the 'un-conquered flame', a looking to oneself in the sexual member and not finding it wanting, a turn towards imaginary narcissism and an image of the 'I'.

Accordingly Wyndham Lewis's refusal of surgery to remove a tumour from the chiasma of the optic nerve owing to the dangers of surgery in old age[14] is countenanced by Pound rather as a stoical dislocation of the eye from the mind, its liberation from the constraints of worldly in favour of transcendental vision :

> Wyndham Lewis chose blindness
> rather than have his mind stop.
>   (*115* : 794)

The mind chooses a divorce from the eye and the world and functions on, whereas the choice of preserving the eye possibly involves, in a cutting off, the loss of both.

With regard to such a continuity between a science of poetry based in observation and the revelations of an amanuensis in divine service, the adoption in the later *Cantos* of the Platonic sign or signature may be understood to be consistent with those earlier structures which can find intelligibility only in the guarantee of an exterior, autonomous subject, and its deliberation of truth. In this sign a perception made by the eye, such as a recognition of colour, makes possible an apprehension of a general nature, and in that nature is held to be the mark or imprint of the divine. In Canto 90 this operation is laid out as follows:

> 'From the colour the nature
>   & by the nature the sign!'
> Beatific spirits welding together
>   as in one ash-tree in Ygdrasail.
>
> (90:605)

The apotheosis of the eye becomes also that of the Luminous Detail, and indeed of all the Poundian epistemological figures which elide the production of representation into the immutable essence of a nature presided over by 'Gods, etc.'

The implication of narcissism or vanity in this assignation of truth to a mythified celestial order extrapolated from the eye is explicitly resisted by Pound, as above in Canto 81:

> Pull down thy vanity, it is not man
> Made courage, or made order, or made grace,
>   Pull down thy vanity, I say pull down.
> Learn of the green world what can be thy place
> In scaled invention or true artistry,
> Pull down thy vanity,
>
> (81:521)

Despite this affirmation, the self-absorption of the subject re-emerges. What man *does* make is the representation of these things in his discourses, forging for himself and for this 'courage' or 'order' or 'grace' identities which have, as Pound here recognizes, to be 'made'. The handing over of the responsibility for production onto the 'green world', with its concomitant establishment of a divine purpose, can only occur by virtue of the production of a discourse, 'I say'.

It has been argued at length above that language does not completely facilitate these representations. In revealing how the signifier comes to function only through its localized context in the signifying chain, multiplication of meanings, for example, seriously disrupts any simple effectivity of the subject in its discourses, such as Pound arrogates at the beginning of the *ABC of Economics:*

Once again, please do not imply. Please do not think I mean one whit more than what I have written. When I want to mean something further I will say it.[15]

Even in this defiant assertion of the possibility of containment of meaning the effects of language overspill that enclosure with the pararhyme 'whit' and 'what'. But such a proclamation is still supported in the confusion of Pisa:

> To communicate and then stop, that is the
>   law of discourse
> To go far and come to an end
>
>   (80:494)

It is even maintained amid the bewildering complexities for intelligibility of Canto 98:

> And as Ford said: get a dictionary
>   and learn the meaning of words.
>
>   (98:689)

The excess capabilities of language work to subvert representation in a splitting of the faces of the sign. In going beyond the securing of a single signified, these multiple effects of a signifier displace repression, and make it possible for what is repressed to return. If repressed capabilities of the signifier reappear in discourse against the circumscription attempted in definition, summoned there by incidental characteristics of the signifying chain in a solicitation of unintended meanings by property of association, then the metonymic implication of metaphor emerges. Other potentialities are elicited by contagious influence. This influence may be described as contagious since it operates by induction between contiguous signifiers. Revelation of multiple meanings by the surplus of the signifier allows to precipitate the very elements which have had to be repressed in order to establish the conditions of precision and definition.

It is now possible to consider once again certain of the symbolic equations which in the course of this analysis of the *Cantos* have been claimed to set up associative paths, tightening as a knot of represented correspondences and identifications. Whilst it was provisionally asserted that these might be grasped in a metaphorical aspect, it is now necessary, following an increasing recognition of the extensive implications of the excess of the signifier, to restore that metaphorical constellation to co-existence with the other great axis of language, metonymy. This is, of course, to challenge Pound's assertion in Canto 82 that what is to be gained from the overlayering of signifiers is knowledge:

> Wisdom lies next thee,
>   simply, past metaphor.   (82:526)

Whilst at one level symbolic equations funnel signifiers into the reduced, allusive counterpoint of the later *Cantos* described above, their surplus agencies resist any such reduction, violating the poem's associative boundaries. Quite apart from the kinds of distilled meaning effected in such continual insistence, different senses of signifiers cross-fertilize one another in a manner so

prolific as to question fundamentally the supposition of any
effective closure.

The acorns of the *Cantos*, which in Canto 39 are offered to
Odysseus in the ingle of Circe, provide a clear instance:

> First honey and cheese
>> honey at first and then acorns
> Honey at the start and then acorns
>> honey and wine and then acorns   (39:194)

These acorns clearly allude to Circe's hospitality resulting in a
transformation of men into pigs, functioning here as an item of
pig diet. But acorns are also the seed of the oak tree, and in
this sense they germinate the path of association in the *Cantos*
which treats trees as emblems of stability, autonomy and rectitude.
In Canto 79 these two opposite investments come together in a
simultaneous allusion to acorns in the context of food, and of
arborial growth:

> Will you trade roses for acorns
> Will lynxes eat thorn leaves?
> . . .
>
>> how many? There are more under the oak trees,
> We are here waiting the sun-rise.   (79:491)

The grapes which in Canto 2 induce the feline companions of
the god Dionysus amid the rigging of the pirates' ship reveal
a similar surplus:

> And where was gunwale, there now was vine-trunk,
> And tenthril where cordage had been,
>> grape-leaves on the rowlocks,
> Heavy vine on the oarshafts,
> And, out of nothing, a breathing,   (2:8)

In Canto 17 these grapes invoke natural fecundity:

> So that the vines burst from my fingers
> And the bees weighted with pollen
> Move heavily in the vine-shoots: (17:76)

But by repetition of the place names Sodom and Gomorrah these grapes may be held to introduce the bitter vines of gall attributed to those towns in the Bible.[16]

When in Canto 45 usury 'stoppeth the spinner's cunning' (45:229), this 'cunning' anticipates the sense of 'cunnus' in Canto 47. But that usage puts into question the kind of knowledge to be gained from copulation (early usages of 'cunning' meant simply 'knowledge' or 'craft') by also alluding to a more regular adoption of 'cunning'. This usage indicates a deviousness or artfulness characterized for Pound as an opposite relation to the phallus and exemplified in the person of Circe. His exaltation of the first sense of 'cunning' cannot exclude the effects upon his hero Odysseus of the second.

The topography of hell provides still another instance. The flame, which is in the *Cantos* and elsewhere in Pound's writings compacted with other representatives of the phallus in a specifically empyrean combustion, is nevertheless, by way of reiterated allusions to Dantesque and Homeric hells, also implicated in infernal fire. These other hells are introduced into the *Cantos* by way of the narrative of *The Odyssey* and through symbolic equations which operate to align usury and buggary. Yet Pound's own hell of Canto 14 and Canto 15 is depicted as a putrid marsh, and is inflammatory only in terms of the law of libel.

The 'fistula' of the letter to Eliot, appearing there as the pan-pipe of the soothsayer ('vates cum fistula') and hence related to the flute by Sulpicia's thigh in Canto 25, clearly functions in this phallic aspect only in terms of a visual representation. The tubular construction (which alongside its sponsorship in the name of Pan of music and coition also appears as a phallic protuberance) relies upon a convention of visual intelligibility governed by an external viewing relation. This convention elides out, as well as the whole question of associative properties generated in the form of the word 'fistula' itself, also the heterogeneity of visual intelligibility.

Such an unthinking elision is pointed out in the adoption of the term 'fistula' in clinical pathology to designate a narrow channel, furrow or leaking duct particularly prevalent as 'fistula in ano', which miscarries faeces away from the anal canal.[17] This amounts to an inversion of the above visual convention, intelligibility now made possible according to the properties of the inner face. Significantly the castration implied in this reintroduction of productivity into representation is reflected here in the abolition of the erectile quality of the phallus, displaced by the anal crevice or fissure of lack.

Consequently 'vates cum fistula' assumes an extra significance, one which accompanying Tiresias and Homer in their blindness serves as a reminder that the persistence of the phallus in incidental appearances can only function to indicate the emergence of a lack. Here the phallus returns from a repression of its signification of difference as precisely the crucial signifier of castration. When in a letter to E. E. Cummings, of February 1935, Pound defends Mairet and Nott, and claims: 'At any rate buggar the castration complex. Mairet, Nott, Newsome have *not* got it', not having it is exactly the term of castration.[18]

Not only, however, is the phallus confronted with its disappearance, but its fluid, the emission spilt on the grass in Canto 25, springing from the Castalian fount in Canto 90, then hovering above the minds of men, and flowing finally into the sea over which it rules, is by a further taxonomic accident a term of generality which embraces those liquids the sea and the flood elsewhere ascribed to women. This is in addition to its etymological derivation from 'fluere', to flow, which relates it to an opposed flowing in the dialectic of Heracleitus.[19]

In Canto 4 the light and the crystal, adamantine emblems of the phallus, are themselves dissolved:

> Thus the light rains, thus pours, *e lo soleills plovil*
> The liquid and rushing crystal
> > beneath the knees of the gods. (4:15)

The liquid torrent and the crystalline phallus are not intertwined in copulative complementarity, but in a mergence which ruptures the boundaries of any restricted signifying economy. The fetishization of the penis can occur only in a recovering, which fact is repeated in this quotation in the instance of crystallization, in as much as this process only occurs as precipitation from solution, a transition from liquid to solid state, the phallus emerging in its turgidity only out of castration.

These and other disruptions of the canalized symbolic chains in which the *Cantos* are structured face the tendentious argument of the poem with an interminable series of contradictions. In this respect they can be understood to subvert authorial domination over language by failing to enclose chosen meanings fully in the fixed discourses of the text. Language recalcitrantly escapes definition, and the orderly systems of the writer are anticipated (in that the symbolic order precedes the entry of the subject who is inscribed there only as an exclusion) and deflected by the radical potency of the Other. To these transgressions of the intention of the writer the insufferable prolongation and yet premature termination of the *Cantos* may be traced. The displacing capabilities of metonymy and desire introduced into the poem will not submit to the limiting intentions of a writer, to that writer's identifications, representations, or particular imaginary.

In Pound's formulation of logopoeia it becomes particularly prominent that his intended practice of language does not take into account any such radical agency of the signifier. Of the three tropes melopoeia, phanopoeia and logopoeia outlined in the essay 'How to Read', logopoeia is that special agency peculiar to the field of language, and most directly faced with the question of any surplus agency of the signifier. Yet Pound's description falls back instantly upon a notion of intention displayed in an attention to the possibility of translation of the tropes. Logopoeia is considered what Pound terms 'paraphrasable' rather than, strictly speaking, translatable:

One might say, you can *not* translate it 'locally', but having determined the original author's state of mind, you may or may not be able to find a derivative or an expedient.[20]

This intention, already as we have seen a pre-empting of the full complexities of the emergence of the subject in the signifying chain in favour of a notion of a fixed, extra-lingual identity, is further run back into a conception of language consisting in direct meanings embellished with a decorative excess. Logopoeia becomes,

'the dance of the intellect among the words', that is to say, it employs words not only for their direct meaning, but it takes count in a special way of habits of usage, of the context we *expect* to find with the word, its usual concomitants, of its known acceptances, and of ironical play.[21]

In this phrase 'not only for their direct meaning' language is considered as a simply effective system of communication in which a user, entering the circuits of transmission and playing upon incidental features of the signifier, patrols the limits of a contemporary acceptance. But also implied in this phrase is that the device's intelligibility is an effect of these contemporary acceptances. A set of linguistic and social relations (like the social semiotics of *Hugh Selwyn Mauberley*) are in this way necessary to make the trope workable. Such a disjunction of an imagined fundamental meaning from additional decoration, and from the network of social relations in which meanings are located, has the effect on the one hand of naturalizing and so maintaining existing ideological relations in so far as these are held at any moment in accepted usages and expected contexts, and on the other (and not unrelatedly) of postulating an autonomous subject outside language. This subject adapts an open linguistic system for personal purchase, and is never in any doubt as to its transmissive efficacy.

Whilst difficulties in such a conception of logopoeia are immediately acknowledged by Pound, these difficulties are only thought to lie in the reconstruction of an original author's intention. They nevertheless ensure that logopoeia is 'the latest come, and perhaps most tricky and undependable mode'.[22] Even this minimal recognition of the far more extensive problems of logopoeia is troubled by the circularity with which it seeks to trace an author's intention from discourse in order to re-inject it there in any new version, intention derived from the text in a reading, and then the text to be re-written according to intention.

If, in addressing itself to usual concomitants and accepted usages as though ideological relations are an unchangeable fact of nature, this practice of logopoeia is to be grasped as a resistance to history, and if the trope actively informs Pound's own writing, then the formulation in the essay 'Date Line' that the epic is 'a poem including history' must be considered to be derived from an opposed or fundamentally different conception of history. Pound obligingly elaborates further what he means by history:

An epic is a poem including history. I don't see that anyone save a sap-head can now think he knows any history until he understands economics.[23]

History here is a set of facts to be learnt, to be known, a set of representations already finished, 'included' in the sense of closed in.

In 'The Liberal, Request for an Effective Burial of Him' Pound indicates that writing is the transmission of this unproblematic knowledge:

I have pledged for a clear definition of terms, for an adequate international news service, and for a knowledge of economic causes and effects, clearly learnable from history.[24]

Since language is a transparent agent of transmission these facts can be learnt and understood from their transcription into a text as exact duplications of the very words known to have had agency in the past, hence the various documents of the *Cantos*.

What is foreclosed from such an inclusion of history (and this folds back upon the question of the subject in the signifying chain) is the fact of those representations as productions, history as a set of articulations in representation at a given historical moment. The presentation of 'history' raises all the questions already argued out above in terms of representation in general —in particular the shift from what is heterogeneous towards a homogeneity which conceals the production on which it is based. The presentation of a history of finished facts closes off this construction, and finds its support (hence the pertinence of the question of the subject in discourse) only in the sutured and dissembling subject of representation, the interloper.

The recurrence Pound finds in history, which underpins the argument of the *Cantos* when expressed as an analysis of the condition of culture at any given moment, and which lies behind all prognoses for a renaissance, is in this way a recurrence produced for history in the articulations of writing. Inscribed in that history is a further unrecognized history, that of the historian which has made possible the conditions of representation. When Pound writes in a letter to Homer, of 11 April 1927, of the ' "repeat in history" ', at one level he is writing about the repetitions of a subjective history which pervades all his discourses, and now articulates his notion of social history.[25] If thought is a general term including unconscious processes, Pound's favoured aphorism borrowed from T. E. Hulme that ' "all a man ever *thought* would go onto a half sheet of notepaper. The rest is application and elaboration" '[26] describes quite accurately this structure of unconscious repetition in many areas of an unremembered psychical conflict.

The promulgation of the fixed subject of representation, the full identity outside history whose claim upon history is charged with the unswerving certitude of empiricism and championed by divine right, has immediate political effects. It predicates practices which can only lead either to an unchanging maintenance of existing social relations in consolidation of our present acceptances as nature, or to a decline into subordination under extreme authoritarian structures. Such a decline rejoins in its turn the historical question of Pound's allegiance to Fascism, by way of the implicit exhortation in the *Cantos* toward a transformative political practice to implement the poem's 'paradiso terrestre' as a consequence of 'understanding history'. Fascism is a likely spin-off from Pound's discursive practices, in so far as it insinuates itself within existing ideological structures, fired as it were by a passion for their preservation. But this preservation exacerbates social divisions and oppressions to the point where, misconceiving historical determination as nature, it argues the vindication of its policies from the self-same extremities to which historical determination can carry subjective inequality.

If the *Cantos* cannot in any way be read as Pound intended, since the emergence of desire everywhere undermines the repression which sponsors conscious, didactic meanings, the question arises if there are any conditions at all in which the poem can be read with pleasure. This is by no means an easy question and only a provisional answer, itself formed as an area only distinguishable as a difference from kinds of reading it is not, may be ventured.

The fundamental danger of readings of a text which work against meanings plainly evident at other levels is not that in doing so they neglect the intention of the author, for reasons which it has been the concern of this analysis to argue. The danger is instead of a formalism in which since language is always operating in excess of what we consciously mean, any text can mean anything to anyone. Clearly, there is a way of reading the *Cantos* whereby exclusive attention is given to these ubiquitous excesses.

But in any such reading there are two main areas of difficulty. The first is that it is not simply a question for such a reader that Pound's particular selected meanings for history and culture are found inacceptable, but that *any* constraint upon the play of meanings is not to be tolerated. The effect of this would be atavistically to return to an aesthetism which incidentally Pound himself opposed in English poetry, and in which writing can only serve the function of a sensory gratification reluctant to accept the evident social conductivity of language. The second reason to some extent explains what is operative and yet ignored (or repressed) in this kind of formalism: although the excesses of language may appear to diffract any single intended meaning into an interminable multiplicity, it is the effect of the unconscious to articulate in these openings what has been repressed, to allow it to return in the discourses from which the subject endeavours to exclude it.

Such a formalism, then, works to deny the force of the unconscious, even if to read the *Cantos* attentive to the surplus of the signifier is continually to encounter the insistences of this return, and in consequence to be held at certain nodes of meaning which circulate there. Relations produced across language by a reader inscribe a further unconscious history which articulates the seemingly unbounded fertility of linguistic possibilities. So whilst a formalistic reading might claim to encounter not the specific meanings of the writer but language itself, this encounter is despite such an affirmation structured first by the unconscious

G*

repetitions of the writer, and secondarily by those of any given reader.

What such readings of the poem attempt is to experience language outside history. But since language and symbolicity in general are only attained in a determinate history of the individual, this experience is never possible. The category of rhythmic pleasure, which has become the index *par excellence* of formalistic renderings of Pound, cannot be isolated in this way from the ritualistically persuasive and rhetorical phrasing which continually imposes the presence of a voice, with its characteristic trace of the history inscribed at all other levels of the poem.[27]

If the poem cannot be read in terms of this kind of gratification, however it is to be read must take into account cultural and political meanings it inscribes. This, however, is not to suggest a reading passively produced as an effect of the structures of the poem, in any way suggesting that to read the poem must be to accept its theses as to artistic and cultural order. Rather to engage the poem is simultaneously to remark produced representations and also features which resist those representations and imply different or other meanings.

The *Cantos* begin by putting cultural and literary meaning in doubt in their claim of an endless and open quest, but in an attempt finally to turn the absence quite explicit in Odysseus's estrangement from Ithaca into the reassuring presence of a home, an identity and a paradise. What the acknowledged failure of the poem to achieve this demonstrates is that comfort in reclaimed presence and identity, and the kinds of certitude that restitution makes possible, can only occur as the effect of an act of production, of making a place to be resided in. It can by no means be taken as any kind of natural condition.

Pound's resistance to this failure, in such forms as 'it coheres all right/even if my notes do not cohere' (*116*: 797), or 'the coherent idea around which my muddles accumulated' of the interview with Donald Hall,[28] reiterates his opposition to such a loss. But whatever pleasure exists in the *Cantos* has to lie precisely there, since despite all protestations to the contrary, the surety of identity is never forged in the poem itself.

It is perhaps here that the *Cantos* may be found readable across and against intention, since the pleasure of constant displacement in certain parts of the poem, and particularly in the sections following the *Pisan Cantos*, outweighs the violence of the disavowal which continues to struggle for coherence. This is, of course, a testimony against the main flow of the poem. For this kind of reading Pound's favoured image of bringing blood to dead spirits has to be emphatically inverted, since the death-touch of desire is instead a losing which kills off the living, and makes forever untenable the certitudes of the egoist.

Notes

1 11 August 1960, quoted in Hugh Kenner, *The Pound Era* (Faber, London, 1971), p. 540.
2 See above, chapter 5, pp. 116–17.
3 Ezra Pound, *Polite Essays* (Faber, London, 1937), p. 51.
4 *Life*, p. 349; *Life* (Penguin), p. 444.
5 *Selected Prose*, p. 227.
6 *Dk: Some Letters of Ezra Pound*, edited with notes by Louis Dudek (DC Books, Montreal, 1974), p. 107.
7 Ezra Pound, *Guide to Kulchur* (London, 1938; reprinted, 1952), p. 77.
8 *Loc.cit.*
9 *Letters*, p. 285.
10 The inhabitants of hell are described as 'powerless' in the Loeb edition. The suggestion of an inadequate genitality is Pound's.
11 *Standard Edition*, vol. XI. The story of Lady Godiva is discussed p. 217.
12 *Ibid.* vol. XVII. The quotation is from p. 231.
13 *Selected Prose*, pp. 29–30.
14 Related in Kenner, *op.cit.*, p. 549.
15 *Selected Prose*, p. 203.
16 Deuteronomy 32. 32.
17 See, for example, the entry for 'fistula' in *Black's Medical Dictionary*.
18 *Letters*, p. 357.
19 'All things are a flowing,/Sage Heracleitus says'; *Collected Shorter Poems*, p. 206.
20 *Literary Essays*, p. 25.
21 *Loc.cit.*
22 *Loc.cit.*
23 *Ibid.* p. 86.
24 Ezra Pound, 'The Liberal, Request for an Effective Burial of Him', *Action*, 27 August 1938, p. 13.
25 *Letters*, p. 285.
26 *Selected Prose*, p. 298.
27 It is not easy to debate the music of Pound's verse except in terms of a purely diagnostic rhythmic analysis, or of an impressionistic attribution of value. The first of these procedures is unable to account for the fact that certain rhythmic patterns are more pleasurable than others (except in terms of variations in established genres). Of the second, the predication of value, Roland Barthes writes: 'The man who provides himself or is

provided with an adjective is now hurt, now pleased, but always *con-stituted*', 'The Grain of the Voice', *Image-Music-Text*, essays selected and translated by Stephen Heath (London, 1977), p. 179. Music establishes an imaginary in the listener when conceived in these terms. Barthes makes the distinction in this essay between vocal performances in which the cantor seeks to trace the grain of the voice, the manifestation of the body as it produces sounds, and those in which passions and feelings are expressed. Listening to recordings of Pound reading the *Cantos* indicates his clear preference for the latter procedure. Generally the rhythms of the poem are those of the speaking voice, a voice of assurance in its rhetorical delivery of meaning.

28 *Paris Review*, 28 (1962), p. 48.

Select Bibliography

Section I: The Writings of Ezra Pound

a) *Poetical Works*
A Lume Spento: And Other Early Poems, 1908 (Faber, London, 1965).
Collected Shorter Poems, 1926, reprinted and enlarged 1952, current edition (Faber, London, 1973).
The Cantos (Faber, London, 1975).

b) *Letters*
The Letters of Ezra Pound: 1907–1941, edited by D. D. Paige (Faber, London, 1951).
EP to LU: Nine Letters Written to Louis Untermeyer by Ezra Pound, edited by J. A. Robbins (Indiana University Press, Bloomington, 1963).
Pound/Joyce: the Letters of Ezra Pound to James Joyce, with Pound's Essays on Joyce, edited by Forrest Read (Faber, London, 1968).
Dk/Some Letters of Ezra Pound, edited with notes by Louis Dudek (DC Books, Montreal, 1974).

c) *Interviews*
D. G. Bridson, 'An Interview with Ezra Pound', *New Directions*, 17 (1961), 159–84.
'Interview with Donald Hall', *Paris Review*, number 28 (1962), 22–51.

d) *Prose Works and Essays*
ABC of Reading (Routledge & Kegan Paul, London, 1934; reprinted Faber, London, 1951).
America, Roosevelt and the Causes of the Present War, 1944, translated by J. Drummond (Peter Russell, London, 1951).
'Britain First', *Action*, 13 August 1938, p. 9.
The Classic Anthology Defined by Confucius, 1955, paperback edition (Faber, London, 1974).

Confucius: The Great Digest and The Unwobbling Pivot, 1947 (Peter Owen, London, 1952).

Gaudier-Brzeska: A Memoir, 1916, reprinted (New Directions, New York, 1970).

Guide to Kulchur (Faber, London, 1938; reprinted New Directions & Peter Owen, London, 1952).

Impact: Essays on Ignorance and the Decline of American Civilization, edited with an introduction by Noel Stock (Chicago, 1960).

Jefferson and/or Mussolini: L'idea Statale, Fascism as I Have Seen It, 1935 (Liveright, New York, 1970).

'The Liberal, Request for an Effective Burial of Him', *Action*, 27 August 1938, p. 13.

Literary Essays of Ezra Pound, edited with an introduction by T. S. Eliot, 1954, reprinted (Faber, London, 1968).

Make It New (Faber, London, 1934).

Patria Mia and the Treatise on Harmony, 1950 (Peter Owen, London, 1962).

Pavannes and Divagations, 1918, paperback edition (New Directions, New York, 1974).

Polite Essays (Faber, London, 1937).

'Race', *New English Weekly*, 15 October 1936, pp. 12–13.

Selected Prose: 1909–1965, edited with an introduction by William Cookson (Faber, London, 1973).

The Spirit of Romance (J. M. Dent, London, 1910; revised edition, New Directions, New York, & Peter Owen, London, 1960).

Ta Hio: The Great Learning (University of Washington Book Store, Seattle, 1928).

The Translations of Ezra Pound, with an introduction by Hugh Kenner (Faber, London, 1953).

Two recent collections of work by Pound require special reference:

'Ezra Pound Speaking': Radio Speeches of World War II, edited by Leonard W. Doob (Greenwood Press, Westport, Connecticut and London, 1978).

Ezra Pound and Music: The Complete Criticism, edited with commentary by R. Murray Schafer (Faber, London, 1977).

Another work requires individual mention:

Les Cahiers de l'Herne: Ezra Pound, edited by Dominique de Roux, 2 vols (Paris, 1965).

These volumes (in French) contain in addition to interviews already cited profiles of Pound by numerous other writers, and much secondary material.

e) *Works with contributions by Pound*
A Negro Anthology 1931–1933, edited by Nancy Cunard (London, 1934).
Authors Take Sides on the Spanish War (Left Books, London, 1941).
Blast: Review of the Great English Vortex, numbers 1–2, 1914–15 (Kraus Reprint Corporation, New York, 1967).
de Gourmont, Rémy, *The Natural Philosophy of Love*, translated with a postscript by Ezra Pound (Casanova Society, London, 1926).
Fenollosa, Ernest, *The Chinese Written Character as a Medium for Poetry* (City Light Books, San Francisco, 1936).
Writers at Work: The Paris Review Interviews (Penguin, Harmondsworth, 1972).

Section II: Secondary Sources Largely or Exclusively Devoted to Pound

Brooke-Rose, Christine, *ZBC of Ezra Pound* (Faber, London, 1971).
———*The Structural Analysis of Ezra Pound's Usura Canto* (Mouton, The Hague and Paris, 1976).
Bush, Ronald, *The Genesis of Ezra Pound's Cantos* (Princeton University Press, 1976).
Davie, Donald, *Ezra Pound: Poet as Sculptor* (Routledge & Kegan Paul, London, 1964).
———'The *Cantos*: Towards a Pedestrian Reading', *Paideuma*, 1 number 1 (1972), 55–62.
———*Pound*, Fontana Modern Masters (Fontana, London, 1975).
Davis, Earle, *Vision Fugitive: Ezra Pound and Economics* (University Press of Kansas, Lawrence, Kansas, 1968).
Dekker, George, *Sailing After Knowledge: The Cantos of Ezra Pound* (Routledge & Kegan Paul, London, 1963).
Ellmann, Maud, 'Floating the Pound: The Circulation of the Subject in Pound's *The Cantos*', *Oxford Literary Review*, 3, number 3 (1979), 16–27.
Heymann, C. David, *Ezra Pound: The Last Rower* (Faber, London, 1976).
Hughes, Glenn, *Imagism and the Imagists: A Study in Modern Poetry* (Stanford, 1931; reprinted Bowes & Bowes, London, 1960).
Kavka, Jerome, 'Ezra Pound's Sanity: The Problems of Public Disclosure', *Paideuma*, 4, numbers 2 and 3 (1975), 527–9.
Kenner, Hugh, *The Poetry of Ezra Pound*, 1951 (New Directions,

Norfolk, Connecticut and Kraus Reprint Corporation, New York, 1974).

Kenner, Hugh, *The Pound Era* (Faber, London, 1971).

Olson, Charles, *Charles Olson and Ezra Pound: An Encounter at St Elizabeths*, edited by Catherine Seelye (Viking Press, New York, 1975).

Pleynet, Marcelin, 'La compromission poétique', *Tel Quel*, 70 (1977), 11–26.

Stock, Noel, *The Life of Ezra Pound* (Routledge & Kegan Paul, London, 1970).

——*The Life of Ezra Pound* (Penguin, Harmondsworth, 1974).

Terell, Caroll F., 'The *Periplus* of Hanno', *Paideuma*, 1, number 2 (1972), 223–8.

Wees, William C., *Vorticism and the English Avant-Garde* (Manchester University Press, Manchester and Toronto University Press, Toronto, 1972).

For records of work in progress on Pound, and latest exegetical and biographical contributions, special reference should be made to *Paideuma: A Journal Devoted to Ezra Pound Scholarship*, Managing Editor, Caroll F. Terell (University of Maine, Orono, Maine). For bibliographical information, see:

Edwards, John Hamilton and Vasse, William W., *Annotated Index to The Cantos of Ezra Pound*, with the assistance of John J. Espey and Frederic Peachy (University of California Press, Berkeley and Los Angeles, 1959).

Gallup, Donald Clifford, *A Bibliography of Ezra Pound*, 1963, second impression, Soho Bibliographies, 18 (Rupert Hart-Davis, London, 1969).

For work in these areas which postdates these studies, see *Paideuma*.

Section III: Other Primary Sources Used

Eliot, Thomas Stearns, *Collected Poems, 1909–1962* (Faber, London, 1963; fifth impression, 1970).

——*The Waste Land: A Facsimile and Transcript of the Original Drafts Including the Annotations of Ezra Pound*, edited by Valerie Eliot (Faber, London, 1971).

Homer, *The Odyssey*, translated by E. V. Rieu (Penguin, Harmondsworth, 1946), reprinted hardback edition (Allen Lane, London, 1973).

Hulme, Thomas Ernest, *Speculations: Essays on Humanism and the Philosophy of Art*, edited by Herbert Read, with a frontispiece and foreword by Jacob Epstein, International Library of Psychology, Philosophy, and Scientific Method (London, 1924).

Joyce, James, *Ulysses* (Egoist Press, London, 1922), revised edition (The Bodley Head, London, Sydney, Toronto, 1969).

Section IV: Works of Psychoanalysis and Semiology

a) *Primary Sources*

Abraham, Karl, *Selected Papers*, with an introductory memoir by Ernest Jones, translated by Douglas Bryan and Alix Strachey, International Psycho-Analytical Library, 13 (Hogarth Press, London, 1927).

Fliess, R. (ed.), *The Psycho-Analytic Reader: An Anthology of Essential Papers with Critical Introductions*, International Psycho-Analytical Library, 38 (London, 1950).

Freud, Sigmund, *The Standard Edition of the Complete Psychological Works of Sigmund Freud*, edited and translated by James Strachey, in collaboration with Anna Freud, and assisted by Alix Strachey and Alan Tyson, 24 vols (Hogarth Press, London, 1953).

Gillespie, W. H., 'A Contribution to the Study of Fetishism', *International Journal of Psycho-Analysis*, 21 (1940), 401–15.

Hunter, Dugmore, 'Object-Relation Changes in the Analysis of a Fetishist', *International Journal of Psycho-Analysis*, 35 (1954), 302–12.

Lacan, Jacques, *Écrits* (Seuil, Paris, 1966).

——*The Language of the Self: The Function of Language in Psychoanalysis*, translated with notes and commentary by Anthony Wilden, second printing (Delta Books, New York, 1968).

——*Le séminaire XI: Les quatre concepts fondamentaux de la psychanalyse* (Seuil, Paris, 1973).

——*Le séminaire XX: Encore* (Seuil, Paris, 1975).

——*Écrits: A Selection*, translated by Alan Sheridan (Tavistock Publications, London, 1977).

——*The Four Fundamental Concepts of Psycho-Analysis*, translated by Alan Sheridan (Hogarth Press and Institute of Psycho-Analysis, London, 1977).

Lacan, Jacques, and Granoff, Wladimir, 'Fetishism: The Symbolic, the Imaginary and the Real', in *Perversions, Psychodynamics, and Therapy*, edited by Sandor Lorand, associate editor, M. Balint (Ortolan Press, London, 1965).

Miller, Jacques-Alain, 'Suture (éléments de la logique du significant)',

Cahiers pour l'analyse, 1 (1966), in English, 'Suture (elements of the logic of the signifier)', translated by Jacqueline Rose, *Screen*, 18, number 4 (1977/8), 24–34.

Safouan, Moustafa, *Études sur l'Oedipe* (Seuil, Paris, 1974).

Sharpe, Ella Freeman, 'An Examination of Metaphor: Psycho-Physical Problems Revealed in Language (1940)', in *The Psycho-Analytic Reader: An Anthology of Essential Papers with Critical Introductions*, edited by R. Fliess, International Psycho-Analytical Library, 38 (Hogarth Press, London, 1950).

b) *Commentaries and Literary and Film Studies*

Barthes, Roland, *Mythologies* (Pierres Vives, Paris, 1957).

——*Image-Music-Text*, essays selected and translated by Stephen Heath (Fontana, London, 1977).

Coward, Rosalind, and Ellis, John, *Language and Materialism: Developments in Semiology and the Theory of the Subject* (Routledge & Kegan Paul, London, Henley and Boston, Massachusetts, 1977).

Derrida, Jacques, 'Structure, Sign and Play in the Discourse of the Human Sciences', in *The Structuralist Controversy: The Languages of Criticism and The Sciences of Man*, edited by Richard Macksey and Eugenio Donato (Johns Hopkins University Press, Baltimore and London, 1970; third printing 1977), pp. 247–72.

——*Of Grammatology*, translated by Gayatri Chakravorty Spivak (Johns Hopkins University Press, Baltimore and London, 1976; second printing 1977).

Heath, Stephen, *The Nouveau Roman: A Study in the Practice of Writing* (Elek, London, 1972).

——'Anata Mo', *Screen*, 17, number 4 (1976), 49–66.

——'Notes on Suture', *Screen*, 18, number 4 (1977/8), 48–76.

——'Sexual Difference and Representation', *Screen*, 19, number 3 (1978), 51–112.

Jones, Ernest, *The Life and Work of Sigmund Freud*, 3 vols (Hogarth Press, London, 1953–7).

MacCabe, Colin, 'Presentation of "The Imaginary Signifier"', *Screen*, 16, number 2 (1975), 7–13.

——*James Joyce and the Revolution of the Word* (Macmillan, London, 1978).

Metz, Christian, *Le Signifiant Imaginaire: psychanalyse et cinéma* (10/18, Paris, 1977).

Mitchell, Juliet, *Psychoanalysis and Feminism* (Penguin, Harmondsworth, 1974; reprinted 1976).

Section V: Other General Works Used

Agassiz, Louis, *Methods of Study in Natural History*, second edition (Boston, Massachusetts, 1864).

Agassiz, Louis and Gould, A. A., *Outlines of Comparative Physiology: Touching the Structure and Development of the Races of Animals, Living and Extinct*, revised edition (London, 1851).

Althusser, Louis, *Lenin and Philosophy: and Other Essays*, translated from the French by Ben Brewster (Monthly Review Press, New York and London, 1971).

Benveniste, Émile, *Problems in General Linguistics* (1966), translated by Mary Elizabeth Meek (Coral Gables, University of Miami Press, Florida, 1971).

Brooke-Rose, Christine, *A Grammar of Metaphor* (Secker & Warburg, London, 1958).

de Saussure, Ferdinand, *Course in General Linguistics*, edited by Charles Bally and Albert Sechehaye, translated by Wade Baskin (New York, Toronto, and Peter Owen, London, 1960).

Foucault, Michel, *The Order of Things: An Archaeology of the Human Sciences*, translated from the French (Tavistock Publications, London, 1970; reprinted 1977).

Frobenius, Leo, *Eine Anthologie*, with a foreword by L. S. Senghor, translated by P. Crampton, Studien zur Kulturkunde, 32 (Wiesbaden, 1973).

Hindess, Barry, and Hirst, Paul, *Mode of Production and Social Formation: An Auto-Critique of Pre-Capitalist Modes of Production* (Macmillan, London, 1977).

Hirst, Paul, *On Law and Ideology* (Macmillan, London, 1979).

Hofstadter, Richard, *Social Darwinism in American Thought: 1860–1915* (Philadelphia, 1944).

Jakobson, Roman, *Selected Writings*, 2 vols (Mouton, The Hague and Paris, 1971).

Ledeen, Michael Arthur, *Universal Fascism: The Theory and Practice of the Fascist International, 1928–1936* (New York, 1972).

Macciocchi, Maria-Antoinetta (ed.), *Élements pour une analyse du fascisme: séminaire de Maria-A. Macciocchi, Paris VIII—Vincennes, 1974–1975*, 2 vols (10/18, Paris, 1976).

——'Sexualité féminine dans l'idéologie fasciste', *Tel Quel*, 66 (1976), 26–42.

Marx, Karl, *Critique of the Gotha Programme*, with appendices by F. Engels and V. I. Lenin, edition authorized by the Marx-Engels-Lenin Institute, Moscow (Martin Lawrence, London, 1933).

——*Capital: A Critique of Political Economy*, translated from the third German edition by Samuel Moore and Edward Aveling, edited by Frederick Engels, 4 vols (Lawrence & Wishart, London, 1954; reprinted 1977).

Reich, Wilhelm, *The Mass Psychology of Fascism*, translated by T. P. Wolfe, third revised and enlarged edition (Orgone Institute Press, third edition, New York, 1946).

Szasz, Thomas, S., *Law, Liberty, and Psychiatry: An Inquiry into the Social Uses of Mental Health Practices* (Routledge & Kegan Paul, London, 1974).

Williams, Raymond, *Marxism and Literature* (Oxford University Press, London, 1977).

Acknowledgements

I would like to thank everyone who has commented or advised during the preparation of this manuscript, which originated in research undertaken at Cambridge University: in particular, Paul Smith, John Rathmell, Adrian Poole, Rebecca Thomas, John Leigh. I owe especial gratitude to the constant encouragement and detailed recommendations of Colin MacCabe.

I am grateful to Faber and Faber Ltd. and to New Directions Publishing Corporation, New York, for permission to reprint extracts from *Selected Prose 1909–1965* by Ezra Pound (edited by William Cookson) © Ezra Pound Literary Property Trust, 1973; for extracts from *The Cantos of Ezra Pound* by Ezra Pound © 1975, Ezra Pound Literary Property Trust, and from *The Letters of Ezra Pound 1907–1941* edited by D. D. Paige © Ezra Pound, 1950.

Index